The Mixed Blessing of Financial Inflows

The International Institute for Applied Systems Analysis

is an interdisciplinary, nongovernmental research institution founded in 1972 by leading scientific organizations in 12 countries. Situated near Vienna, in the center of Europe, IIASA has been for more than two decades producing valuable scientific research on economic, technological, and environmental issues.

IIASA was one of the first international institutes to systematically study global issues of environment, technology, and development. IIASA's Governing Council states that the Institute's goal is: *to conduct international and interdisciplinary scientific studies to provide timely and relevant information and options, addressing critical issues of global environmental, economic, and social change, for the benefit of the public, the scientific community, and national and international institutions.* Research is organized around three central themes:

– Global Environmental Change;
– Global Economic and Technological Change;
– Systems Methods for the Analysis of Global Issues.

The Institute now has national member organizations in the following countries:

Austria
The Austrian Academy of Sciences

Bulgaria*
The Bulgarian Committee for IIASA

Finland
The Finnish Committee for IIASA

Germany**
The Association for the Advancement
of IIASA

Hungary
The Hungarian Committee for Applied
Systems Analysis

Japan
The Japan Committee for IIASA

Kazakstan*
The Ministry of Science –
The Academy of Sciences

Netherlands
The Netherlands Organization for
Scientific Research (NWO)

Norway
The Research Council of Norway

Poland
The Polish Academy of Sciences

Russian Federation
The Russian Academy of Sciences

Slovak Republic*
The Slovak Committee for IIASA

Sweden
The Swedish Council for Planning and
Coordination of Research (FRN)

Ukraine*
The Ukrainian Academy of Sciences

United States of America
The American Academy of Arts and
Sciences

*Associate member
**Affiliate

The Mixed Blessing of Financial Inflows

Transition Countries in Comparative Perspective

Edited by

János Gács
International Institute for Applied Systems Analysis, Laxenburg, Austria

Robert Holzmann
Ludwig Boltzmann Institute for Economic Policy Analysis, Vienna, Austria, and The World Bank, Washington, DC, USA

Michael L. Wyzan
International Institute for Applied Systems Analysis, Laxenburg, Austria

Edward Elgar
Cheltenham, UK • Northampton, MA, USA

IIASA
International Institute for Applied Systems Analysis
Laxenburg, Austria

In association with the Ludwig Boltzmann Institute for Economic Policy Analysis, Vienna, Austria

© International Institute for Applied Systems Analysis 1999

Published by
Edward Elgar Publishing Limited
Glensanda House
Montpellier Parade
Cheltenham
Glos GL50 1UA
UK

Edward Elgar Publishing, Inc.
6 Market Street
Northampton
Massachusetts 01060
USA

A catalogue record for this book
is available from the British Library

Library of Congress Cataloguing in Publication Data
The mixed blessings of financial inflows : transition countries in
  comparative perspective / edited by János Gács, Robert Holzmann,
  Michael L. Wyzan.
     "In association with the International Institute for Applied
  Systems Analysis."
     Includes index.
     1. Capital movements. 2. Investments, Foreign. 3. International
  finance. I. Gács, János. II. Holzmann, Robert. III. Wyzan,
  Michael L. IV. International Institute for Applied Systems
  Analysis.
  HG3891.M585   1999   98–31843
  332'.042—dc21   CIP

ISBN 1 84064 038 3

Printed and bound in Great Britain by
Biddles Ltd, Guildford and King's Lynn

Contents

List of Figures

List of Tables

Contributors

Velimir Bole
Economic Institute at School
  of Law (EIPF)
University of Ljubljana
Ljubljana, Slovenia

Timothy James Bond
International Monetary Fund (IMF)
Washington, DC, USA

Vittorio Corbo
Institute of Economics
Catholic University of Chile
Santiago, Chile

Marta de Castello Branco
International Monetary Fund (IMF)
Washington, DC, USA

Paweł Durjasz
National Bank of Poland
Warsaw, Poland

János Gács
International Institute for Applied
  Systems Analysis (IIASA)
Laxenburg, Austria; also
KOPINT-DATORG Rt. Institute for
  Economic and Market Research
  and Informatics
Budapest, Hungary

Robert Holzmann
The World Bank
Washington, DC, USA; also
Ludwig Boltzmann Institute for
  Economic Policy Analysis
Vienna, Austria

Ryszard Kokoszczyński
National Bank of Poland
Warsaw, Poland

Gábor Oblath
KOPINT-DATORG Rt. Institute for
  Economic and Market Research
  and Informatics
Budapest, Hungary

Helmut Reisen
OECD Development Centre
Paris, France

Marcelo Soto
Catholic University of Chile
Santiago, Chile

Salvador Valdés-Prieto
Catholic University of Chile
Santiago, Chile

Charles Wyplosz
Graduate Institute of International Studies
Geneva, Switzerland

Michael L. Wyzan
International Institute for Applied
  Systems Analysis (IIASA)
Laxenburg, Austria

Introduction

János Gács, Robert Holzmann, and Michael L. Wyzan

Due to a variety of systemic features, the centrally planned economies were, as a rule, characterized by chronic shortages (see, e.g., Kornai, 1980). The hunger for resources also included an insatiable appetite for convertible currency, which was partly reflected in these countries' meager international reserves.

In the Central and East European countries (CEECs) in the early 1990s, the establishment of currency convertibility, realistic exchange rates, and market-based interest rates, along with the liberalization of foreign trade transactions, essentially eliminated enterprises' insatiable hunger for foreign exchange. The need for investable resources from abroad, however, did not disappear. This demand was fueled by the impending privatization of a great number of state-owned enterprises, the need to restructure most of these firms, and weak and undiversified domestic financial systems unable to select prospective investment projects and channel domestic savings toward them.

Even during the era of central planning, the governments and central banks of the CEECs were present on western capital markets; with the exception of Czechoslovakia, they borrowed heavily from abroad, especially in the second half of the 1980s, and most accumulated large debts. As *Table I.1* shows, the major form of this capital inflow was long-term public or publicly guaranteed debt. Before 1989–1990, in the absence of autonomous private firms and in the face of stringent state regulation, domestic enterprises could not raise capital on international capital markets, and for similar reasons, foreign direct investment (FDI) was also not a feasible source of finance.

In the first years of economic transformation, even the sources of debt creation that had been available under communism became blocked. This was due to the inability of most of the countries to service their inherited debts and the decisions

Table I.1. Debt level in selected Central and East European countries, 1985–1990 (US$ million).

	1985	1986	1987	1988	1989	1990
Bulgaria						
Total debt	3,852	5,866	8,266	8,944	10,137	10,890
Of which long-term public or publicly guaranteed	3,802	5,806	7,915	8,315	9,283	9,834
Total debt/GNP (%)	22.0	29.1	29.4	84.7	114.2	239.7
Czechoslovakia						
Total debt	4,608	5,568	6,658	7,281	7,915	8,363
Of which long-term public or publicly guaranteed	2,689	2,877	3,582	3,875	4,328	5,460
Total debt/GNP (%)	11.7	12.1	12.8	14.2	15.7	18.4
Hungary						
Total debt	13,955	16,907	19,585	19,609	20,397	21,277
Of which long-term public or publicly guaranteed	9,965	12,383	15,673	15,612	16,634	18,006
Total debt/GNP (%)	70.6	74.3	78.1	71.4	73.4	67.2
Poland						
Total debt	33,336	36,670	42,603	42,103	43,077	49,162
Of which long-term public or publicly guaranteed	29,763	31,932	36,038–	33,627	34,500	39,059
Total debt/GNP (%)	48.7	51.5	69.8	63.9	54.5	88.4
Romania						
Total debt	7,008	6,983	6,580	2,960	1,087	1,173
Of which long-term public or publicly guaranteed	5,805	5,653	5,343	2,117	199	263
Total debt/GNP (%)	n.a.	n.a.	17.4	7.3	2.6	3.1

Abbreviation: n.a., not available.
Source: World debt tables 1993–1994 and 1996, The World Bank, Washington, DC.

by all the indebted CEECs except Hungary to reschedule payments on those debts. In this environment, western official lending increased, while private capital was hesitant (Lankes and Stern, 1997). In addition, in several countries, uncertainties in the early phase of the transformation (1990–1991), combined with a more liberal trade regime and looser capital controls, led to capital flight. Capital accounts switched into the red and international reserves fell to low levels (UN/ECE, 1997).

All CEECs suffered a "transformational recession" during 1990–1993, which was reflected in an average 20% decline in GDP and a 40% drop in industrial production (Holzmann *et al.*, 1995). The subsequent recovery, combined with the increased credibility of the local currencies and improved prospects for political stability, attracted foreign capital in gradually increasing amounts. The pick-up in

Table I.2. Private capital flows to emerging markets (US$ billion).

	1990	1991	1992	1993	1994	1995	1996
Emerging markets							
Total private capital inflows	45.7	139.8	133.4	161.0	147.0	192.8	235.2
Net foreign direct investment	18.8	32.1	37.9	56.9	75.5	78.3	105.9
Net portfolio investment	17.0	39.7	59.2	106.8	97.2	31.6	58.7
Net other investment	90.9	68.0	36.3	−2.7	−25.7	73.9	70.6
Africa							
Total private capital inflows	2.9	5.5	5.7	4.7	12.7	13.6	9.0
Asia							
Total private capital inflows	21.4	37.7	22.4	59.5	75.1	98.9	106.8
Middle East and Europe							
Total private capital inflows	7.0	73.3	42.8	24.1	−1.1	15.3	22.2
Western hemisphere							
Total private capital inflows	10.3	24.9	55.5	61.7	44.9	35.7	77.7
Countries in transition							
Total private capital inflows	4.2	−1.6	7.1	10.9	15.4	29.1	19.4
Net foreign direct investment	0.0	2.4	4.2	6.0	5.4	13.1	11.3
Net portfolio investment	n.a.	0.8	−0.8	3.4	2.7	3.4	1.6
Net other investment	4.1	−4.8	3.8	1.5	7.3	12.6	6.6

Abbreviation: n.a., not available.
Source: International capital markets, 1998, International Monetary Fund, Washington, DC.

growth occurred in economies that had been partly restructured, so that they were now characterized by predominantly private ownership, reoriented foreign trade, and increasing shares of services and those industrial sectors that corresponded to the new demand conditions on CEEC markets. In addition, capital markets were being created, the liberalization of capital flows progressed, and in several countries foreign investors were invited to take part in the privatization of state enterprises and utilities.

Just as in other emerging markets, in CEECs the coincidence of domestic recovery with declining interest rates in the developed world in the first half of the 1990s provided an impetus for private investors to turn toward the region. As *Table I.2* indicates, the broad group of transition economies, although they represented a minor share of the private capital attracted by emerging economies in 1990, have significantly increased that share in recent years. This tendency is even more pronounced for the transition countries in Central Europe (see *Table I.3*).

The CEECs have shown many similarities in the timing and manner in which they have attracted investments from abroad. If we compare, for instance, capital inflows in 1992 and 1995 (see *Table I.4*), we see that the combined inflows

Table I.3. Balance of payments items as a percentage of GDP.

	1990	1991	1992	1993	1994	1995	1996
Croatia							
Current account		−3.2	2.6	0.9	0.7	−9.5	−7.8
Capital account		3.2	−1.3	3.0	4.8	12.2	10.0
Reserves		−	−1.3	−3.9	−5.5	−2.7	−2.2
Czech Republic							
Current account	−0.4	7.1	−1.6	−0.2	−2.1	−2.9	−8.1
Capital account	−1.3	−5.5	1.6	9.9	8.6	18.7	6.7
Reserves	2.9	−2.5	0.3	−9.7	−6.6	−15.8	1.6
Hungary							
Current account	0.4	0.8	0.9	−8.9	−9.4	−5.7	−3.8
Capital account	−1.9	7.3	1.2	15.8	7.8	16.0	0.5
Reserves	1.6	−8.1	−2.0	−6.8	1.6	−10.4	3.3
Poland							
Current account	1.2	−1.8	1.0	−0.7	2.4	4.6	−1.0
Capital account	2.5	0.7	−0.2	0.9	−1.0	2.3	4.0
Reserves	−3.7	1.2	−0.6	−	−1.9	−7.6	−2.3
Slovakia							
Current account				−4.8	5.2	2.2	−11.0
Capital account				4.9	3.5	8.1	13.0
Reserves				−0.1	−8.8	−10.3	−2.0
Slovenia							
Current account	3.0	1.0	7.4	1.5	3.8	−0.2	0.3
Capital account	−3.0	−0.2	−2.4	−0.6	0.7	1.4	9.0
Reserves	−	−0.8	−5.1	−0.9	−4.5	−1.2	−3.2
Estonia							
Current account			3.4	1.4	−7.4	−5.1	−9.7
Capital account			1.9	7.4	8.7	8.1	12.1
Reserves			−5.3	−8.8	−1.3	−2.9	−2.3
Latvia							
Current account			1.8	7.0	−0.2	−3.4	−4.1
Capital account			8.0	7.9	4.1	1.3	8.7
Reserves			−9.9	−14.8	−3.8	2.1	−4.7
Lithuania							
Current account			n.a.	−3.0	−2.2	−10.2	−9.1
Capital account			n.a.	11.1	5.0	13.0	9.1
Reserves			n.a.	−7.9	−2.8	−2.8	−0.1

Notes: All capital account data here include net errors and omissions. A negative sign (−) in reserves data indicates an increase in reserves.

Abbreviation: n.a., not available.

Sources: UN/ECE, 1997; *Balance of Payments Statistics Yearbook 1997*, International Monetary Fund, Washington, DC, and *Table 7.2* in this volume.

increased from $234 million to $21,829 million, and a substantial increase was experienced in almost all of the countries listed.

At the same time, there were notable differences with respect to the evolution of the structure of these investments and the impact that these inflows had on major macroeconomic indices and policy-making. The reasons for this divergence include differences in exchange rate regime, geographical location and trade orientation, privatization policy (which has affected the nature and intensity of FDI), fiscal position, perceived political risk, and other elements of economic policy.

Exchange rate regimes, for instance, showed great variation, including the strictest fixed rate regimes based on currency board arrangements (Estonia, Lithuania), fixed regimes within narrow bands (Latvia, Hungary until March 1995, the Czech Republic until February 1996), crawling pegs and bands (Poland, Hungary from April 1995), and managed floats (Slovenia, Czech Republic from May 1997). Accordingly, the unexpected inflow of capital in some countries has put upward pressure on the domestic money supply, while in others it is the exchange rate that has been the most directly affected.

Some countries (especially Estonia and Hungary) have shown a relatively high degree of openness and a positive attitude toward FDI, including allowing and even routinely inviting foreign business to participate in bids for companies being privatized. This explains why these countries have achieved high shares of FDI in their inflows in certain years (see *Table I.4*). Where mass privatization was based on vouchers distributed only among residents (as in the Czech Republic and Latvia), the likelihood that FDI will play a major role in the inflows has been substantially lower.

The liberalization of capital movements progressed in the various CEECs at different paces. Estonia, for example, started very early with liberalization and moved much further than the other countries. In 1995 and 1996, the Czech Republic, Hungary, and Poland made substantial steps to liberalize capital movements in order to meet the requirements for acceding to the OECD. Slovenia, however, has been lagging behind, its reintroduction of certain capital controls resulting in a critical reaction from the European Commission (Horváth *et al.,* 1997).

The impact of the sudden capital inflows to CEECs has unfolded in many ways. The most frequently emphasized positive impact of financial inflows is that they complement customarily low indigenous savings and thereby augment investment. The most straightforward and favorable impact of these flows was that nonacquisition ("greenfield") FDI directly contributed to gross investment and, within it, to gross fixed capital formation. As experience in other parts of the world shows, this direct impact is usually small. For the Visegrád countries, Hunya (1998) found that in 1993–1996 the direct contribution of FDI to gross fixed capital formation amounted to 10–16% in Hungary, 2–3% in the Czech Republic and Slovenia, and

Table I.4. Capital account[a] and major components as a ratio.

	1990	1991	1992	1993	1994	1995	1996
Croatia							
Capital account (US$ million)		589	−162	345	685	2,203	1,871
FDI (%)			−9.9	21.4	14.3	3.7	18.7
Medium-, long-term funds (%)		−101.9	−15.4	28.4	69.5	−1.8	23.2
Short-term funds (%)		24.3	161.1	28.1	1.5	39.0	14.2
Errors and omissions (%)		177.6	−35.8	22.0	14.7	59.1	43.9
Czech Republic							
Capital account (US$ million)	−335	−1,110	376	3,083	3,116	8,820	3,657
FDI (%)	−39.4	−46.2	261.4	17.9	24.0	28.6	38.0
Portfolio (%)	0.0	0.0	−6.9	51.9	27.4	15.4	19.9
Medium-, long-term funds (%)	−110.4	−102.9	85.1	26.5	35.6	38.2	85.0
Short-term funds (%)	−0.6	269.3	−339.1	1.8	21.1	11.0	25.3
Errors and omissions (%)	250.7	−19.9	99.5	1.9	−8.2	6.7	−22.8
Hungary							
Capital account (US$ million)	−689	2,453	436	6,090	3,254	7,011	219
FDI (%)	−45.1	59.5	337.4	38.2	33.7	62.9	906.8
Portfolio (%)	−133.7	47.5	224.1	64.4	75.7	29.1	−393.2
Medium-, long-term funds (%)	149.2	18.1	−462.6	−10.1	−38.9	−12.2	−874.0
Short-term funds (%)	129.6	−25.2	1.1	7.5	29.5	20.1	−462.1
Errors and omissions (%)	n.a.	n.a.	n.a.	n.a.	n.a.	n.a.	−851.1
Poland							
Capital account (US$ million)	1,461	551	−186	790	−937	2,749	5,268
FDI (%)	0.7	21.2	−152.7	73.4	−57.8	41.3	52.0
Portfolio (%)	0.0	0.0	0.0	0.0	66.6	42.6	3.6
Medium-, long-term funds (%)	−252.2	−774.4	681.7	−75.7	47.4	−45.1	−4.5
Short-term funds (%)	−204.0	−209.6	941.9	−146.5	93.2	61.6	38.0
Errors and omissions (%)	24.6	−129.4	−26.9	74.6	24.3	−1.0	9.1
Slovenia							
Capital account (US$ million)	−519	−22	−302	−81	102	257	540
FDI (%)	0.4	−186.4	−37.4	−137.0	128.4	66.1	33.3
Portfolio (%)	−0.6	0.0	3.0	−3.7	−32.4	−3.9	118.1
Medium-, long-term funds (%)	−49.7	222.7	−1.0	−156.8	−8.8	202.7	43.9
Short-term funds (%)	59.2	804.5	39.7	414.8	11.8	−112.8	−92.2
Errors and omissions (%)	90.6	−736.4	95.7	−12.3	4.9	−46.7	−2.2
Estonia							
Capital account (US$ million)			20	125	202	291	524
FDI and portfolio (%)			394.8	123.2	98.2	63.9	48.7
Medium-, long-term funds (%)			47.5	67.5	3.6	16.4	30.7
Short-term funds (%)			−130.7	−65.9	−19.8	9.3	28.1
Errors and omissions (%)			−27.7	−40.7	13.1	10.9	−4.0
Latvia							
Capital account (US$ million)			110	171	149	61	466
FDI and portfolio (%)			39.2	29.8	104.2	400.5	86.3
Medium-, long-term funds (%)			30.1	57.3	58.5	104.1	13.2
Short-term funds (%)			0.0	21.6	21.5	−94.4	27.5
Errors and omissions (%)			30.8	−8.8	−84.1	−310.2	−27.0
Lithuania							
Capital account (US$ million)			n.a.	296.3	210.7	783.6	718.4
FDI and portfolio (%)			n.a.	10.1	16.9	11.2	29.9
Medium-, long-term funds (%)			n.a.	53.2	61.1	37.6	67.1
Short-term funds (%)			n.a.	5.6	36.4	19.4	−5.3
Errors and omissions (%)			n.a.	31.1	−20.6	36.7	7.6

[a]Capital account data here include net errors and omissions.

Abbreviation: n.a., not available.

Sources: UN/ECE (1997); *Balance of Payments Statistics Yearbook 1997*, International Monetary Fund, Washington, DC; and *Table 7.2* in this volume.

1% in Slovakia. In any case, both nonacquisition and acquisition FDI brought indirect positive synergies to the region, especially by strengthening market institutions and competition, enforcing market behavior of the enterprises, and furthering the restructuring process by bringing imported advanced technology and know-how to companies dominated by obsolete equipment and inefficient management.

In those CEECs with underdeveloped banking systems, capital inflows (in the broader sense, not just FDI) improved enterprises' access to finance and induced competition among banks. Furthermore, in some of the countries, capital inflows helped to alleviate the foreign exchange constraint on development by financing net imports, increasing international reserves to desired levels, and/or facilitating paying off excessive external debt.

CEEC policymakers soon realized, however, that the much desired inflow of foreign capital was having worrisome side effects. Depending on the environment, recently stabilized prices may face renewed inflationary pressures; the exchange rate may appreciate in real terms (and in the case of floating exchange rates, even in nominal terms), leading to a deterioration in international competitiveness of domestic products and current account deficits; if the inflows increasingly finance consumption, that may also lead to current account deficits; and if subject to sudden reversals, inflows may have serious destabilizing effects.

The mixed blessing character of the capital inflows derives, however, not only from the unavoidable combination of benefits and disadvantages of those flows, but also from the fact that there is not a single, reliable policy instrument, nor even a policy mix, that would treat the detrimental effects of the inflows in a straightforward manner. The policies usually advised have strong side effects, such as limiting the effectiveness of the monetary policy, saddling the government and national bank with quasi-fiscal costs, contributing to an increase in domestic interest rates (thereby further encouraging inflows), and bringing into question the government's commitment to keeping to its liberalization course.

The world has had striking experiences with capital flows that suddenly switch from being beneficial to leading to economic disasters. The financial crises in Latin America at the beginning of the 1980s, in Mexico and subsequently in the rest of Latin America in the mid-1990s, and recently in East Asia, have all had painful repercussions for the real economy.

Capital inflows are crucial for transition economies in the process of catching up with the developed world, thus the search for the most appropriate policy options for tempering the detrimental effects of these flows is imperative. One of the goals of this volume is to assist in this search by attempting to grasp the nature and characteristics of the recent inflows to Eastern Europe.

In order to study this important question, the International Institute for Applied Systems Analysis (IIASA, Laxenburg) and the Ludwig Boltzmann Institute for Economic Policy Analysis (Vienna) jointly organized a project on "Financial Inflows to Transition Economies".[1] Two workshops were held at IIASA in December 1996 and May 1997, respectively. When the seminars took place, the emerging crisis in East Asia was not yet clearly visible to the participants, who came from international institutions, universities, and research centers in America and Europe. The papers and the discussion, however, anticipated many of the emerging policy issues, and clearly indicated the need for a strong and consistent micro- and macroeconomic policy if the beneficial effects of capital flows are to be harvested.

The chapters in the first part of the volume summarize the experience of the Latin American and East Asian countries. In addition to clarifying the macroeconomic problems brought about by capital inflows and the advantages and disadvantages of possible policies, these studies also make quantitative assessments of certain critical macroeconomic developments and policy actions. The macroeconomic development issue dealt with in Chapter 2 is the buildup of unsustainable and "excessive" current account deficits. Employing an intertemporal approach, the author analyzes relationships that help determine when the nature and size of a current account deficit calls for correction or resistance to capital inflows. With the example of two Asian countries, Chapter 3 examines the possibilities for effective monetary policy actions, with special emphasis on sterilized intervention in the face of massive capital inflows. Chapter 4 analyzes the virtues and drawbacks of capital controls by modeling and providing an econometric analysis of the effects and limitations of a certain capital control measure applied in Chile.

In the second part of the book, the CEE cases are presented. The reader will realize that each country is a special case. In view of the countries' varying histories and geographical locations, institutional arrangements, and economic policies, capital flows and the problems that they engender differ across countries, raising the need for differing policy responses. While the chapters seem to suggest that eventually each government had developments under control, recent events in East Asia and their tangible repercussions (in the CEECs as elsewhere in the world), suggest that policymakers can never be content with past achievements in wrestling with capital flows.

The book closes with a summary assessment of the nature of capital inflows in today's world in general, and in the transition countries in particular. The author recalls the debates that surround this phenomenon and tries to identify those issues where experts have come to some sort of consensus and those still open to discussion and policy experiment.

The authors and editors hope that this book will contribute to the understanding of, and efficient policy-making toward, the puzzling phenomenon of capital

---

[1]The organizers of the workshop are grateful for the scientific advice of Richard N. Cooper (Harvard University) and acknowledge the financial support of Bank Austria and Girocredit.

inflows. This phenomenon seems to be in continuous flux, rejecting the application of any ready recipe.

References

Holzmann, R., Gács, J., and Winckler, G., eds., 1995, *Output Decline in Eastern Europe: Unavoidable, External Influence or Homemade?* Kluwer Academic Publishers, Dordrecht, Netherlands.

Horváth, Á., Dvorsky, S., Backé, P., and Radzyner, O., 1997, EU opinions: The qualifying round for applicants, *Focus on Transition*, No. 2, Österreichische Nationalbank, Vienna, Austria.

Hunya, G., 1998, Integration of CEEC manufacturing into European corporate structures by direct investments, paper presented at the Phare-ACE workshop on "Impact of Foreign Direct Investment on Efficiency and Growth in CEEC Manufacturing", 29–30 May, Vienna Institute for International Economic Studies (WIIW), Vienna, Austria.

Kornai, J., 1980, *Economics of Shortage*, North-Holland, Amsterdam, Netherlands.

Lankes, H.P., and Stern, N., 1997, Capital flows to Eastern Europe and the former Soviet Union, paper presented at the NBER Conference on International Capital Flows, Woodstock, Vermont, 16–18 October.

UN/ECE, 1997, *Economic Bulletin for Europe*, **49**, United Nations Economic Commission for Europe (UN/ECE), New York and Geneva.

Part I

The Background: Capital Inflow Episodes and Their Lessons in Asia and Latin America

Chapter 1

Macroeconomic Policy Issues Raised by Capital Inflows

Vittorio Corbo

1.1 Introduction

To the surprise of many, in the early 1990s, less than a decade after the initiation of the Third World debt crisis, significant flows of private capital surged into many developing countries. As shown in *Table 1.1*, total capital flows to developing countries increased from an annual average of $8.8 billion in the period 1983–1989, to an annual average of $163.4 billion in the period 1990–1996. During the 1990s the flows reached $158.0 billion in 1994, and $231.1 billion in 1996. They then declined to $202.7 billion in 1997, the year of the Asian crisis (IMF, 1998).

The capital flows of the early 1990s are different from those of the late 1970s in two important respects. First, in the late 1970s the flows went mostly to the public sector to finance ambitious public expenditure programs and current account deficits, whereas the capital flows of the early 1990s were mostly channeled toward the private sector. Second, while syndicated bank lending dominated the flows of the late 1970s, foreign direct investment (FDI) and portfolio investment dominate the new wave of capital inflows.

Table 1.1. Capital flows to developing countries (US$ billion).

	1977–1982	1983–1989	1990–1996	1994	1995	1996	1997
Developing countries total	30.5	8.8	163.4	158.0	226.9	231.1	202.7
Net FDI	11.2	13.3	63.1	75.4	84.3	105.0	119.4
Net portfolio flows	−10.5	6.5	54.1	85.0	20.6	42.9	40.6
Other flows	29.8	−11.0	46.2	−2.4	122.0	83.2	42.7
Asia	15.8	16.7	64.3	69.3	96.9	111.5	56.2
Latin America	26.3	−16.6	47.5	43.4	57.7	67.1	83.8
Other	−11.6	8.7	51.6	45.3	72.3	52.5	62.7

Abbreviation: FDI, foreign direct investment.
Source: IMF (1995) for figures up to 1989 and IMF (1998) for other years.

Another characteristic of the flows is their regional concentration. A substantial portion of the flows has been directed to Asia and Latin America (see *Table 1.1*). More importantly, the distribution of flows has been more even across developing regions in the 1990s than in the 1970s. While in the 1970s about 86% of the net flows went to Latin America and 52% to Asia (with –38% going to other regions), in the period 1990–1996, 29% of the total flows went to the former and 39% to the latter (and 32% to other regions).

Not surprisingly, the increase in inflows to developing countries has been accompanied by a decline in the interest rate spreads over comparable US Treasury securities, reflecting a reduction in recipient countries' risk premia. However, after the Asian crisis, spreads increased again all across emerging markets.

Capital inflows are expected to bring many benefits to the recipient country, such as facilitating an increase in the pool of investable funds and the diversification of risks. But they also change the effectiveness of macroeconomic policies. Thus, because capital markets in the 1990s have become increasingly integrated, macropolicies must be designed in such a way as to take into account their implications for, and feedback from, the capital account; otherwise unexpected outcomes may ensue. For example, a tight monetary policy to dampen aggregate demand may turn out to be ineffective if it leads to larger capital inflows. This area of inquiry will not be pursued here, as much has been written on macroeconomic management under conditions of an open capital account.[1]

The recent crisis in Southeast Asia has reopened the debate on the costs and benefits of integration into world capital markets. In particular, some observers have attributed an important role to capital account liberalization both in the origin of the crisis and in its spread to other countries. However, it is important to understand that the revolution in telecommunications and information and financial technology has resulted in and facilitated a substantial integration of world capital markets. The challenge to any country that wants to be part of the international community is how best to maximize the benefits and minimize the risks associated with this integration.

Many reasons have been advanced to explain the crisis that originated in Thailand and spread to Indonesia, the Philippines, Malaysia, and through Hong Kong to Latin America. Among the typical explanations, one can single out the following: (i) a sharp real appreciation of their currencies and a resulting slowdown in their export growth; (ii) a large current account deficit as a share of GDP that made their economies vulnerable to external and internal shocks; (iii) a weak financial system; and (iv) the low quality of their investment activity. Although all the above reasons had some role to play in the initiation and propagation of the crisis, it is clear that a weak financial system and low investment quality were particularly important (Claessens and Glaessner, 1997; Krugman, 1998).

The purpose of this chapter is to review the factors that account for the inflows, the potential problems that they may cause, and the most effective way to benefit from inflows while reducing some of their potential costs.

1.2 The Liberalization of Capital Flows and Potential Problems

At a time when the contagion effects of a crisis that originated in Thailand are finding their way to Latin America, it is important to reassess the case for capital account liberalization and to restate some of the associated risks. Better access to international capital markets allows a country to choose an optimal level of investment and an optimal path for consumption. Specifically, the optimal policy is to invest up to the point where the marginal return to investment is equal to the cost of capital, and to select a consumption path that distributes consumption optimally over time subject to the intertemporal budget constraint. Furthermore, the FDI component of capital flows has a set of benefits, realized through access to technology and markets.

In a given time period, a country should import capital to smooth consumption or to finance profitable investment opportunities if the optimal level of national savings is insufficient to finance the desired level of investment. The above considerations represent the case for net flows. In a competitive market economy, with no distortions in the intermediation of foreign saving, individual market decisions will lead to the optimal level. Gross flows also serve an important economic purpose:

they expand the opportunities for portfolio diversification. Through this channel, gross flows provide investors with an opportunity to improve on the risk–return trade-off that they would face under financial autarky.[2]

However, surging capital inflows have some macroeconomic repercussions. First, the macroeconomic effect of the adjustment to accommodate a higher level of net capital inflows is an appreciation of the real exchange rate. The mechanism that generates this real appreciation works through the increase in aggregate expenditures that the capital inflow will ultimately entail. Given the pattern of aggregate demand, some of the increase in expenditures will go into tradable goods (i.e., both exports and domestically produced goods competing with imports) and nontradable goods. The increase in expenditures on tradable goods will increase the size of the trade deficit and will help to absorb the capital inflow directly.

If this were the only adjustment required, there would be no grounds for concern, because the higher trade deficit would be financed directly by the capital inflow, with no disequilibrium created in the market for nontradable goods. The only reason to worry about capital inflows would be whether the debt/GDP ratio is sustainable. Part of the increase in expenditures, however, will be spent on nontradable goods, creating, at the initial value of the real exchange rate (the relative price of tradables and nontradables), an excess demand for nontradable goods. This excess demand will result – independently of the exchange rate regime – in an increase in the relative price of nontradable goods. This increase will, in turn, create incentives for a reallocation of factors from the tradables to the nontradables sector, and for a switching of expenditures toward tradable goods. The final result is a real appreciation, a larger nontradable sector, and a smaller tradable sector.

A real appreciation is the mechanism that accompanies the increase in expenditures and permits the eventual absorption of the capital inflow into the domestic economy through a larger trade deficit. This is the standard macroeconomics of the transfer problem. The same type of process would be triggered by an oil discovery or a large trade gain. The only difference is that, in the latter case, the export good that benefits from the increase in price will end up with an increase in production, while the rest of the tradable sector will lose resources to the expanding export good and to the nontradable sector. This is the well-known "Dutch disease" problem analyzed by, for example, Corden and Neary (1982) and Corden (1984).

Capital flows may be very sensitive to developments in the local economy, which may trigger a sudden reversal, forcing a costly adjustment process on the country. The best line of defense against this reversal is through appropriate macroeconomic policies and a sound financial system. Still, contagion effects will develop and a country must be ready to adjust to them. The globalization of the world economy is a fact of life. The only choice that individual countries have is in deciding on the best ways to maximize the net benefits of this reality.

1.3 Factors Behind the Recent Surge in Capital Flows: A Preliminary Analysis

Many factors have contributed to the recent surge in capital flows, including the following: (i) pull factors resulting from reforms introduced by the recipient countries; (ii) push factors resulting from lower interest rates and a deceleration of growth in the industrial countries; (iii) the emergence of large institutional investors in industrial countries; and (iv) the worldwide liberalization of current account transactions and financial flows. We will discuss each of these developments in turn.

Pull Factors Resulting from Reforms Introduced in Recipient Countries

In recent years, many developing countries have carried out radical changes in their economic policies and institutions aimed at raising long-term economic growth and reducing poverty. Improved macroeconomic and incentive frameworks in these recipient countries have increased rates of return and reduced country risks. As a result, risk-adjusted returns have increased, *ceteris paribus*, resulting in larger inflows of capital.[3]

This change has been assisted by an emerging consensus, both in academic and policy-making circles, on the types of policies that promote growth with equity. A development model has emerged from this new consensus that emphasizes the following: macroeconomic stability; competitive market structures; integration into the world economy (outward orientation); and a government sector responsible for creating the institutions necessary for the functioning of a market economy, for the provision of public goods, and for improving access to social services (i.e., education, health, nutrition, and housing) for the poorest groups in the population.[4]

To achieve macroeconomic stability in this new model, the public finances must be put in order and the monetary and exchange rate policy must have as its main objective the achievement of a credible and sustainable reduction in inflation.[5] The creation of an independent central bank has been part of the institution-building effort to facilitate macroeconomic stability. In this new model, the role of the public sector has drastically changed. The government is deemed responsible for delivering macroeconomic stability – in the form of a low and predictable rate of inflation and a sustainable current account deficit – and for creating the conditions for fostering an open and competitive private economy.

In order to create these conditions, the state is supposed to gradually dismantle trade protection, deregulate labor and financial markets, and cease its involvement in the production and distribution of private goods. Furthermore, it must create an appropriate regulatory framework to promote both competition and private ownership in public utility services and the development of a sound financial system. The state must also concentrate its efforts on developing a system where property rights are clearly defined and enforced and where the poorest groups of the population have proper access to basic social services.

Some of these policy actions were part of the Washington consensus, a concept introduced by Williamson (1990); however, as the recent experiences of Argentina, Peru, Poland, and the Czech Republic illustrate, some of the new reformers have gone far beyond that consensus in completely overhauling their policies and institutions.[6]

Push Factors Resulting from Lower Interest Rates and Deceleration of Growth in Industrial Countries

These factors are related to movements in short-term interest rates in industrial countries and the state of the business cycle in these countries (Calvo *et al.*, 1993). In particular, lower interest rates in industrial countries "push" capital toward developing countries in search of better rates of return. Also, a slowdown in economic activity in industrial countries reduces company profits, making opportunities in other countries more attractive.

Emergence of Large Institutional Investors in Industrial Countries

These investors need international diversification of their portfolios (IMF, 1995).

Worldwide Liberalization of Current Account Transactions and Financial Flows

The substantial movement toward current account convertibility has generally been accompanied by the elimination of the discrimination against FDI, and by improvements in the enforcement of property rights. An additional factor in many countries has been the liberalization of financial flows, and, in some countries, a reduction in country risk following the successful reduction of their debt on a nonconfrontational basis.

1.4   Should Governments Tamper with the Workings of the Normal Transfer Mechanism?

Although capital flows may play an important role in improving the welfare of the recipient country, under some circumstances they can be a matter of serious concern.[7] Some of these concerns are as follows:

- In the presence of micro-distortions, these resources may be misused or their inflow encouraged beyond the optimal level. For countries with weak banks (ones with low or negative net worths and large shares of connected lending) and poor banking regulation and supervision, access to capital inflows can exacerbate the moral hazard problems arising from the presence of deposit insurance. These problems may result in a financial bubble and eventually a costly financial crisis.

- Suppose that a country is reducing inflation from the moderate (20–30% per annum) to the single-digit level using high domestic interest rates and restricting the appreciation of the nominal exchange rate. In such a case, free access to international capital markets would result in large inflows and a temporary increase in monetary aggregates and inflation. An attempt to sterilize the monetary effects of the inflows would leave the original cause of the inflows (i.e., the difference between the domestic and the international interest rate, adjusted for the expected rate of depreciation) untouched and result in a costly accumulation of foreign reserves. In this case, a change in the macroeconomic mix toward a tighter fiscal policy and a less restrictive monetary policy would be the appropriate response. Attempts to reduce the size of the inflows through capital controls are of limited and temporary effectiveness, since private agents quickly develop methods of evading such controls.
- For countries that have initiated trade reforms, a large temporary level of capital inflows (or a temporary improvement in the terms of trade) would result in a substantial real appreciation, which may work against the reform of the trade regime. In such a case, the government might try to implement policies to minimize the size of the real exchange rate appreciation. Successful trade reforms will be the ones that combine initial reductions in the mean tariff and in the variance of tariffs with an initial real depreciation, accompanied by a fairly stable real exchange rate adjusted for fundamentals (Thomas *et al.*, 1990).
- A country may be concerned about the volatile and temporary nature of some inflows, due to the possible costs resulting from a sudden reversal of the inflows. These costs may be especially high in the presence of downward real wage rigidity.
- Access to capital flows increases the financial system's lending capacity and may result in a larger gap between domestic spending and output. The resulting current account deficit could become excessively large, making the country vulnerable to a sudden reversal of capital inflows.

The rest of this chapter illustrates each of these potential problems and the methods of dealing with them. First, however, we briefly summarize the main features of the microeconomic distortions that have played a major role in generating the recent surge in capital inflows to emerging markets. It should be stated from the outset that the best protection against some of these problems is an appropriate macroeconomic framework and a well capitalized, regulated, and supervised financial system.

1.5   Microeconomic Distortions and Capital Inflows

In countries with weak banks and poor systems of banking regulation, private returns are quite different from social returns, resulting in undue risk-taking on the part of banks and excessive capital inflows. This is particularly so in countries with explicit or implicit deposit insurance systems, where moral hazard problems may encourage more risk-taking than is socially optimal. Moreover, access to capital inflows allows financial intermediaries to pursue risky strategies. In this case, there may be improper financial intermediation, leading to bubbles in asset markets.

Micro-distortions may also result from reforms of a more macroeconomic nature (e.g., trade liberalization or stabilization). Excessive borrowing may also result when the borrowing itself creates negative externalities associated with the cost of default on an international loan contract. Real sector distortions, such as wage rigidities, may necessitate a costly adjustment to a reversal of inflows.

1.6   Macroeconomic Management and Capital Inflows

Without micro-distortions, a higher level of capital inflows is a good thing, although macroeconomic adjustments may create unwelcome effects.

A typical macroeconomic objective is to achieve a target for the inflation rate, while providing some stability to the nominal exchange rate through the use of a currency band or target-zone exchange rate system. In these types of arrangements, the main monetary policy tool is the trajectory of the interest rate. However, with an open capital account and uncovered interest rate parity, movements in the domestic interest rate result in movements in the nominal exchange rate within its band. The domestic monetary authority may wish to constrain the exchange rate's movements within the band to lower its volatility; it may also be interested in defending the band. Because the interest rate instrument is already tied to the inflation target, the absence of a second instrument to respond to exchange rate movements may lead the authorities to restrict capital inflows through taxes or outright capital controls. In this case, a more efficient instrument would be fiscal policy. The motivation for the formulation of a policy response to capital inflows is often the fear that such flows may result in a loss of monetary control and a real appreciation.

In countries pursuing a preannounced path for the exchange rate as an anchor for inflation and inflationary expectations, capital inflows result in a monetary expansion. The monetary expansion would then result in upward pressure on asset prices, an expansion of the domestic demand for nontradable and tradable goods, and an overheating of the economy. The increase in domestic demand, in turn, would generate a real exchange rate appreciation and a deterioration in the current account. To the extent that capital inflows are themselves unstable, their presence increases the degree of macroeconomic instability.

Thus, in a country that is in the expansionary phase of its business cycle, and that has a predetermined nominal exchange rate, capital flows will severely reduce the efficiency of a tight monetary policy (according to the well-known Mundell-Fleming model). The best policy here is a more active use of fiscal policy for stabilization purposes. If the stabilization program is in its early stages (and credibility is just being built up) and/or an appropriate system of banking regulation and supervision is not in place, a country without the capacity to alter fiscal policy may decide to restrict capital flows or the amount of foreign borrowing.

Restrictions on capital flows in different countries and in a single country over time may act in many ways, including the following:

(i)   Restricting the net inflow of capital, either by restricting gross inflows or promoting gross outflows.
(ii) Restricting foreign exchange accumulation by increasing exchange rate risk, by encouraging a current account offset, or by allowing the exchange rate to appreciate.
(iii) Accepting the reserve accumulation, but trying to limit its effects on the monetary base.
(iv) Accepting the increase in the monetary base, but attempting to restrain its effects on broader monetary aggregates.
(v)   Accepting the monetary expansion, but attempting to offset its expansionary effects on aggregate demand.

With respect to these options, one could ask the following questions: are these policies feasible? And, if so, are they optimal? The answers are given below.

(i) Policies to Reduce Net Capital Inflows

As long as it is profitable to bring capital into a country as a result of a margin in uncovered interest parity, capital will flow in despite the controls. Evading the controls may take place through many types of current or capital account transactions. However, these policies may work in the short run, while the private sector is investing in methods of evading the controls. These policies are second-best solutions (when compared to those below), but may increase welfare if the inflow results from a domestic distortion in the form of a weak and poorly regulated and supervised banking system. Indeed, many distortions become more costly in the presence of capital inflows (e.g., distorted intertemporal prices, or moral hazard in banking). These types of restrictions may also be justified in the presence of a financial bubble or of bandwagon effects in international lending.

Related policies aimed at increasing capital outflows may not be effective (Mathieson and Rojas-Suarez, 1993). Furthermore, the removal of controls on outflows may not result in lower net capital inflows and may even lead to larger inflows (see Labán and Larraín, 1993; or Bartolini and Drazen, 1997).

(ii) Policies to Restrict Foreign Exchange Accumulation

These are the best policies when the central bank is offering free insurance through currency swap facilities. The introduction of an exchange rate band to replace a fixed exchange rate system increases exchange rate risk, creates a wedge between domestic and foreign interest rates, and discourages capital inflows.

Policies that try to limit foreign exchange accumulation by accelerating the opening of the economy and, in this manner, generating a current account off- set, have limited efficacy at most. The current account deficit is a macroeconomic phenomenon. Thus, the effect of trade liberalization on the current account is am- biguous and depends upon the macroeconomic policy stance that accompanies that liberalization. Indeed, in some models, trade liberalization improves the current account. The empirical evidence for the relation between trade liberalization and the size of the current account shows the most common case to be an improvement in the current account, as a result of the accompanying macroeconomic policies (Michaely *et al.*, 1991).

If the inflow is believed to be temporary, there are problems in allowing the exchange rate to appreciate, as doing so will generate high adjustment costs later. The exchange rate's role as a nominal anchor is thereby weakened.

(iii) Policies to Control Monetary Effects of Reserve Accumulation

The standard policy here is sterilized intervention. However, such a policy works only as long as capital mobility is less than perfect. Sterilization of the inflow has clear quasi-fiscal costs. Moreover, as long as there is a spread between the domestic interest rate and the foreign interest rate augmented by the devaluation expectation, the capital flows will continue.

(iv) Policies that Attempt to Restrain Effects on Monetary Aggregates

These policies are effected through the deposits held by public institutions at the central bank. The need for such policies can be partially avoided through disin- termediation, but that has real costs in terms of efficiency and economic growth. If banks are poorly supervised and regulated and are taking undue credit risks, an increase in reserve requirements is only a secondary solution. The best policy is to

Table 1.2. Measures for dealing with capital inflows.[a]

	Restrictions on capital inflows (i)	Liberalization of outflows (i)	Exchange rate adjustment (ii)	Liberalization of current account (ii)	Sterilization/ open market (iii)	Selective sterilization (iii)	Increasing reserve requirements (iv)	Fiscal adjustment (v)
Argentina							x	x
Chile	x	x	x	x	x		x	
Colombia	x	x	x	x	x	x	x	
Indonesia	x		x		x	x	x	x
Rep. of Korea		x	x	x	x			
Malaysia	x	x	x	x	x	x		x
Mexico	x	x	x	x	x		x	
Philippines	x	x	x	x	x	x		x
Thailand	x	x	x	x	x	x	x	x

[a] Numbers in parentheses correspond to those in the text.
Source: Corbo and Hernández (1996), Montiel (1996), and unpublished material.

restrict the activities of the banks taking the credit risks and to eliminate the causes of the moral hazard problem.

(v) Policies that Attempt to Offset Expansionary Effects on Aggregate Demand

In this instance the authorities let the interest rate adjust until uncovered interest rate policy is fulfilled and use fiscal policy tools to control potential overheating of the economy. The main problems with this are the usual lags in the preparation of fiscal actions and their effects once implemented: fiscal policy may be too inflexible to be available at the needed time.

Table 1.2 summarizes the different measures that a number of countries have taken recently to deal with capital inflows.

Montiel (1996) summarizes macroeconomic performance in these same countries, all of which experienced capital outflows (see *Table 1.3*).

1.7 Conclusion

For countries with weak financial systems that are concerned with the side effects of capital inflows, the first best strategy should be to upgrade the quality of financial supervision and regulation, with increasing use of incentive regulation. For countries that are following a restrictive monetary policy with limited exchange rate flexibility, sterilized intervention can work temporarily, but its quasi-fiscal costs are

Table 1.3. Macroeconomic outcomes.

	Base money growth	Money multiplier	Stock market boom	Real exchange rate	Inflation	Current account deficit	Investment rate
Argentina	Lower	Increased	1991–1993	Large appreciation	Much lower	Higher	Higher
Chile	Increased	Increased	1989–1993	Small appreciation	Much lower	Stable	Higher
Colombia	Temporary increase	Stable	1991–1993	Appreciation	Temporary increase	Higher	Higher
Indonesia	Restrained	Increased	1990–1993	Depreciation	Stable	Stable	Stable
Rep. of Korea	Restrained	Decreased	–	Depreciation	Temporary increase	Higher	Higher
Malaysia	Increased	Decreased	1988–1993	Stable	Increased	Much higher	Much higher
Mexico	Temporary increase	Increased	1989–1993	Large appreciation	Much lower	Much higher	Higher
Philippines	Temporary increase	Stable	1993	Stable	Temporary increase	Higher	Higher
Thailand	Stable	Increased	1988–1993	Stable	Much lower	Much higher	Much higher

Source: Montiel (1996).

high. Moreover, such a policy is not sustainable, as the difference between domestic interest rates and foreign ones (adjusted for expected depreciation) encourages the inflows to continue.

Capital controls may work temporarily – especially if applied across the board – while more permanent corrections in policies are made. Controls that stay in place for too long, however, encourage the investment of resources in ways to avoid them. As a result, such controls become ineffective and resources are wasted in rent-seeking. For countries trying to reduce inflation by relying on monetary policy and simultaneously using a fixed exchange rate or a narrow band, fiscal policy must play an active role.

Moving toward a more flexible exchange rate regime, such as an exchange rate band, has many advantages: it helps to restore the effectiveness of monetary policy; it increases the exchange rate risk faced by market participants, thereby discouraging short-term capital flows; and finally, it helps to accommodate changes in the fundamentals through time via appreciation in equilibrium real exchange rates.

Notes

[1] For macroeconomic management in the presence of capital inflows, see, among others, Schadler *et al.* (1993), IMF (1995), Montiel (1995), and Corbo and Hernández (1996).

[2] When liberalization of capital flows is accompanied by the entrance of foreign banks into the domestic financial system, the increased competition also benefits local producers and consumers in terms of lower spread and product innovation in banking.

[3] One area in which the change in policy has been particularly pronounced is the treatment of FDI. Awareness of FDI's potential contribution to growth – through the introduction of new technologies, higher quality design, and access to market channels – has led to a substantial reduction or outright elimination of restrictions on capital and dividend repatriations.

[4] For an assessment of the consensus on policy reforms, see Williamson (1990) and Corbo and Fischer (1995).

[5] In many countries, the creation of an independent central bank and the upgrading of institutionality and accountability in budgetary matters have been integral parts of an institution-building effort aimed at facilitating the attainment and maintenance of macroeconomic stability.

[6] On the evaluation of the results of reforms, see Corbo and Fischer (1995). The consensus on policies that promote growth with equity has been supported by at least three separate factors: (i) a better understanding of the factors that contribute to long-term growth (achieving and maintaining macroeconomic stability, a high level of human capital accumulation, and the promotion of export-led growth; see Edwards, 1993 and Fischer, 1993); (ii) the favorable record of such recent adjusters as Chile, Poland, and

the Philippines; and (iii) the collapse of the central planning model in the ex-Soviet Union and the former socialist countries of Central and Eastern Europe.

[7] For a more detailed discussion of these concerns, see Calvo *et al.* (1994), Corbo and Hernández (1996), and Montiel (1996).

References

Bartolini, L., and Drazen, A., 1997, Capital-account liberalization as a signal, *American Economic Review*, **87**(1):138–154.

Calvo, G., Leiderman, L., and Reinhart, C., 1993, Capital inflows to Latin America: The role of external factors, *IMF Staff Papers*, **40**(1):108–151.

Calvo, G., Leiderman, L., and Reinhart, C., 1994, The capital inflows problem: Concepts and issues, *Contemporary Economic Policy*, July:54–66.

Claessens, S., and Glaessner, T., 1997, Are financial sector weaknesses undermining the East Asian miracle? *Directions in Development*, The World Bank, Washington, DC, USA.

Corbo, V., and Fischer, S., 1995, Structural adjustment, stabilization and policy reform, in J. Behrman and T.N. Srinivasan, eds., *Handbook of Development Economics*, North-Holland Publishing Company, Amsterdam, Netherlands.

Corbo, V., and Hernández, L., 1996, Macroeconomic adjustment to capital inflows: Lessons from recent Latin American and East Asian experience, *World Bank Research Observer*, **11**(1):61–85.

Corden, W.M., 1984, Booming sector and Dutch disease economics: Survey and consolidation, *Oxford Economics Papers*, **36**:359–380.

Corden, W.M., and Neary, J.P., 1982, Booming sector and de-industrialization in a small open economy, *Economic Journal*, **92**:825–848.

Edwards, S., 1993, Openness, trade liberalization, and growth in developing countries, *Journal of Economic Literature*, **31**(3):1358–1393.

Fischer, S., 1993, Role of macroeconomic factors in growth, *Journal of Monetary Economics*, **32**(December):485–512.

International Monetary Fund (IMF), *World Economic Outlook*, various issues, IMF, Washington, DC, USA.

Krugman, P., 1998, What happened to Asia? mimeo, Massachusetts Institute of Technology, Cambridge, MA, USA.

Labán, R., and Larraín, F., 1993, Can a liberalization of capital outflows increase net capital inflows? Working Paper No. 155, Instituto de Economía, Universidad Católica de Chile, Santiago de Chile, Chile.

Mathieson, D.J., and Rojas-Suarez, L., 1993, *Liberalization of the Capital Account: Experiences and Lessons*, IMF Occasional Paper No. 103, International Monetary Fund, Washington, DC, USA.

Michaely, M., Papageorgiou, D., and Choksi, A.M., eds., 1991, *Liberalizing Foreign Trade: Lessons of Experience in the Developing World*, Volume 7, Basil Blackwell, Cambridge, MA, USA.

Montiel, P.J., 1995, The new wave of capital inflows to developing countries: Country policy chronologies, The World Bank, Washington, DC, USA.

Montiel, P.J., 1996, Policy responses to surges in capital inflows: Issues and lessons, in G. Calvo, M. Goldstein and E. Hochreiter, eds., *Private Capital Flows to Emerging Markets After the Mexican Crisis*, Institute for International Economics and Austrian National Bank, Institute for International Economics, Washington, DC, USA.

Schadler, S., Carkovic, M., Bennett, A., and Kahn, R., 1993, *Recent Experiences with Surges in Capital Inflows*, IMF Occasional Paper No. 108, International Monetary Fund, Washington, DC, USA.

Thomas, V., Martin, K.M., Nash, F., 1990, Lessons in trade policy reforms, *Policy Research Paper 2*, The World Bank, Washington, DC, USA.

Williamson, J., 1990, *Latin American Adjustment*, Institute for International Economics, Washington, DC, USA.

Chapter 2

Sustainable and Excessive Current Account Deficits

Helmut Reisen

2.1 The Shortcomings of the Lawson Doctrine

The current account deficits analyzed in this chapter share three important features. First, they are 'private-sector driven' in the (non-Ricardian) sense that they do not reflect government budget deficits. The chapter examines the experiences of four Asian and four Latin American countries that have not had public-sector deficits during the 1990s, but have received sizable capital imports. With the public budget in balance and private capital mobile in these countries, the current account is determined by private-sector saving–investment decisions. Second, the current account deficits are 'overfinanced' (except just prior to currency crises), implying a positive overall balance of payments and rising levels of foreign exchange reserves. Third, a part of the deficit is financed by cyclical capital flows, as has been generally the case for a large share of emerging-market flows during the 1990s (see, e.g., Calvo *et al.*, 1996). Their cyclical determination makes these flows subject to reversal.

Commenting on concerns about the United Kingdom's balance of payments in a speech to the International Monetary Fund (IMF), the UK Chancellor Nigel Lawson concluded in September 1988 (a year before a deep crisis with falling output and surging unemployment set in): "We are prisoners of the past, when UK current

An earlier version of this chapter was published in *Empirica*, Volume 25, Number 1, 1998, Kluwer Academic Publishers.

account deficits were almost invariably associated with large budget deficits, poor economic performance, low reserves and exiguous net overseas assets. The present position could not be more different". What came to be known internationally as the Lawson doctrine is a proposition that has been most eloquently expressed by Max Corden (1977, and, with some qualifications, 1994):

> The current account is the net result of savings and investment, private and public. Decentralized optimal decisions on private saving and investment will lead to a net balance – the current account – which will also be optimal. There is no reason to presume that governments or outside observers know better how much private agents should invest and save than these agents themselves, unless there are government-imposed distortions. It follows that an increase in a current account deficit that results from a shift in private sector behavior should not be a matter of concern at all. On the other hand, the public budget balance is a matter of public policy concern and the focus should be on this. [Corden, 1994]

The fact, however, that large current account deficits primarily reflected a private-sector saving–investment imbalance did not prevent private capital markets from attacking currencies in Chile (early 1980s), in the UK and the Nordic countries (late 1980s), in Mexico and Argentina (mid-1990s), and in several Asian countries (1997). So what was wrong with the Lawson doctrine? Five issues can be identified.

- First, in a forward-looking rational-expectations framework, current account balances are always the result of private-sector decisions, with or without public-sector deficits. With Ricardian equivalence, a public budget deficit immediately stimulates private savings to pay for future taxes. People who subscribe to the Lawson doctrine are thus saying that they do not believe in Ricardian equivalence (i.e., they believe in optimal private-sector decisions, but not in rational expectations). In fact, the Ricardian offset coefficient has been estimated to average 0.5 for developing countries (Edwards, 1995); other things being equal, a deterioration in the current account worth 5% of GDP thus requires the public-sector deficit to worsen by 10% of GDP.
- Second, current private-sector liabilities are often contingent public-sector liabilities. Foreign creditors may force governments to turn private-sector debt into public-sector obligations, as happened in Chile after 1982. Furthermore, private-sector losses tend to be absorbed eventually by the public sector, either in terms of tax revenue forgone or through costly resolutions of banking crises, in particular when financial institutions are deemed 'too large to fail'. Balance of payments and financial crises are often caused by common factors, such as domestic financial liberalization, implicit deposit insurance, or exchange rate-based stabilization plans (Kaminsky and Reinhart, 1996).

- Third, observed and expected returns to saving and investment can be distorted by various market failures. One such failure is termed the Harberger externality. In this, private borrowers may not internalize the rising marginal social cost of their external borrowing that arises from the upward-sloping supply of foreign capital (Harberger, 1985). Another failure involves excessively optimistic expectations about permanent income levels after major changes in the policy regime. These expectations can lead to overborrowing, because financial market institutions fail as efficient information conduits between depositors and borrowers (McKinnon and Pill, 1995). Financial market bubbles may add to this boom mentality by discouraging private savings through wealth effects.
- Fourth, a worsening current account deficit may lead to an unsustainable appreciation in the real exchange rate. Such an appreciation can conflict with development strategies based on the expansion of exports and efficient import substitution, which rely on a reliable and competitive exchange rate. Overvalued exchange rates cause suboptimal investments that are costly to reverse, undermine active trade promotion, export diversification and productivity growth, and breed capital flight. Large swings in real exchange rates, often a result of temporary capital flows, have been found to significantly depress machinery and equipment investment and thus long-run growth performance (Agosin, 1994).
- Fifth (as also stressed by Corden, 1994), markets are concerned with country risk and look at a country's total debt ratio. Therefore, the current account as a whole, and not just the sources of its change, become relevant. Once debt ratios and current account deficits exceed certain levels (see Section 2.2), decentralized decision making can lead to excessive borrowing from a national point of view (again, due to the Harberger externality), particularly when increased borrowing is for consumption rather than for investment into the tradables sector.

Table 2.1 displays three hard-landing episodes in Latin America where the required switch in the current account was accompanied by sharp drops in real GDP, even sharper cuts in private per capita consumption, and often strong depreciation in the real exchange rate. During the bust, the benefits of consumption-smoothing and growth enhancement through foreign savings did indeed ring hollow. As the Lawson doctrine has been repeatedly discredited, there is a need to define when private-sector driven current account deficits might be considered either sustainable or excessive. This is all the more important as demographic divergences between the aging OECD area and the emerging countries can be predicted to stimulate massive net capital flows from North to South (MacKellar and Reisen, 1998).

The chapter is structured as follows. First, various long-term sustainability measures of debt-augmenting capital flows are presented. As large current account

Table 2.1. Macroeconomic adjustment in selected countries.

Country	Year (period average)	Current account/ GDP (%)	Real GDP growth (%)	Real private consumption growth (%)	Real exchange rate apprecia- tion (%)
Chile	1980	−7.1	7.8	1.5	22.0
	1981	−14.5	5.6	2.4	8.4
	1982	−9.5	−14.1	−12.4	−20.6
	1983	−5.6	−0.7	−5.1	−20.4
Mexico	1993	−6.5	0.6	−2.1	5.8
	1994	−7.8	3.5	3.7	−3.7
	1995	−0.3	−6.9	−9.2	−28.1
Argentina	1993	−2.9	6.0	1.2	7.4
	1994	−3.5	7.4	3.7	1.7
	1995	−0.8	−4.4	−9.2	0.4

Sources: *International Financial Statistics*, IMF; J.P. Morgan, *World Financial Markets*; author's calculations.

deficits will not be financed by foreigners forever, authorities need to know the required magnitude and time profile of the subsequent adjustment back to the payments balance. As an unsustainable deficit is not necessarily an "excessive" deficit, the size of the current account deficit does not give rise to normative judgments; what matters, rather, is the source of the deficit. Second, an intertemporal approach is applied to the current account for a prediction of how the 'equilibrium' current account should respond to a reform-induced productivity rise and a drop in the world interest rate. This productivity rise and interest rate drop are two impulses that have figured prominently in the discussion on the determinants of recent capital flows to emerging markets. The final section of the chapter presents a case for resisting part of foreign savings when unsustainable currency appreciation, excessive risk-taking in the banking system, and a sharp drop in private savings coincide (for how to resist, see Reisen, 1996). Thus the appropriate policy response is to strike a balance between the benefits of consumption-smoothing and of financing viable investment versus the economic costs of excessive private borrowing. A case can be made that foreign direct investment (FDI) is less likely than other capital flows to stimulate excessive private consumption and a real appreciation problem.

2.2   Long-term Sustainability

A large external deficit will not be financed by foreigners indefinitely. At one point there will inevitably have to be an adjustment back to the payments balance. It is thus not only important to know the sources of the current account deficit (see Section 2.3), but also the size and the time profile of the balancing adjustment.

That makes long-term sustainability of the current account deficit a benchmark of which authorities should be aware. This section presents a conventional debt dynamics equation to arrive at a notion of intertemporal solvency, emphasizing the role of potential GDP growth, the real exchange rate, and the desired level of foreign exchange reserves.[1] The section builds on recent work by Milesi-Ferretti and Razin (1996) and Edwards *et al.* (1996).

Let us first consider an economy in steady state, with liabilities as a fraction of the country's GDP that foreigners are willing to hold in equilibrium, denoted by d. This d can be interpreted as an 'equilibrium portfolio share'. In equilibrium, that is, with d held constant, the country accumulates net liabilities, equal to the current account deficit *CAD* plus the net accumulation of international reserves *FX*, both as fractions of GDP, in proportion to its long-run GDP growth, γ, thus

$$CAD + \Delta FX = \gamma d. \tag{2.1}$$

Long-run GDP growth also exerts two indirect effects on the steady state current account that is consistent with a stable debt-to-GDP ratio. First, as the economy expands, the desired level of international reserves also grows. The literature on the demand for international reserves has empirically identified two important determinants (Heller and Khan, 1978). The first is the level of imports. The second is the variability in the balance of payments which, by creating uncertainty, increases the demand for reserves. In the following, uncertainty in the balance of payments is ignored. In principle it can be incorporated into the analysis, by making predictions about the coefficient of variation from the time trend in the foreign reserve ratio. Denoting real annual import growth by η, the change in the desired reserve ratio can be expressed as:

$$\Delta FX = [(1+\eta)/(1+\gamma)]FX - FX. \tag{2.2}$$

Incorporating (2.2) into (2.1) yields:

$$\gamma d = CAD + [(\eta - \gamma)/(1+\gamma)]FX. \tag{2.3}$$

A second channel through which GDP growth indirectly impacts on debt dynamics is the Balassa–Samuelson effect.[2] In the long run, relative growth leads to real exchange rate appreciation, largely driven by the evolution of productivity differentials between traded and nontraded goods in the domestic economy and in the rest of the world. Real exchange rate appreciation per unit of GDP growth, denoted by ε, reduces both debt and foreign exchange reserves as a fraction of GDP, so that equation (2.3) becomes:

$$(\gamma + \varepsilon)d = CAD + [(\eta + \varepsilon - \gamma)/(1+\gamma)]FX. \tag{2.4}$$

Table 2.2. Current account deficits (CAD) in steady state (in %).

Country	CAD	$= (\gamma + \varepsilon)d^*$	$- [(\eta + \varepsilon - \gamma)/(1+\gamma)]FX^*$	Memo: d	FX
Argentina	1.6	$= (0.043 + 0.007)50$	$- [(0.318 + 0.007 - 0.043)/1.043]\ 3.5$	34	6.1
Chile	2.0	$= (0.042 + 0.006)50$	$- [(0.069 + 0.006 - 0.042)/1.042]11.4$	30	20.2
Mexico	1.9	$= (0.052 + 0.008)50$	$- [(0.126 + 0.008 - 0.052)/1.052]14.0$	51	5.4
Peru	3.8	$= (0.078 + 0.009)50$	$- [(0.152 + 0.009 - 0.078)/1.078]\ 6.5$	51	13.6
Indonesia	3.0	$= (0.061 + 0.004)50$	$- [(0.073 + 0.004 - 0.061)/1.061]\ 9.9$	45	8.7
Malaysia	1.7	$= (0.065 + 0.014)50$	$- [(0.111 + 0.014 - 0.065)/1.065]39.6$	38	28.3
Philippines	2.1	$= (0.057 + 0.004)50$	$- [(0.112 + 0.004 - 0.057)/1.057]16.6$	56	13.5
Thailand	2.8	$= (0.072 + 0.010)50$	$- [(0.133 + 0.010 - 0.072)/1.072]19.7$	50	20.0

Note: See text and Appendix for explanation.

Equation (2.4′) describes the steady-state current account deficit that can be sustained over the long run if the debt ratio remains constant and desired reserves rise in proportion to import growth:

$$CAD = (\gamma + \varepsilon)d - [(\eta + \varepsilon - \gamma)/(1+\gamma)]FX. \qquad (2.4')$$

Table 2.2 provides numerical estimates of equation (2.4′) for four Latin American and four Asian countries. The variables d (total external debt/GDP) and FX (international reserves/GDP) refer to 1996 estimates as given in J.P. Morgan, *World Financial Markets*, 28 March 1997. The parameters γ, ε, and η are estimated as described in the Appendix.

Table 2.2 displays the results of calibrating equation (2.4′) for the long-run steady-state current account ratio, implying constant debt and reserve levels relative to GDP. As a high debt ratio can be sustained by a larger deficit in the current account than a smaller debt ratio, it is assumed for all sample countries that foreign investors are comfortable with tolerating a debt ratio of 50%, i.e., $d^* = 50$. The target level of foreign exchange reserves for all countries (FX^*) is assumed to be equal to half the import ratio (six months of imports). The sustainable steady-state deficits on the current account displayed in *Table 2.2* are essentially driven by potential growth rates. Their size, as a percentage share of GDP, is relatively small, fluctuating between 1.6 (Argentina) and 3.8 (Peru).

While the steady-state simulations in *Table 2.2* are relevant for those countries close to the external debt threshold of 50% of GDP, Argentina and Chile reported debt stocks greatly below this level. For a certain period, therefore, countries with low levels of debt or high foreign exchange reserves can run a higher current account deficit. *Table 2.3* considers a hypothetical adjustment of the current debt–GDP ratio to 50% and of foreign exchange reserves to a target level of half the import–GDP ratio (m). The resulting 'transitional' current account deficits

Helmut Reisen 35

Table 2.3. Transitional current account deficits (CAD; five-year adjustment to $d^* = 50$ and $FX^* = 0.5m$).

Country	1/5CAD	=	$1/5[d^* - (1 - \gamma - \varepsilon)d$	−	$FX^* - ((1 - \eta - \varepsilon)/1 + \gamma)FX]$
Argentina	3.67	=	18.65	−	0.27
Chile	5.15	=	−17.63	+	8.13
Mexico	−5.16	=	−16.78	−	9.02
Peru	1.36	=	3.44	+	3.38
Indonesia	−0.45	=	−0.49	−	1.73
Malaysia	−0.87	=	11.32	−	15.69
Philippines	−3.30	=	−7.41	−	9.08
Thailand	0.32	=	5.94	−	4.35

Note: See text for explanation.

vary greatly between countries. To reach the targeted debt–GDP and reserve levels within five years, Mexico would have to run a current account *surplus* worth more than 5% of GDP. Chile, by contrast, could enjoy a five-year period of current account *deficits* of 5% of GDP to find itself at the imposed levels of debt stocks and foreign exchange levels.

A largely unresolved issue is whether net FDI flows should be included in the calculations for sustainable current account deficits. From 1970 to 1982, Singapore ran on average a current account deficit equal to 12.1% of GDP; in the early 1970s, the deficit peaked at around 20% of GDP several times. Almost one-half of the corresponding net capital inflows consisted of FDI. Real GDP growth averaged 8.6% per year over the period, and the domestic saving rate doubled from 21% in 1970 to more than 40% in 1982, but a balance of payments crisis never developed. This anecdotal evidence – which supports the view that FDI lessens the possibility of later balance of payments problems – is supported by Frankel and Rose (1996). They find in a panel of annual data for over 100 developing countries from 1971 to 1991 that a high ratio of FDI to debt is associated with a low likelihood of a currency crash. This raises the question of whether FDI is special with respect to its macroeconomic implications. There is a strong presumption that it is, for the following reasons:

- First, FDI is largely determined by noncyclical considerations. Being governed rather by long-term profitability expectations, it is less subject to sudden shifts in investor sentiment. While, on an annual basis, large fluctuations of FDI *flows* are regularly observed, FDI *stocks* are largely illiquid and irreversible. FDI is less dependent on financial market sentiment. This observation is reinforced by Mexico's experience in 1995, when its capital account showed only a slightly reduced net inflow of FDI after the crisis in 1994.

- Second, the Harberger externality does not apply to FDI. Even if the supply schedule of FDI is upward-sloping, FDI is likely to produce positive external spillovers, comparable to agglomeration benefits. This conjecture implies that higher inflows of FDI carry positive externalities, by improving the host country's production function (Borensztein *et al.*, 1995). Moreover, returns to FDI are contingent on corporate profits and sovereign risk seems to apply less to FDI than to other forms of foreign capital inflows. As a result, foreign investors do not observe an upper limit of engagement, in contrast to debt flows.
- Third, to the extent that FDI is not induced by privatization (which represents, other things being equal, just a change in ownership), FDI inflows exert less upward pressure on the real exchange rate, minimizing the risk of 'Dutch disease'. Since FDI is likely to crowd in domestic investment, to the extent that it is 'green field' investment, it will stimulate a corresponding movement in the demand for foreign exchange by stimulating imports. Moreover, by stimulating investment rather than consumption, FDI creates an *ex ante* home goods excess supply in the recipient country. Equilibrium in the home goods market requires a depreciation of the real exchange rate to stimulate the demand for home goods (Artus, 1996).
- Fourth, in the absence of financial sector and foreign exchange distortions, FDI can improve the current account balance. Fry (1996) has shown that, despite the fact that FDI increases domestic investment, the positive direct and indirect (through accelerated growth) effects of FDI on national saving actually lead to an improvement in the current account in the long run. While the FDI impulse leads to a worsening of the current account in the first three years (for an average of six Asian countries), it induces growth and saving effects so as to improve the current account thereafter.

Capital is fungible, however, and the distinction between FDI and other capital account items (notably portfolio equity flows) can be blurred. Net FDI will also change the level of a country's net external liabilities just as any other capital flow.

When suggesting measures for judging whether actual current account deficits are sustainable in the long term, one conclusion can be made: actual deficit numbers alone cannot provide information about long-term sustainability. Any judgment needs to consider debt–GDP levels (current versus that tolerated by investors), official foreign exchange reserves (current versus targeted), the potential GDP growth rate, import growth, the Balassa–Samuelson effect, and the structure of capital inflows. Sustainability considerations do not make sense for FDI flows, as long as there is no widely held notion about the sustainability of net foreign liabilities for the stock of FDI invested in a country.

Table 2.4. Account effects predicted by the intertemporal approach.

Shock	Temporary			Persistent		
	Saving	Invest-ment	Current account	Saving	Invest-ment	Current account
Drop in the world interest rate						
below permanent average rate						
Net debtor countries	+	0	+	n.a.	n.a.	n.a.
Net creditor countries	–	0	–	n.a.	n.a.	n.a.
Rise in productivity						
Country-specific	+	0	+	–	+	–
Global	+	0	+	+	+	0

Abbreviation: n.a., not applicable.
Sources: See discussions in Obstfeld and Rogoff (1994); Glick and Rogoff (1995); and Razin (1995).

The size of the current account deficit does not give rise to normative judgments; a deficit worth 3% of GDP may be "excessive" in one country, while a deficit worth 12% of GDP may be justified for another country. What distinguishes such deficits is not so much whether they are driven by public-sector or private-sector decisions, as there is some evidence for a Ricardian offset and because private debt is a contingent public-sector liability. Rather, what matters for governments is the source of the current account deficit.

2.3 The Intertemporal Approach: Defining "Excessive" Deficits

In principle, the intertemporal approach to the current account is able to provide a benchmark for defining "excessive" current account deficits in the context of models that yield predictions about the equilibrium path of external imbalances (Milesi-Ferretti and Razin, 1996). International capital mobility opens the opportunity to trade off present levels of absorption against future absorption. If saving falls short of desired investment, foreigners have to finance the resulting current account deficit, leading to a rise in the country's net foreign liabilities. The intertemporal approach views the current account as the outcome of forward-looking dynamic saving and investment decisions (Obstfeld and Rogoff, 1994), which are driven by expectations of future productivity growth, interest rates and other factors.

We do not describe here the whole maximization problem for the representative consumer (among the many assumptions necessary to produce behavioral predictions are intertemporal separability of preferences and perfect foresight; see Obstfeld and Rogoff, 1994; Glick and Rogoff, 1995; and Razin, 1995). *Table 2.4* shows some important predictions of the intertemporal approach about how the 'equilibrium' (first-period) current account should respond to a drop in the world interest rate and a reform-induced productivity rise (the two capital-flow determinants emphasized in the literature).

The results in the table imply the following:

- Capital-importing countries, as net foreign debtors, should raise the saving rate in response to cyclical portfolio flows, which are interest-driven. The current account deficit should decline (or move into surplus) as people smooth consumption in the face of temporarily low interest payments. For net creditor countries, temporarily low interest rates should result in opposite current account effects. If a net debtor country widens its current account deficit in response to temporary interest rate reductions, the response may destabilize rather than smooth the intertemporal consumption path.
- The intertemporal approach does not necessarily predict an increasing current account deficit when capital flows are attracted by country-specific productivity surges. The 'equilibrium' response of the current account depends crucially on the expectation of whether the productivity surge is temporary or permanent. In both cases, the productivity surge raises output immediately, but only a persistent rise in productivity raises permanent income. The reason for this is that only a permanent productivity surge induces investment and a higher future capital stock. The rise in permanent income also causes consumption to rise more than output, resulting in a strong current account deficit as a result of lower saving and higher investment. In contrast, a transitory increase in productivity should result in an opposite current account effect (a lower deficit), because there is no effect on investment and agents save part of any transitory increase of income (in the permanent-income model of consumption).
- Productivity surges should not necessarily be interpreted as country-specific in origin, but could be part of a broader global shock. A persistent productivity-enhancing shock common to all countries raises the world rate of interest. This should dampen consumption in net debtor countries sufficiently to offset the consumption effects arising from higher permanent income brought about by higher investment. Since all countries cannot improve their current accounts, world interest rates rise until global savings and investment are balanced. A global transitory productivity shock produces excess world saving and thereby exerts downward pressure on interest rates. A temporary drop in world interest rates results in lower current account deficits for net debtor countries, as analyzed above.

How well then does the intertemporal approach explain actual current account balances in our eight sample countries? It is still too early, in view of the limited

Table 2.5. Panel estimates on current account equations, 1988–1993 (t-values in brackets).

1. $CAD_t = b_1 I_{t-1} + b_2 \Delta\theta_t^c + b_3\theta_t^w + b_4 CAD_{t-1} + b_5 TOT_t + b_6 r_t^w$

-0.2	-0.02	-0.06	$+0.6$	-0.001	$+0.01$
(-0.87)	(-0.14)	(-1.7)	(2.52)	(-1.02)	(0.31)

Estimation: Fixed effect model using OLS framework;
number of observations: 48; $R^2 = 0.59$; DW = 2.53

2. $BD_t = b_1(S^{pr} - I)_t$

-0.4
(-10.2)

$R^2 = 0.84$; DW = 1.48; number of observations = 48

$CAD_t = b_1 I_{t-1} + b_2 \Delta\theta_t^c + b_3\theta_t^w + b_4 CAD_{t-1} + b_5 TOT_t + b_6 r_t^w$

-0.1	$+0.1$	-0.1	$+0.5$	-0.001	$+0.003$
(-0.45)	(1.16)	(-2.54)	(3.42)	(-0.48)	(0.89)

$R^2 = 0.58$; DW = 2.62; number of observations = 48

Estimation: Simultaneous equation system with Generalized Method of Moments estimation (equivalent to 3 Stages Least Square method).

Sources: The instrumental variable method was used; residuals were heteroskedastic-consistent. Current account, gross domestic investment, and terms of trade index are from the World Bank database. US treasury bill interest rate minus change in CPI index, and private savings are from the IMF. Domestic productivity and global productivity (GDP-weighted average for G7 countries) are Solow residuals from Cobb-Douglas production functions and are from the World Bank database and national accounts.

number of reliable observations of productivity developments in the sample countries for the recent capital inflow period, to estimate investment and current account equations for the individual sample countries. We therefore present for the period 1988–1993 panel estimates for the current account equation:

$$CAD_t = b_0 + b_1 I_{t-1} + b_2 \Delta\theta^c t + b_3\theta^w t + b_4 CAD_{t-1} + b_5 TOT_t + b_6 r^w t \qquad (2.5)$$

where CAD is the current account deficit as a fraction of GDP, I is gross domestic investment as a fraction of GDP, θ^c and θ^w are domestic and global productivity (the Solow residual derived from Cobb-Douglas production functions), TOT is the terms of trade index, and r^w is the real US treasury bill interest rate (see *Table 2.5*, first panel).

The second panel estimate in *Table 2.5* introduces a government budget reaction function similar to Summers (1988), where

$$BD_t = b_0 + b_1(S^{pr} - I)_t. \tag{2.6}$$

The government budget deficit BD_t responds to changes in the balance between private savings S^{pr} and investment (all variables as a fraction of GDP). Equation (2.6) can be taken as evidence of current account targeting, so that equation (2.5) has to be estimated in a simultaneous equation system.

As seen in *Table 2.5*, there is a strong negative correlation between the size of the private current account and the size of the budget deficit. The results for the current account equation are largely the same, however, in the direct and the simultaneous panel estimate. All parameters show the expected sign as predicted in *Table 2.4*, but only global productivity enters significantly among the determinants stressed by the intertemporal approach.

The results in *Table 2.5* lead to the tentative conclusion that econometric tests derived from the intertemporal approach to the current account cannot explain actual current account deficits in major capital-flow recipient countries. This means either that the observed current account deficits have been excessive, or that the benchmark (derived from the intertemporal approach) is ill-defined or insufficiently represented in our estimates. While global productivity (as defined in *Table 2.5*) has stagnated during the observation period 1988–1993, country-specific productivity surges were observed in Argentina and Peru. These countries could be predicted by the intertemporal approach to run current account deficits, due to transitorily higher investment levels (and possibly lower saving rates), assuming that the productivity surges were permanent.

Tables 2.6 and *2.7* explore the issue in more detail. A comparison is made from 1987 to the year when foreign capital started to flow in with the capital inflow period. *Table 2.6* shows that the capital inflow period coincided with a strong surge in efficiency (the inverse of the incremental capital–output ratio) in Argentina and Peru only. Efficiency rose also slightly during the inflow period in Mexico, Indonesia, and more recently, in the Philippines. By contrast, much higher investment rates in Malaysia and Thailand resulted in declining levels of capital productivity; in a milder form, the same phenomenon was visible in Chile, reflecting the law of diminishing marginal returns of investment (and probably indicating unproductive 'excess' investment).

The sharpest deterioration in current account balances was seen in Malaysia, Mexico, and Thailand, and not in those countries (Argentina, Peru) where country-specific productivity surges were particularly important (*Table 2.7*). In Argentina, Mexico, Malaysia, and the Philippines private consumption (as a share of GDP) rose by more than 3% of GDP on average during the inflow period, often reflecting

Table 2.6. Investment, growth, and productivity.[a]

	First year of inflow	Investment ratio		Real GDP growth rate		Efficiency[b]	
		Before inflow	After inflow	Before inflow	After inflow	Before inflow	After inflow
Argentina	1991	16.9	18.3	−1.4	7.5	−9.0	41.0
Chile	1990	20.9	23.3	8.0	7.0	37.8	30.6
Mexico	1989	18.8	19.7	1.7	3.0	8.8	15.6
Peru	1992	17.8	20.4	−2.7	4.8	−14.8	28.4
Indonesia	1990	32.7	34.1	6.0	7.0	18.3	20.6
Malaysia	1989	23.6	35.1	7.2	8.7	30.2	23.5
Philippines	1992	19.6	23.2	3.8	4.2	20.1	16.2
Thailand	1988	27.6	39.8	9.6	9.0	34.7	23.6

[a]Data are annual averages for the first period from 1987 to the year that preceded the first year of inflow and for the second period from the year after the inflow started to 1995 (investment, efficiency) or to 1996 (growth). For Argentina and Mexico, the second period stops in 1994.
[b]Efficiency is defined as the inverse of the investment rate to the real GDP growth rate.
Sources: J.P. Morgan, *World Financial Markets*; IMF, *International Financial Markets*; author's calculations.

a strong rise in public savings. As noted above, a rise in private consumption can be validated by higher investment rates (indicating expectations of higher permanent income levels) or by current income levels being below potential. In Argentina and Mexico, however, the size of the switch in private consumption relative to the switch in investment looks excessive.

The evidence suggests that the intertemporal approach fails to predict the macroeconomic responses of most capital-flow recipient countries. In the case of Chile, the existence of effective capital controls may provide part of the explanation for the failure of the intertemporal approach (which assumes full capital mobility). In the case of the other sample countries (for which full openness can be assumed), the change in macroeconomic aggregates must be explained by determinants not captured by the consumption-smoothing approach.

The predictive power of the intertemporal approach to the current account may remain very limited for developing countries, despite their higher financial openness. Heymann (1994) raises some important questions, notably in the context of recurrent episodes of private-sector overindebtedness; e.g., How plausible is the assumption of rational expectations during a period when there is a 'regime change' in the economy? How correct can forecasts be about the expected value of future prices and quantities, and how realistic and binding is the intertemporal budget constraint to induce agents to plan according to these forecasts? Such questions raise deep doubts about the claim that 'The intertemporal approach to the current account offers a viable framework for assessing macroeconomic policy' (Obstfeld and Rogoff, 1994).

Table 2.7. Change in foreign reserves and current account balances (in % of GDP).

	Change[a]				Memo		
	Foreign reserves	Current account	Saving	Private consumption	First year of inflow	Peak year current account deficit	Peak current account deficit
Argentina	1.4	−1.9	−0.5	4.5	1991	1994	3.5
Chile	5.7	1.2	3.7	1.2	1990	1996	3.3
Mexico	−0.7	−6.9	−6.0	3.1	1989	1994	7.8
Peru	5.9	0.1	2.8	0.7	1992	1995	7.2
Indonesia	−0.2	−0.5	0.9	−0.3	1990	1996	3.7
Malaysia	8.8	−11.8	−0.7	3.4	1989	1995	8.1
Philippines	3.4	−1.6	1.9	3.8	1992	1994	4.5
Thailand	8.2	−5.8	6.4	−4.9	1988	1995	8.2

[a]Changes are calculated as the annual average changes between the first period from 1987 to the year that preceded the first year of inflow and the second period from the year after the inflow started to 1995 (for Argentina and Mexico, 1994). Saving rates were derived as residual.

Sources: IMF, *International Financial Statistics*; J.P. Morgan, *World Financial Markets*; World Bank, *Global Development Finance*; author's calculations.

2.4 When Should Large Current Account Deficits Be Resisted?

With theory providing little guidance as to when precisely a current account deficit is considered 'excessive', policymakers will have to rely on first principles and on hard empirical evidence from balance of payments crises. The first principle is that current account deficits should be seen to finance productive investment, preferably into the exportable sector, in order to prepare for the amortization of rising foreign liabilities, which is inevitable. The empirical link between large current account deficits, consumption booms, surges in bank lending, and subsequent banking crises is well documented (Gavin and Hausmann, 1996). Therefore, payments deficits owing to private spending booms suggest great risks to the public sector – risks of tax revenue losses and costly bank crisis resolutions, as shown in *Table 2.8*.

It seems obvious that such costs imposed on the public sector suggest that governments should engage in some stabilizing measures to moderate private spending booms (by restrictive fiscal policies or credit restrictions for private borrowers). However, it is less obvious that resistance to large current account deficits should be included in these measures. Distortions should be corrected at the source; the twin payment and banking crises seem to originate in: (i) domestic financial

Table 2.8. Episodes of systemic banking crises with heavy capital inflows.

Country	Scope of crisis	Cost of rescuing banks (% of GDP)
Argentina (1980–1982)	16% of assets of commercial banks; 35% of total assets of finance companies	55.3
Chile (1981–1983)	45% of total assets	41.2
Israel (1977–1983)	Entire banking sector	30.0
Finland (1991–1993)	Savings banks affected	8.2
Mexico (1995–?)	Commercial banks' (past due loans)/(gross loans) ratio reaches 9.3% in February 1995	12–15

Sources: Bank for International Settlements, Basle, 63rd Annual Report (1993); and Caprio and Klingebiel (1996).

deregulation; (ii) implicit deposit insurance; or (iii) protracted exchange rate-based stabilization plans.

(i) Since the 1980s, the link between banking crises and balance of payments crises has strengthened. Kaminsky and Reinhart (1996) trace 71 balance of payments crises and 25 banking crises during the period 1970–1995. While they report only 3 banking crises on 25 balance of payments crises during 1970–1979, they find 22 banking crises on 46 payments crises over 1980–1995. They find that financial liberalization (which occurred mostly from the 1980s) plays a significant role in explaining the probability of a banking crisis preceded by a private lending boom. A banking crisis, in turn, helps to predict a currency crisis. There is also clear evidence for the OECD countries that rapid and extensive financial deregulation has tended to lower household savings by lessening liquidity constraints (Blundell-Wignall and Browne, 1991). While most of that drop in private savings could be interpreted as a temporary stock adjustment to a higher consumption path, there is evidence that household saving rates have remained low (Andersen and White, 1996).

(ii) Information asymmetries, reinforced by the lack of institutions that monitor and supervise credit risk, produce moral hazard and adverse selection. Firms with a high risk-return profile have an incentive to borrow heavily, as their exposure is limited by bankruptcy laws. Consumers incur excessive debt when they feel that their debt is not comprehensively monitored. In principle, banks and other intermediaries may attempt to reduce credit risk through credit rationing. This limits the extent to which liberalization can ease liquidity constraints. But when the government insures deposits against adverse outcomes, it alters how the banking system views the risks associated with making loans – it introduces moral hazard. This results in higher bank lending, which in turn can underpin excessively optimistic expectations about the success of reform (McKinnon and Pill, 1995).[3]

(iii) Exchange rate-based stabilization plans have often been accompanied by a boom in bank lending, which in turn fuels a boom in consumption spending. Disinflation, unlike money-based stabilization, produces a rise in real-money balances. This is a result of central bank intervention to peg the currency, and of money demand rising as domestic wealth holders convert their assets back into domestic currency. As long as foreign exchange intervention is unsterilized, the capital inflows are fully intermediated through the banking system. This allows a boom in credit to agents who have been rationed previously as a result of inflation and financial repression (Reisen, 1993). Subsequently, overvaluation due to inflation inertia causes a recession and a deterioration of bank assets as a result of nonperforming loans and lower asset prices.

Although the source of these private spending booms is domestic, one must question whether foreign savings worsen the boom (Corden, 1994). In the absence of foreign capital inflows, the spending boom would manifest itself not in a current account deficit, but in higher interest rates. The critical question then is what kind of investment would be crowded out by the rise in domestic interest rates? With ineffective bank supervision (e.g., as a result of too rapid financial deregulation), the average productivity of borrowing may decline as risk-averse investors withdraw from the pool of potential borrowers. The failure to finance productive investment would be the cost of the decision not to accept capital inflows; the excess of the risk-adjusted domestic interest rate over the world interest rate would act as a measure of the distortion created by that decision. The result of the decision to accept or resist inflows would be ambiguous.

In the McKinnon–Pill model the closed economy financial market failure is reflected in higher financial yields, but its effect on quantities – borrowing and consumption – is ambiguous, depending on offsetting income and substitution effects. Excessively optimistic expectations about future permanent income levels, resulting in both overconsumption and overinvestment, are financed by excessive borrowing from the rest of the world. This distortion is reinforced by foreign savings. The McKinnon–Pill solution to the distortion is similar to a Pigou–Harberger tax (specifically, a reserve requirement on foreign deposits) that achieves the optimal balance of consumption-smoothing and excessive borrowing.

The first best solution to the boom distortion triggered by exchange rate-based stabilization is to announce, at the start of the stabilization plan, that the peg will be temporary, and will be followed by more nominal exchange rate flexibility. While this is easier said than done, it does not do away with the immediate remonetization and real exchange rate appreciation that characterize the first phase of disinflation.

Temporary support from selective controls on short-term capital controls may well be needed (Hausmann and Reisen, 1996). If an unsustainable currency appreciation, excessive risk-taking in the banking system, and a sharp drop in private savings coincide, there is a case for resisting foreign capital inflows. The appropriate policy response then must balance the benefits of consumption-smoothing and financing viable investment and the risks of excessive borrowing.

A case can be made for an open economy to accept all FDI, unless it creates new distortions as a result of new trade restrictions, and as long as it can be absorbed by the existing stock of human capital. From the perspective of the investor, FDI is less constrained by considerations of sovereign risk and portfolio limits than other types of capital flows. By crowding in domestic investment and having a minor initial effect on consumption (possibly unless privatization-induced), FDI is unlikely to generate a real appreciation problem.

Acknowledgments

I thank Guillermo Larraín and Julia von Maltzan for valuable assistance, as well as Guillermo Calvo, Max Fry, Reuven Glick, Robert Holzmann, 'Butch' Montes, and Assaf Razin for helpful comments on an earlier version.

Notes

[1] Interest payments on outstanding debt are ignored to keep the focus on the sustainable current account deficit. The loss of information is minor to the extent that average interest costs do not vary much across the sample countries.

[2] Measures of equilibrium real exchange rates are especially difficult to calculate for the transition countries, because their production structures and productivity levels are undergoing substantial changes (see Halpern and Wyplosz, 1996).

[3] In other words, bank lending supports excess credibility of liberalization and stabilization programs. For liberalization programs perceived as temporary (a hypothesis that does not seem apt to describe existing policy regimes in most capital-importing countries), it was a lack of credibility that was used to explain temporary spending booms as residents exploited a 'window of opportunity' (Calvo, 1987).

References

Agosin, M.R., 1994, Saving and Investment in Latin America, UNCTAD Discussion Papers, No. 90.
Andersen, P.S., and White, R.W., 1996, The Macroeconomic Effects of Financial Sector Reforms: An Overview of Industrial Countries, Bank for International Settlements, Basle, Switzerland (mimeo).

Artus, P., 1996, Le financement de la croissance par endettement extérieur, Document de travail No. 1996-05/T, Caisse des dépôts et consignations, Paris, France.

Blundell-Wignall, A., and Browne, F., 1991, Macroeconomic Consequences of Financial Liberalisation: A Summary Report, ESD Working Paper No. 98, Organisation for Economic Co-operation and Development, Paris, France.

Borensztein, E., De Gregorio, J., and Lee, J.-W., 1995, How Does Foreign Direct Investment Affect Economic Growth? NBER Working Paper No. 5057, National Bureau of Economic Research, Cambridge, MA, USA.

Calvo, G., 1987, On the costs of temporary policy, *Journal of Development Economics*, **27**:147–169.

Calvo, G., Leiderman, L., and Reinhart, C., 1996, Inflows of capital to developing countries in the 1990s, *Journal of Economic Perspectives*, **10**(2):123–140.

Caprio, Jr., G., and Klingebiel, D., 1996, *Bank Insolvency: Bad Luck, Bad Policy, or Bad Banking?* The World Bank, Washington, DC, USA.

Corden, W.M., 1977, *Inflation, Exchange Rates and the International System*, Oxford University Press, Oxford, UK.

Corden, W.M., 1994, *Economic Policy, Exchange Rates and the International System*, Clarendon Press, Oxford, UK.

Edwards, S., 1995, Why are Saving Rates So Different Across Countries? An International Comparative Analysis, NBER Working Paper No. 5097, National Bureau of Economic Research, Cambridge, MA, USA.

Edwards, S., Steiner, R., and Losada, F., 1996, Capital inflows, the real exchange rate and the Mexican crisis of 1994, in H. Sautter and R. Schinke, eds., *Stabilization and Reform in Latin America: Where Do We Stand?* Vervuert, Frankfurt, Germany.

Frankel, J., and Rose, A.K., 1996, Currency Crashes in Emerging Markets: Empirical Indicators, NBER Working Paper No. 5437, National Bureau of Economic Research, Cambridge, MA, USA.

Fry, M., 1996, How foreign direct investment in Pacific Asia improves the current account, *Journal of Asian Economics*, **7**(3):459–486.

Gavin, M., and Hausmann, R., 1996, The Roots of Banking Crises: The Macroeconomic Context, Working Paper Series 318, Inter-American Development Bank, Washington, DC, USA.

Glick, R., and Rogoff, K., 1995, Global versus country-specific productivity shocks and the current account, *Journal of Monetary Economics*, **35**(1):159–192.

Halpern, L., and Wyplosz, C., 1996, Equilibrium Exchange Rates in Transition Economies, IMF Working Paper 96/125, November.

Harberger, A., 1985, Lessons for debtor-country managers and policymakers, in G.W. Smith and J.T. Cuddington, eds., *International Debt and the Developing Countries*, pp. 236–257, The World Bank, Washington, DC, USA.

Hausmann, R., and Reisen, H., eds., 1996, *Securing Stability and Growth in Latin America: Policy Issues and Prospects for Shock-Prone Economies*, Organisation for Economic Co-operation and Development, Paris, France.

Heller, H.R., and Khan, M.S., 1978, The demand for international reserves under fixed and floating exchange rates, *IMF Staff Papers*, **25**(4):623–649.

Heymann, D., 1994, En la interpretacion de la cuenta corriente, *Economía Mexicana*, **3**(1).

Kaminsky, G., and Reinhart, C.M., 1996, The Twin Crises: The Causes of Banking and Balance-of-Payments Problems, Working Paper No. 17, Center for International Economics, University of Maryland, College Park, MD, USA.

Larraín, G., 1996, Productividad del gasto publico y tipo de cambio real, in F. Morande, ed., *Estudios Empiricos de Tipo de Cambio Real in Chile*, CEP/ILADES Georgetown University, Santiago, Chile.

MacKellar, L., and H. Reisen, 1998, A Simulation Model of Global Pension Fund Investment, IR-98-34, International Institute for Applied Systems Analysis, Laxenburg, Austria.

McKinnon, R., and Pill, H., 1995, Credible Liberalizations and International Capital Flows, Stanford University, Stanford, CA, USA (mimeo).

Milesi-Ferretti, G.M., and Razin, A., 1996, Sustainability of Persistent Current Account Deficits, NBER Working Paper No. 5467, National Bureau of Economic Research, Cambridge, MA, USA.

Obstfeld, M., and Rogoff, K., 1994, The Intertemporal Approach to the Current Account, NBER Working Paper No. 4893, National Bureau of Economic Research, Cambridge, MA, USA.

Razin, A., 1995, The dynamic-optimizing approach to current account, in P. Kenen, ed., *Understanding Interdependence: The Macroeconomics of the Open Economy*, Princeton University Press, Princeton, NJ, USA.

Reisen, H., 1993, Integration with disinflation: Which way? in R. O'Brien, ed., *Finance and the International Economy: 7, The Amex Bank Review Prize Essays*, pp. 128–145, Oxford University Press, Oxford, UK.

Reisen, H., 1996, Managing volatile capital inflows: The experience of the 1990s, *Asian Development Review*, **14**(1):72–96.

Sachs, J., and Warner, A., 1995, Economic reform and the process of global integration, *Brookings Papers on Economic Activity*, **1**:1–118.

Summers, L., 1988, Tax policy and international competitiveness, in J.A. Frenkel, ed., *International Aspects of Fiscal Policies*, University of Chicago Press, Chicago, IL, USA.

Appendix: Estimation of Parameters γ, ε, and η

GDP can be seen as the result of a transformation of key factors of production. Thus a theoretically appropriate way to estimate potential GDP and its growth, γ, is to estimate the available volume of factor inputs in the business sector into a numerically specified production function. However, even small estimation errors for the individual parameters of the production function (e.g., output elasticities, rate of technical progress, or degree of slack) can lead to rather implausible estimates for potential output. Instead, a simpler approach can be employed – the peak-to-peak method, which uses actual GDP data only for the derivation of potential GDP estimates.

This method is implemented by first identifying the peak of actual GDP in each cycle and connecting these data points by interpolation. The procedure is applied for two different observation periods, for 1960–1995 (for Malaysia 1970–1995) and for the period since "openness" reform as classified by Sachs and Warner (1995) until 1995. For Argentina and Peru, Sachs and Warner classify the year of opening as 1991, for the Philippines 1988, for Mexico 1986, and for Chile 1976; the other countries were accounted as open from 1960 on. Annual GDP data are used, except for Peru and the Philippines where good quarterly data are available and where the reform period is relatively short. The resulting GDP series can be seen as an approximation of the highest attainable level of output at any given point in time.

In a second step, the average ratio of actual GDP to the highest attainable GDP for each cycle is calculated – a measure of the 'normal' degree of slack in the eight economies. This ratio is then used to scale the series of highest attainable GDP to derive estimates for potential GDP. The annual growth rate of potential GDP is then obtained by regressing the potential GDP series on a time trend. The results give largely plausible estimates, except possibly for Mexico and the Philippines, where potential growth for the period since openness reform is lower than for a full period. The results reported in *Table 2.2* use the growth rates of potential GDP obtained for the period since reform, except for Mexico and the Philippines where estimated and forecast GDP growth rates, based on J.P. Morgan, have been taken.

Estimates of the real exchange rate appreciation effect of GDP growth relative to the USA are obtained from Larraín's (1996) instrumental variables analysis of the determinants of real exchange rates (viz. the dollar) for a sample of 28 Asian and Latin American countries over the period 1960–1990. These estimates control for the effects of other determinants, i.e., government spending, degree of openness, and the terms of trade. The parameter ε is calculated by scaling these figures by the annual growth rate of potential GDP. Note that since the relationship between real exchange rates and relative GDP levels is nonlinear, a given estimate of the growth rate of potential GDP implies a greater real equilibrium exchange rate appreciation at higher relative income levels; witness the difference between Malaysia and Indonesia, for example.

Finally, estimates of the future annual real import growth rate, η, are simply extrapolated out of the reform period sample for each country. Argentina's annual import growth may seem implausibly high, but it must be recognized that Argentina is still a very closed economy in terms of the import ratio, m, and that the potential for natural trade through, for example, the Mercosur free trade agreement is far from exhausted.

Chapter 3

Capital Inflows to Asia:
The Role of Monetary Policy

Timothy James Bond

3.1   Introduction

The magnitude of private capital inflows to developing countries has increased sharply in recent years. Owing to the macroeconomic pressures that these inflows generate, economists have devoted substantial attention to the issue of designing an appropriate policy response. The Asian experience with capital inflows offers some important lessons in this area. This chapter reviews the capital inflow episode in Asia, and focuses in more detail on the experience of two countries: Indonesia and Thailand.[1] Monetary policy played a key role in these countries, both as a response to capital inflows, when sterilization was used to limit the expansion of monetary aggregates, and as a cause, when increases in interest rates to counter overheating attracted additional inflows. For this reason, and because the importance of monetary policy has been underemphasized in the literature,[2] this chapter analyzes the relationship between monetary policy and capital flows in some detail. It concludes that the Asian experience with capital inflows illustrates the difficulty of maintaining monetary independence with an exchange rate target and an open capital account. Under these conditions, monetary policy will decline in

An earlier version of this chapter was published in *Empirica*, Volume 25, Number 1, 1998, Kluwer Academic Publishers.

usefulness as capital mobility rises, and macroeconomic management will become more difficult. Consequently, countries should develop other means of responding to capital flows, such as fiscal policy or increased exchange rate flexibility.

The Asian experience with capital inflows can provide valuable lessons to policymakers in other countries, for several reasons. First, capital inflows began earlier in Asia, and have endured longer. In Thailand, for example, the capital inflow episode has lasted nearly a decade. Inflows to Asia showed little tendency to slow after the 1994 crisis in Mexico, in contrast to the pattern of capital flows to many Latin American countries. This experience offers valuable evidence to countries in which capital inflows have only recently begun. Second, inflows to Asian countries have been strong: Thailand has experienced average inflows of nearly 10% of GDP per year since 1988. The causes and effects of inflows of this magnitude are often more readily apparent. Third, faced with strong capital inflows, the countries considered here fashioned strong policy responses. They adopted conventional policies, such as tightening the fiscal stance, as well as unconventional policies, such as innovative means of monetary management, measures to limit credit growth, and measures to raise the cost of short-term capital movements. Fourth, and possibly as a result of the strong policy response, Asian countries avoided some of the concerns associated with large capital inflows. In particular, the inflows had a limited impact on inflation and the real exchange rate; most importantly, the inflows financed a surge in investment rather than consumption. The effect of capital inflows was not completely benign, however, as by 1995 many of these countries faced higher levels of external debt, as well as concerns over the intermediation of external borrowing through the domestic financial system.

The Asian experience demonstrates an additional, extremely important point: that in countries with pegged exchange rates, an increase in capital flows complicates monetary management. Over a longer horizon, policymakers were concerned with the potential effects of inflows on final targets such as economic activity and inflation, while on a day-to-day basis, they attempted to manage the economy by controlling intermediate targets such as interest rates and monetary aggregates. Many countries experienced downward pressures on interest rates and upward pressures on monetary aggregates as the pace of capital inflows increased, and policymakers often felt that their ability to control these key variables had declined. In this way, capital flows complicated the task of central banking.

This fact illustrates an important link between monetary policy and capital flows under pegged exchange rates, familiar from standard texts on open economy macroeconomics. Capital flows constrain monetary policy because monetary policy draws capital flows. In particular, an attempt either to contract monetary policy, or to sterilize a reserve inflow, will raise interest rates and attract more capital inflows.[3] This chapter relies on a simple model to illustrate this relationship. The model, developed over 20 years ago by Kouri and Porter (1974), provides useful insights into the causes of capital flows to countries with pegged exchange rate regimes. It can be used to quantify empirically both the constraints that international capital mobility imposes on monetary management, and the proportion of capital inflows due to contractionary monetary policy.

This chapter uses the cases of Indonesia and Thailand to demonstrate the importance of these links in practice. There are important similarities between these two countries' experiences with capital inflows. Each country, after undergoing a period of structural adjustment and economic liberalization in the mid-1980s, received a surge in capital inflows around the turn of the decade. Each country maintained a fairly open capital account and an exchange rate target,[4] and thus had a limited number of policy instruments to respond to the surge in inflows. Despite the exchange rate regime, each country tightened monetary policy to limit the effects of capital flows, and periodically sterilized inflows of reserves; these policies were important sources of additional inflows. Finally, each of these countries, concluding that a monetary response alone was insufficient, also relied on other policies to maintain macroeconomic control. In brief, both countries tightened fiscal policy, while Indonesia gradually increased exchange rate flexibility – standard policy prescriptions in response to a rise in capital inflows. The experiences of Indonesia and Thailand during the capital inflow episode thus provide examples of the use, effectiveness, and limitations of some of the most important policy instruments.

The chapter is organized in the following way. The next part of this section defines some of the terminology used throughout the chapter. Section 3.2 discusses the overall Asian experience with capital inflows, and reviews the main results and policy conclusions of the literature on the subject. Section 3.3 reviews a simple model that clarifies the relationship between monetary policy and capital flows. To illustrate the points the model makes, Section 3.4 discusses the Indonesian experience with capital inflows, while Section 3.5 discusses the Thai experience. Section 3.6 provides quantitative estimates of the constraints capital mobility imposes on monetary management, and the contribution of monetary policy to capital flows in Indonesia and Thailand. Section 3.7 offers a summary and conclusion.

Some discussion of the terminology used here is in order, given the recent changes in balance of payments accounting methodology.[5] As in previous literature on the subject, the term "capital inflow" in this chapter refers to a decrease in the net national asset position of the private and public sectors (excluding the central bank) over a certain period of time. Thus, increases in external debt or net sales of equity will be recorded as capital inflows. In practice, capital inflows are measured by the surplus on the financial account in the new presentation of the balance of payments, plus errors and omissions.[6] The financial account equals the sum of net flows of foreign direct investment (FDI), portfolio investment (in debt and equity securities), and other investment, of which banking flows are an important element. Errors and omissions belong to a residual category that ensures that the balance of payments sum to zero; it is included in measures of capital flows under the assumption that movements in this category are more likely to represent unrecorded international asset transactions, rather than mismeasurement of official reserve transactions or items on the current account.

Using this definition, the familiar balance of payments accounting identity implies that capital inflows equal the current account deficit plus the increase in official international reserves.[7] Higher capital inflows correspond to higher current account deficits, increases in reserves, or both. The exchange rate regime determines the extent to which capital inflows will increase reserves. Under a purely floating exchange rate, where the central bank does not intervene in the foreign exchange market, a capital inflow will not be associated with an increase in reserves. In contrast, under pegged exchange rates, the central bank will intervene to keep the currency from appreciating, and capital inflows will generally be associated with increases in reserves. This relationship will be important in the analysis below.

3.2   An Overview of the Asian Experience

The features and macroeconomic effects of capital inflows to Asia have been discussed in the literature in some detail;[8] consequently, this section presents only a brief overview of these issues as a backdrop for the analysis to follow. *Figure 3.1* shows the average balance on the financial account (plus errors and omissions) for five Asian countries. These countries – Indonesia, Korea, Malaysia, the Philippines, and Thailand – account for about two-thirds of total capital flows to developing Asia during 1990–1995, and will be the focus of this section.[9] As a comparison, the figure also graphs average capital flows to four Latin American countries: Argentina, Brazil, Chile, and Mexico.

The figure clearly shows the surge in capital inflows around the turn of the decade, and demonstrates several other points as well. First, inflows as a percentage of GDP were substantial in this sample of Asian countries, reflecting the fact that some countries experienced several years of large capital inflows. In Malaysia, inflows exceeded 15% of GDP in 1992 and 1993; in Thailand, inflows exceeded 10% of GDP during 1989–1991, and again in 1995. The increase in inflows was also large in dollar terms. Over the period 1985–1988, this sample of Asian countries received a total of $3.0 billion in capital inflows, or $0.8 billion per year; during 1989–1995, in contrast, they received a total of $219.6 billion, or $31.4 billion per year. Second, the countries in the Asian sample were less capital constrained than the Latin American countries before the inflow episode began, receiving positive inflows on average in the years before 1989. Third, average capital inflows began

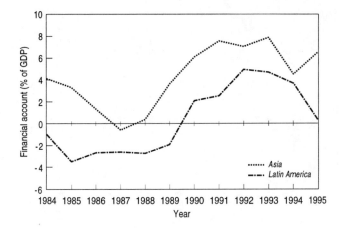

Figure 3.1. The financial account: Average of selected Asian and Latin American countries (as percent of GDP; includes errors and omissions). Source: International Monetary Fund, *International Financial Statistics*, various issues.

to increase in 1989, one year before the corresponding increase in the Latin American sample. The initial year of the capital inflow episode differed from country to country, however. Capital inflows to Indonesia first surged in 1990; to Korea, in 1991; to Malaysia, in 1989; to the Philippines, in 1990; and to Thailand, in 1988. Finally, capital inflows to the countries in the Asian sample increased in 1995. Several countries briefly experienced contagion effects after the Mexican financial crisis in 1994, but these were relatively quickly contained.

More detail on the balance of payments accounts appears in *Table 3.1*, which compares average statistics from the Asian sample over the capital inflow period (1989–1995) to those of the preceding four years (1985–1988). The average financial account surplus increased to over 6% of GDP, reflecting an increase in net FDI, which rose in all countries except Korea,[10] and a substantial increase in other investment, which included bank lending.[11] Portfolio investment increased only slightly; however, the average figure masks sharp increases in portfolio flows in several countries after 1993.[12] Along with the rise in the financial account, the average current account slipped from surplus into deficit, and the rate of accumulation of reserves increased, indicating a heavy degree of foreign exchange intervention.

The behavior of key macroeconomic variables across countries was mixed, with two exceptions. Each of the countries experienced a dramatic rise in investment during the capital inflow period, which reached 34% of GDP on average. Inflation also rose in each country, although the increase was not large. Among other variables, private consumption fell slightly on average, although it rose in Malaysia

Table 3.1. Balance of payments and macroeconomic statistics for selected Asian countries.[a]

	Average, selected Asian countries[b]		Indonesia		Thailand	
	1985–1988	1989–1995	1988–1989	1990–1995	1984–1987	1988–1995
Balance of payments (% of GDP)						
Financial account	1.0	6.1	2.9	4.1	3.0	9.6
Foreign direct investment	0.8	2.2	0.7	1.2	0.6	1.6
Portfolio investment	0.5	0.6	-0.1	0.9	0.8	1.5
Other investment	-0.3	3.3	2.3	2.0	1.6	6.4
Current account balance	0.6	-3.5	-1.4	-2.5	-2.3	-5.9
Reserve transactions[c]	-1.7	-2.7	-0.2	-1.1	-1.3	-4.1
Errors and omissions	0.2	0.1	-1.2	-0.5	0.6	0.4
Key macroeconomic variables						
As % of GDP						
Private consumption	59.0	57.7	55.1	55.4	61.8	55.0
Public consumption	11.1	10.6	9.2	8.8	12.7	9.7
Investment	26.1	33.6	33.4	34.4	27.9	39.6
In % per year						
Real GDP growth	5.7	7.2	6.6	7.1	6.4	9.9
Real M2 growth	10.4	13.3	22.8	15.2	13.9	13.8
Inflation	4.7	7.0	7.2	8.7	1.9	4.9
Real exchange rate appreciation[d]	-7.9	0.4	-1.5	-1.3	-7.9	-0.3
Official reserves	End-1988	End-1995	End-1989	End-1995	End-1987	End-1995
US$ (billion)	8.8	16.1	5.5	13.7	4.0	36.0
Months of imports	4.4	5.4	4.9	5.1	5.2	7.9

[a]Period averages.
[b]Indonesia, Korea, Malaysia, the Philippines, and Thailand.
[c] A negative sign indicates an increase in reserves.
[d] A positive sign denotes the appreciation of a CPI-based, trade-weighted real effective exchange rate.
Source: *International Financial Statistics*, and Information Notice System, IMF.

and the Philippines; and public consumption also declined, reflecting in part fiscal tightening in response to the capital inflows, as discussed below. GDP growth increased in each of the five countries except Korea, and although real M2 growth rose on average, it did not show a clear pattern across countries. The real exchange rate depreciated on average during the years preceding the capital inflow episode, partially reflecting devaluations in Indonesia and Thailand. During the capital inflow episode, however, the real exchange rate showed little tendency to appreciate.

Asian countries experienced well-documented movements in asset prices as capital inflows increased. Stock prices increased sharply, but only well after the inflows began: Asian stock markets experienced a region-wide boom in the second half of 1993. Domestic interest rates, however, tended to increase during the inflow period, while international interest rates were declining. This fact provides important clues about the causes of the inflows, and the policy responses to them.

In summary, the distinguishing macroeconomic features of the Asian experience were the lack of real exchange rate appreciation; the large increase in FDI; the recent rise in portfolio inflows and associated boom in equity markets; and the marked rise in investment, combined with the absence of upward pressure on consumption. These features give rise to two questions: first, what caused Asia's large capital inflows; and second, how did Asian countries avoid real appreciation of their currencies?

Previous studies provide a partial answer. For the first question, most work finds that movements in external variables, such as the decline in international interest rates in the 1990s, were an important cause of recent capital inflows to developing countries (see for example Calvo *et al.*, 1993; Chuhan *et al.*, 1993; and Fernández-Arias, 1994). External factors, however, differ in importance across regions, typically explaining 50% of the variation in capital flows in Latin American countries, compared to 30% in Asian countries. This suggests that domestic factors were important determinants of capital flows to Asia, perhaps reflecting the larger role of direct investment, which characteristically responds to longer-term considerations. For the second question, the literature focuses on the role of conservative fiscal policies (Schadler *et al.*, 1993) and the regional surge in FDI from Japan after the appreciation of the yen in 1985–1987 (Frankel and Wei, 1996). Assuming that FDI has a low nontraded goods component, FDI inflows will tend to increase domestic investment without increasing demand for nontraded goods and without thereby inducing an appreciation of the real exchange rate.

Previous work has, however, underemphasized the role of monetary policy in the capital inflow episode. A standard empirical model of international finance shows that domestic monetary conditions can be an important cause of capital flows under pegged exchange rates. In addition, tight monetary and sterilization policies may have limited the effect of capital inflows on domestic expenditure and the real exchange rate,[13] as long as monetary policy retains some independence under capital mobility. To investigate these and other issues, the next section outlines a simple, macroeconomic model of capital flows.

3.3   A Standard Model of Capital Flows

As discussed above, Asian countries accumulated large amounts of reserves in the 1990s. This reflects frequent intervention in foreign exchange markets, generally to prevent currency appreciation in the face of capital inflows. All of the countries considered here managed their exchange rates in some fashion; Indonesia and Thailand, for example, maintained fairly tight exchange rate targets throughout much of the capital inflow episode.

Under these conditions, monetary policy can be an important source of capital flows. The literature on the "offset coefficient", initially developed by Kouri and Porter (1974), provides a useful framework to examine this issue. The approach is based on a simple model, which combines a money demand function with a portfolio balance model expressing demand for domestic assets. The model assumes the exchange rate is pegged, and takes the current account as given. It yields the following well-known equation for capital flows:

$$KF = -\alpha \Delta NDA - b\Delta i^* - cCA + d\Delta F + \varepsilon, \tag{3.1}$$

where *KF* denotes capital flows (the financial account plus errors and omissions); i^* denotes world interest rates; *NDA*, the net domestic assets of the central bank; *CA*, the current account; and *F* represents a collection of other variables that influence capital flows.[14] Among other things, *F* includes factors that affect money demand, such as the level of economic activity. The key coefficient in this equation is α, the offset coefficient, which measures the independence of monetary policy as well as the impact of monetary policy on capital flows. As Kouri and Porter (1974) show, $0 \le \alpha \le 1$.

This equation does not provide a complete determination of capital flows, as it treats the current account as exogenous. Nevertheless, it provides some important insights into the nature and determinants of capital flows.

3.3.1   The causes of capital flows

According to equation (3.1), movements in international interest rates can generate capital flows – a major conclusion of empirical work to date. The equation also shows that movements in net domestic assets are a potential source of capital flows. The mechanism linking the two variables is the following. A contraction of net domestic assets – through an open-market sale of bonds, for example – will place upward pressure on domestic interest rates. Higher interest rates attract foreign funds, generating a capital inflow that relieves the pressure on domestic interest rates. The size of the inflow depends on the degree of substitutability of domestic and foreign assets. If assets are close substitutes, a small rise in domestic interest rates will generate a large capital inflow, and the offset coefficient will approach one in value. At the other extreme, if the degree of substitutability is low, the capital inflow will be smaller, and the offset coefficient will approach zero. The offset coefficient thus measures the size of the impact of movements in net domestic assets on capital flows.

3.3.2   Monetary independence

Using the balance of payments identity $CA + KF = \Delta NFA$, equation (3.1) can be rewritten as:

$$\Delta NFA = -\alpha \Delta NDA - b\Delta i^* + (1 - c)CA + d\Delta F + \varepsilon. \tag{3.2}$$

This equation illustrates the limits placed on monetary policy by capital flows; once again, the offset coefficient is the key parameter. When $\alpha = 1$, a reduction of net domestic assets to lower the monetary base will attract an equal and opposite capital inflow, raising net foreign assets and completely offsetting the initial monetary contraction. In this case, the central bank will be unable to control monetary aggregates. When $\alpha < 1$, the offset will be incomplete, and the central bank will retain some monetary control.

Equation (3.2) also demonstrates a major concern central banks faced during the capital inflow episode. As capital inflows rose, driven by falling world interest rates or movements in the elements of F, the resulting expansion in net foreign assets threatened to derail monetary targets. Central banks often emphasized monetary targets as a means to control final targets, such as output growth or inflation. In this way, increasing capital flows complicated the task of central banking.

3.3.3   Monetary and sterilization policy

Many Asian countries heavily sterilized inflows of foreign exchange, in an attempt to limit their impact on monetary aggregates. This policy has received substantial attention in the literature. Several studies conclude that while sterilized intervention insulates the economy from the macroeconomic effects of capital inflows, it keeps domestic interest rates high, perpetuating the incentives for inflows. To illustrate this last point, consider a typical central bank reaction function:

$$\Delta NDA = -\beta \Delta NFA + zG, \tag{3.3}$$

where $0 \leq \beta \leq 1$. According to this equation, the central bank contracts net domestic assets when net foreign assets rise. The coefficient β is a simple measure of the extent of sterilization: when $\beta = 1$, reserve inflows are sterilized completely. Monetary policy may react to a range of other variables, contained in G, such as inflation, the rate of economic growth, or the degree of capacity utilization.

Equations (3.2) and (3.3) together illustrate the criticism of sterilization policy voiced above. If, for example, world interest rates fall, sterilization of the resulting reserve inflow [by equation (3.3)] will attract additional inflows [by equation (3.2)], which require additional sterilization, and so on. To quantify this process, insert equation (3.3) into equation (3.2) to obtain:

$$\Delta NFA = (1 - \alpha\beta)^{-1}[zG - b\Delta i^* - cCA + d\Delta F + \varepsilon]. \tag{3.4}$$

Sterilization thus magnifies the response of reserve inflows to the exogenous variables in equation (3.2) by the factor $(1 - \alpha\beta)^{-1} \geq 1$. The size of the magnification effect depends on the values of the offset and sterilization coefficients. The closer these coefficients are to unity, the larger the magnitude of capital inflows. However, even with full sterilization, capital inflows will be limited as long as the offset is incomplete; thus, sterilization will not necessarily perpetuate an inflow indefinitely. As long as assets are imperfect substitutes, the inflow will eventually cease once investor demand for domestic assets is satiated.

Equation (3.4) demonstrates a second concern for central banks during the capital inflow period. Sterilizing large capital inflows, which were magnified by sterilization policy itself, often required the issuance of large amounts of interest-bearing domestic securities. This became costly when the central bank paid a higher interest rate on these instruments than it earned on foreign exchange reserves. Consequently, central banks often resorted to nontraditional means of sterilization, such as the manipulation of government and state enterprise deposits.

The simple model reviewed in this section highlights a potential link between monetary policy and capital flows. Despite a simultaneous exchange rate target, Indonesia and Thailand used monetary policy as a tool of macroeconomic management; their experience demonstrates the importance of this link in practice.

3.4   The Indonesian Experience

Table 3.1 displays several key macroeconomic variables for Indonesia and Thailand. Indonesia set the stage for capital inflows in the mid-1980s. At that time, Indonesia's main exports were energy products and primary commodities. In 1984–1986, the prices of oil and several commodities fell; as a result, the terms of trade deteriorated, economic growth slowed, and external government debt mounted. In the face of these developments, the government devalued the rupiah in October 1986, and began implementing a series of deregulation measures aimed at liberalizing the economy and promoting non-oil exports. In addition, tax reform and expenditure cuts helped to improve the government's fiscal position. These efforts began to bear fruit in the late 1980s, as investment increased and non-oil export growth surged. In 1988, a financial deregulation package lowered entry barriers in the commercial banking sector, and reduced the required reserve ratio from 15% to 2% of deposits. This measure led to rapid growth in monetary aggregates: M2, for example, grew by over 40% in 1990.

The capital inflow episode began in 1990: the current account deficit reached $3.0 billion (3% of GDP), and official reserves rose by $2.0 billion. The deterioration in the current account, along with mounting inflation and high monetary growth rates, convinced the government that the economy was overheating. In response, the Ministry of Finance engineered a monetary contraction in early 1991 by ordering state enterprises to remove their deposits from the banking system and purchase debt instruments issued by Bank Indonesia (the central bank). The move caused a sharp fall in M2, and raised domestic interest rates to 25%. Later in the year, limits were imposed on offshore borrowing by state enterprises.

Indonesia maintained an open capital account and an exchange rate target. The rupiah was depreciated against the dollar to offset inflation differentials, thereby maintaining a relatively stable real exchange rate. Under these circumstances, as the previous section argued, contractionary monetary policy should attract capital inflows. This indeed was the case: the increase in domestic interest rates in 1991 attracted a flood of capital inflows, and net foreign assets of the central bank rose rapidly over the next few years (*Figure 3.2*).

In the years after the initial monetary contraction, sterilization was the main defense against capital inflows.[15] As equation (3.3) shows, sterilization involves contracting net domestic assets to offset increases in net foreign assets. Thus, in a situation of strong capital inflows, sterilization implies that net foreign assets and net domestic assets will tend to move in opposite directions. This tendency can be seen in *Figure 3.2*. The mirror image path of net domestic and net foreign assets after 1990 is striking evidence of the central bank's sterilization practice.

The main instruments of sterilization were bonds issued by the central bank – called SBIs (Sertifikat Bank Indonesia) – at relatively high interest rates. As the amount of outstanding SBIs grew, the interest rate costs to the central bank rose sharply. Bank Indonesia sterilized a large proportion of reserve inflows throughout 1993. In addition, Bank Indonesia widened the exchange rate intervention band in several stages, beginning in 1992, with the objectives of increasing the independence of monetary policy, discouraging capital inflows by increasing exchange rate risk, and encouraging the development of the foreign exchange market. In practice, however, the exchange rate remained near the appreciated end of the band, and the widening of the band provided little additional freedom to tighten monetary policy.

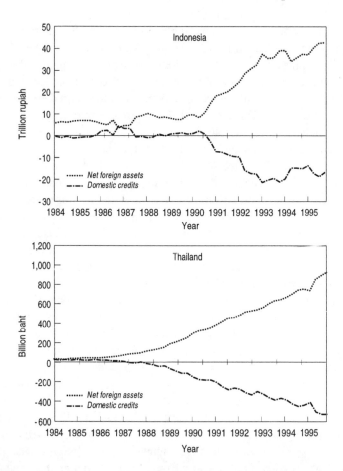

Figure 3.2. Net foreign assets and domestic credit of the central bank for Indonesia and Thailand. Source: International Monetary Fund, *International Financial Statistics*, various issues.

In 1995, sterilization policy was relaxed somewhat, and the central bank introduced a credit plan as an alternative tool to slow the growth of monetary aggregates. Under this plan, Bank Indonesia attempted to achieve an aggregate credit growth rate by specifying credit growth targets for individual banks, and exerted "moral suasion" to induce banks to adhere to these targets. Credit growth, however, slowed only marginally in 1995 and 1996.

There are several broad similarities between the Indonesian and the "average" Asian experience with capital inflows.[16] Investment increased, while both public and private consumption declined. GDP growth picked up during the capital inflow period, as did inflation, but the real exchange rate remained stable. Indonesian companies enjoyed increasing access to offshore capital markets; this fact, together with growing interest in emerging stock markets from developing countries, contributed to a surge of portfolio inflows starting from 1993.

3.5 The Thai Experience

Thailand, like Indonesia, pursued a sustained adjustment effort in the years preceding the capital inflow episode, including a large depreciation of the baht in 1984, trade and financial sector reform, and an improvement in the fiscal balance, which swung from consistent deficit in the early 1980s to surplus by 1988. These internal developments positioned the economy to take full advantage of the fall in world interest rates and the wave of FDI from Japan in the late 1980s.

The initial surge in capital inflows to Thailand took place during 1988–1991. There are two distinctive features of this initial stage. First, it was sudden and large. Capital inflows increased from 2.6% of GDP in 1987 to 12.3% in 1991; concurrently, the current account deficit deteriorated from 2.7% to 7.7% of GDP. Foreign direct investment, averaging 2.2% of GDP over 1988–1991, formed an important part of these inflows and helped fuel a boom in investment, which increased from 28% of GDP in 1988 to 41% in 1991. The investment boom, in turn, supported rapid output and export growth: real GDP grew at an average rate of 11.4% over the period. The second distinctive feature of this stage was the government's strong fiscal response. The central government balance improved from a deficit of 0.3% of GDP in 1987 to a surplus of 4.1% in 1991, reflecting measures on both the revenue and expenditure sides.

Thailand maintained the value of the baht in the foreign exchange market against a basket of currencies, in which the dollar carried a heavy weight. In line with this policy, the central bank intervened heavily to keep the baht from appreciating, and accumulated large quantities of foreign reserves in 1988–1991. The central bank actively sterilized these inflows throughout the period, both by repurchasing government bonds and by issuing its own bonds when the supply of government bonds dried up. In addition, the government's fiscal surpluses resulted in rising treasury deposits at the Bank of Thailand, helping to offset the effect of capital inflows on the monetary base.[17] As with Indonesia, the sterilization activities of the central bank were reflected in the inverse behavior of net foreign and net domestic assets (*Figure 3.2*). Interest rates remained close to international levels until 1990, when monetary policy was tightened to slow the rapid economic expansion, while international interest rates declined.

Capital inflows moderated somewhat in subsequent years, reflecting domestic political uncertainties following a coup in 1992, a decline in FDI due to infrastructure bottlenecks, and a reorientation of foreign interest toward other economies in the region. In addition, monetary conditions were eased as GDP growth moderated and the interest rate differential declined. Nevertheless, the level of capital inflows over 1992–1993 remained high, averaging 8.4% of GDP. An increasing share of these inflows was in the form of nonresident baht accounts, which financed equity and other portfolio investment.

The Bangkok International Banking Facility (BIBF) was established in 1993, in an effort to mobilize foreign savings and develop Thailand as a regional financial center. Under this initiative, licensed BIBF banks accept foreign deposits and relend them either domestically or abroad; several tax incentives were granted to encourage banks to seek licenses. In practice, the vast majority of BIBF loans were extended to domestic borrowers. As a result, capital inflows surged again, reaching 12% of GDP in 1995; about two-thirds of this was intermediated through the BIBF. The resulting credit expansion helped to finance extensive construction of offices and condominiums in the Bangkok area. Economic activity picked up, the current account deficit widened over the next two years, and the central bank raised interest rates in response.

The increase in interest rates and a sharp slowdown in the export sector contributed to a moderation of economic growth in 1996. As the economy slowed, vacancy rates in the property market increased. A large share of credit in preceding years had directly financed construction, or was collateralized by real estate assets. Consequently, the property market downturn gave rise to concerns over the health of the financial sector, concerns that were strengthened by the collapse of the Bangkok Bank of Commerce, a medium-sized bank, in the middle of the year. Believing that the vulnerability of financial institutions would prevent the central bank from raising interest rates to defend the currency, markets launched a series of increasingly serious speculative attacks against the baht near the end of the year. These attacks further eroded market confidence; capital inflows declined, and liquidity problems began to emerge among smaller financial institutions.[18]

3.6   A Quantitative Assessment

To assess the role of monetary policy in capital inflows to Indonesia and Thailand, this section provides empirical estimates of the simple model presented in Section 3.3. The key parameter is α, the offset coefficient, which can be estimated using standard techniques. *Table 3.2* contains estimates of equation (3.1), which regresses capital flows, defined as the financial account plus errors and omissions, on the current account (CA) and the first difference of the net domestic assets of

Table 3.2. Regression results for Indonesia and Thailand. Dependent variable: capital inflows.[a]

	1984–1995		1984–1989	1990–1995
	OLS	IV	OLS	OLS
Indonesia				
ΔNDA	−0.29	−0.29	−0.21	−0.33
	(−4.92)[b]	(−1.63)	(−3.26)[b]	(−3.74)[b]
CA	−0.94	−0.94	−0.57	−0.91
	(−7.26)[b]	(−6.23)[b]	(−2.95)[b]	(−4.82)[b]
R^2	0.68	0.68	0.52	0.68
DW	1.80	1.79	1.80	1.79

	1984–1995		1984–1987	1988–1995
	OLS	IV	IV	IV
Thailand				
ΔNDA	−0.62	−0.33	−0.21	−0.41
	(−7.66)[b]	(−2.50)[c]	(−0.76)	(−3.27)[b]
CA	−1.24	−1.32	−0.72	−1.21
	(−18.26)[b]	(−16.16)[b]	(−3.35)[b]	(−11.50)[b]
R^2	0.93	0.91	0.46	0.87
DW	2.13	2.08	2.90	2.26

Abbreviations: OLS, ordinary least squares; IV, instrumental variables; ΔNDA, net domestic assets; CA, current account; DW, Durbin-Watson coefficient.
[a]Defined as the financial account plus errors and omissions.
[b]Significant at the 1% level.
[c]Significant at the 5% level.

the central bank (ΔNDA).[19] Several other potentially important variables, including international interest rates and real domestic output, were insignificant in the estimated equations and dropped from the reported results.[20] As Kouri and Porter (1974) point out, ΔNDA will be endogenous under a policy of sterilizing reserve movements, and thus ordinary least squares (OLS) estimates of the offset coefficient may be biased. Consequently, equation (3.1) is estimated under both OLS and instrumental variables (IV), using as instruments a constant term, the exogenous variables, and the endogenous variables with two lags.

For Indonesia, OLS estimates over the period 1984–1995 yield a statistically significant value of 0.29 for the offset coefficient. This value remains virtually unchanged under IV, suggesting that simultaneity bias is not a problem.[21] An increase in the offset coefficient is one explanation for the perceived loss of monetary independence in recent years. This would occur if there was an increase in capital mobility, or more precisely, in the presence of substitutability of domestic and foreign assets. To test this hypothesis, the sample was split into the capital inflow period (1990–1995) and the period preceding it (1984–1989). OLS was used to estimate the model over each subperiod, given the apparent absence of simultaneity bias.[22] The offset coefficient, 0.21 in the first period, rises to 0.33 in the capital inflow period; and the coefficient on *CA* rises in absolute value.[23] The conventional Chow test rejects the null hypothesis of parameter stability across the two periods at the 10% level (the f-statistic is 2.60).

For Thailand, OLS estimates produce an offset coefficient of 0.62 over the period 1984–1995. This falls to 0.33 under IV, suggesting some simultaneity bias in the OLS estimates. For this reason, the offset coefficient is estimated with IV over the capital inflow period (1988–1995) and the period preceding it (1984–1987). The Chow test rejects parameter stability across the two periods at the 5% level, with an f-statistic of 3.71. The offset coefficient, at 0.21, is insignificant in the first period. It rises to 0.41 during the capital inflow period, and becomes statistically significant.

These results indicate an important link between capital flows and movements in net domestic assets, which reflect monetary and sterilization policy. Since the model does not attempt to explain current account deficits, perhaps the best assessment of the importance of this link can be obtained by inserting the estimated offset coefficient into equation (3.2). Indonesia, for example, accumulated a total of $8.8 billion of reserve assets over 1990–1995. Of this amount, $2.6 billion, or 29.6%, was due to a contraction of *NDA* over the period.[24] This proportion increased in 1991–1993, the period in which monetary policy was substantially tightened and offsetting reserve inflows were sterilized. The corresponding contraction of *NDA* attracted $2.9 billion in reserves, 69.2% of the total $4.2 billion reserve accumulation in these three years.

Taking the results literally, these figures imply that if monetary policy were passive (*NDA* were constant) and exchange market intervention were unsterilized, reserve accumulation would have totaled only $6.2 billion over 1990–1995, and $1.3 billion over 1991–1993. The estimated parameters also quantify the "magnification effect" associated with sterilization of reserve inflows. With an offset coefficient of 0.33, a policy of full sterilization would magnify reserve inflows by a factor of 1.5 [see equation (3.3)].

In Thailand, movements in *NDA* generated capital inflows of $8.9 billion over 1988–1995, or 26.5% of the $33.7 billion in reserve accumulation over the period. Once again, passive monetary and sterilization policy would yield reserve accumulation of $24.8 billion, while the estimated 0.41 value for the offset coefficient during the capital inflow episode implies a magnification factor of 1.7 under full sterilization.

In summary, the empirical work of this section indicates a significant link between capital flows and movements in *NDA*. The importance of this link increased during the capital inflow episode. Monetary and sterilization policy attracted higher offsetting inflows, and consequently decreased in effectiveness.

3.7 Conclusions

This chapter describes the Asian experience with capital inflows, and argues that monetary policy played an important role. Central banks used monetary policy to contain the expansionary tendencies associated with large inflows. Under fixed exchange rates, however, contractionary monetary policy will attract more capital inflows, and these inflows will offset the effects of the contraction. In addition, sterilization policy magnifies the size of inflows due to other sources. In practice, these relationships were important sources of capital flows.

In conclusion, the large capital flows to Asia are partly a reminder of a textbook lesson: that maintaining monetary independence with a pegged exchange rate and an open capital account is difficult at best. If capital mobility to developing countries rises significantly, independent monetary policy may become impossible. For this reason, countries should develop other means to respond to capital flows, such as fiscal policy or increased exchange rate flexibility.

Acknowledgments

Mahmood Pradhan and James Morsink provided helpful comments on an earlier draft. The views expressed are those of the author, and do not necessarily reflect those of the International Monetary Fund.

Notes

[1] The chapter deals with capital inflows to Asia between 1988 and 1995. It does not discuss the period of sharp capital outflows during the regional financial crisis that began in 1997.

[2] Several papers by Reisen (1993a, b) are important exceptions.

[3] The literature on capital inflows often mentions this conclusion in discussions of sterilization. See Schadler *et al.* (1993) or Calvo *et al.* (1994).

[4] Indonesia targeted a broadly constant real exchange rate, depreciating the nominal rate to offset inflation differentials vis-à-vis trading partners. Thailand pegged the nominal exchange rate to a basket of currencies in which the dollar, yen, and the German mark carried heavy weights.

[5] See International Monetary Fund (1993:3–5) for a brief summary of these changes.

[6] See Calvo *et al.* (1993, 1994), for example. Of course, earlier work used the previous definition of the capital account in place of the financial account.

[7] This discussion ignores the newly defined capital account, which refers mainly to capital transfers. It was not significant in magnitude in any of the countries considered here.

[8] See Calvo *et al.* (1993, 1994); Reinhart and Khan (1995); and Corbo and Hernández (1996), among others.

[9] Several other countries, such as China, India and Sri Lanka, began to receive capital inflows in recent years, but it is difficult to draw clear lessons from their experience at this stage. China, in particular, has received huge inflows of direct investment since 1993.

[10] Foreign direct investment from Japan to Indonesia, Malaysia, and Thailand rose sharply in the late 1980s; see Frankel and Wei (1996).

[11] See Folkerts-Landau *et al.* (1995) for a discussion of the role of the banking system in the capital inflow episode.

[12] Ishii and Dunaway (1995) discuss the increase in portfolio capital flows to Asia-Pacific Economic Co-operation (APEC) countries.

[13] Tight domestic monetary conditions would probably have little effect on FDI, however.

[14] Equation (3.1) can be specified in levels, rather than differences, with cumulated capital flows as the dependent variable.

[15] Fiscal policy in Indonesia is strongly influenced by a balanced budget rule, which limits (but does not eliminate) its role as a countercyclical policy tool.

[16] *Table 3.1* reports the balance of payments accounts for two years previous to the capital inflow episode (rather than four years). Large surpluses on the financial account and corresponding current account deficits in 1986–1987 reflect government borrowing, and would mask the rise in private capital flows beginning in 1990.

[17] The decline in net claims on the government offset about one-half of the contribution of net foreign assets to reserve money growth during this period.

[18] These developments continued to increase in severity, inducing Thailand to seek IMF and multilateral assistance in August 1997 (after the first draft of this chapter was written).

[19] All data are quarterly, from IMF, *International Financial Statistics. NDA* is calculated by subtracting net foreign assets from the monetary base. The variables are in nominal terms; coefficients on price indices and other variables intended to capture scale effects were insignificant.

[20] The insignificance of world interest rates in these equations may reflect the fact that, when reserve inflows are sterilized, inflows caused by declining world interest rates will cause *NDA* to fall. Thus, *NDA* and i^* will be positively correlated. Through this mechanism, these results are consistent with previous work that emphasized declining world interest rates as a cause of capital inflows.

[21] The dynamics of sterilization may account for this result. Bond (1996) estimates that only partial sterilization takes place within the first quarter, limiting the bias of ordinary least squares. Full sterilization occurs after four quarters.

[22] IV estimates give similar results; however, the estimated offset coefficients are insignificant in both periods.

[23] The model predicts that the coefficient on *CA* will increase in absolute value when the offset coefficient rises; see Kouri and Porter (1974), equation (3.19).

[24] This calculation uses the estimated value of 0.33 for the offset coefficient over the capital inflow period.

References

Bond, T., 1996, Macroeconomic policy and capital flows, unpublished PhD thesis, Harvard University, Cambridge, MA, USA.

Calvo, G., Leiderman, L., and Reinhart, C., 1993, Capital inflows to Latin America: The role of external factors, *IMF Staff Papers*, **40**:108–151.

Calvo, G., Leiderman, L., and Reinhart, C., 1994, The capital inflows problem: Concepts and issues, *Contemporary Economic Policy*, **XII**:54–66.

Chuhan, P., Claessens, S., and Mamingi, N., 1993, Equity and bond flows to Latin America and Asia: The role of external and domestic factors, unpublished paper, The World Bank, Washington, DC, USA.

Corbo, V., and Hernández, L., 1996, Macroeconomic adjustment to capital inflows: Lessons from recent Latin American and East Asian experience, *World Bank Research Observer*, **11**(1):61–85.

Fernández-Arias, E., 1994, The New Wave of Private Capital Inflows: Push or Pull? World Bank Policy Research Working Paper 1312, Washington, DC, USA.

Folkerts-Landau, D., Schinasi, G., Cassard, M., Ng, V., Reinhart, C., and Spencer, M., 1995, The effect of capital flows on the domestic financial sector in APEC developing countries, in M. Khan and C. Reinhart, eds., *Capital Flows in the APEC Region*, IMF Occasional Paper No. 122, International Monetary Fund, Washington, DC, USA, pp. 31–57.

Frankel, J., and Wei, S.-J., 1996, ASEAN in a regional perspective, paper prepared for the Conference on Macroeconomic Issues Facing ASEAN Countries, held in Jakarta, Indonesia.

International Monetary Fund, 1993, *Balance of Payments Manual*, fifth edition.

Ishii, S., and Dunaway, S., 1995, Portfolio capital flows to the developing country members of APEC, in M. Khan and C. Reinhart, eds., *Capital Flows in the APEC Region*, IMF Occasional Paper No. 122, International Monetary Fund, Washington, DC, USA, pp. 3–14.

Kouri, P., and Porter, M., 1974, International capital flows and portfolio equilibrium, *Journal of Political Economy*, **82**(3):443–467.

Reinhart, C., and Khan, M., 1995, Macroeconomic management in APEC economies: The response to capital inflows, in M. Khan and C. Reinhart, eds., *Capital Flows in the APEC Region*, IMF Occasional Paper No. 122, International Monetary Fund, Washington, DC, USA, pp. 15–30.

Reisen, H., 1993a, Capital flows and their effect on the monetary base, *CEPAL Review*, **51**(December):113–122.

Reisen, H., 1993b, South-East Asia and the "Impossible Trinity", *International Economic Insights*, **4**(2):21–23.

Schadler, S., Carkovic, M., Bennett, A., and Kahn, R., 1993, *Recent Experiences with Surges in Capital Inflows*, IMF Occasional Paper No. 108, International Monetary Fund, Washington, DC, USA.

Chapter 4

The Effectiveness of Capital Controls: Theory and Evidence from Chile

Salvador Valdés-Prieto and Marcelo Soto

4.1 Introduction

For many countries in Eastern Europe, Latin America, or East Asia (prior to 1997), persistent increases in capital *inflows* have caused a real appreciation of the currency, which may undermine competitiveness and slow investment and economic growth. An unexpected surge in inflows also raises problems for monetary policy, leading to either higher inflation or a large nominal appreciation. When the authorities have reacted with large sterilized purchases of foreign reserves, the result has been painful quasi-fiscal deficits. Selective capital controls have been suggested to deal with these problems.

Conversely, countries that suffer unexpected surges in capital *outflows* must choose between high interest rates and the inflation fueled by a devaluation, as in the speculative attacks on some of the currencies included in the European Monetary System (EMS) in 1992 and 1993, and in Southeast Asia during 1997. Again, selective capital controls have been proposed.

An earlier version of this chapter was published in *Empirica*, Volume 25, Number 1, 1998, Kluwer Academic Publishers.

The policy objectives that would justify a selective capital control are the following:

(i)   To improve the policy tradeoffs available to the central bank. In small open economies receiving large inflows, the central bank's choice set is bounded by political pressure from either workers and others hurt by inflation, or exporters hurt by the real appreciation.

(ii) To reduce the scope of volatile short-term foreign credits in relation to the economy. This relates to the stability of capital inflows, the possibility of domestic repercussions if these flows are suddenly reversed, and the management of speculative attacks.

(iii) To act as a substitute for mediocre banking supervision.

In this chapter, we argue that a form of capital control employed in Chile – the unremunerated reserve requirement (URR) – cannot attain objective (ii), because it has operated on a permanent basis. Therefore this experience is not directly applicable to countries that merely want to buy a few weeks time while responding to speculative attacks. Objective (iii) does not apply to Chile, because since 1986 it has had some of the best banking supervision in the western hemisphere. Thus, we concentrate on objective (i).

Chile has experienced large inflows and appreciation during the 1990s, even though it adopted a URR in June 1991, which was gradually extended to cover a larger proportion of the loans from nonresidents. This Chilean capital control has been promoted internationally as a success. For example, at the September 1995 meeting of the Group of Río, which comprises 12 democratically elected Latin American heads of state, one of the resolutions adopted was as follows: in order to "prevent the damaging effect of volatile capital flows on the members' economies", the signatories promised "to establish specific regulations to preclude the entry of flight capital".[1] Similarly, at the 1996 Asia Pacific Economic Cooperation (APEC) summit, "several presidents agreed to include the topic of capital controls on the APEC agenda".[2]

This chapter tries to go beyond such rhetoric and offer an empirical evaluation of the Chilean URR. The first part of the chapter presents a conceptual framework for evaluating the general effectiveness of selective capital controls. It has been argued in the literature that capital controls are irrelevant after a few weeks or months because the private sector always finds ways to avoid them. Our framework allows for the possibility of limiting avoidance, so that the capital control is relevant in the sense that the taxed sectors continue to exist and yield positive revenue. However, the framework also allows for the possibility that the capital control may not have an impact on aggregate flows. If sectors that are exempt from the control or able to avoid it determine the level of aggregate flows at the margin, the control is unable to affect the macroeconomy. We also discuss the implications of this framework under fixed and freely floating exchange rate regimes.

The remainder of the chapter analyzes the Chilean evidence during the period 1987–1996. Revenue data show that the URR was relevant, in that it collected substantial revenue. We also study quarterly data on total short-term credit inflows to the private sector. The URR was positive for 27 quarters out of 40.[3] To test whether the URR tax was effective at the macroeconomic level, an econometric model is proposed that attempts to explain net short-term credits to the private sector. The model controls for factors such as international interest rates and such policy measures as the sterilization of capital inflows.

We find that for URR rates below 450 basis points per year for a 180-day credit, aggregate net short-term credit inflows to the private sector were not discouraged. Short-term credits that were exempt (legally or otherwise) from the URR, *ceteris paribus*, increased in response to the capital control to such an extent as to render the URR ineffective. The selective capital control influenced the composition of net short-term credits, but not the overall level of such credits. This result is similar to other results in the empirical literature on financial taxation. For example, Gravelle (1991) found that tax-advantaged individual retirement accounts in the USA had a significant influence on the composition of financial saving, but no measurable impact on aggregate savings. Because total short-term credits were not affected, the relative magnitude of short-term and long-term credit was also unchanged.

We also find that when the URR tax rate is raised to about 600 basis points per year on 180-day credits, there is a negative relationship between that rate and the volume of short-term credits, but that relationship is not statistically significant. A threshold effect may be present, but has not been established. The URR's effectiveness is also put in doubt because other short-term inflows not officially classified as short-term credits increased significantly during the period of high URR tax rates (1995–1996). In addition, the apparent threshold effect may in reality be picking up the impact of other factors that shifted the supply of foreign funds to Chile in those 2 years.

Section 4.2 contains the framework that defines macroeconomic effectiveness. Section 4.3 shows its implications under fixed and freely floating exchange rate regimes. Section 4.4 provides a description of the policy objectives in Chile, the specific capital control used, and evidence on the amount of tax revenue collected. Section 4.5 presents the econometric procedure employed to test for the macroeconomic impact of the URR, data definitions, and the results. Section 4.6 concludes by offering a policy evaluation of selective capital controls.

4.2 A Theoretical Framework for Evaluating a Selective Capital Control

4.2.1 Framework

Consider a partial equilibrium model concerned only with credit flows. In this economy, residents engage in financial transactions with nonresidents at some given term (e.g., one week, one month, one quarter). There are two groups of resident borrowers. The first is subject to a selective capital control, which is represented as a percentage tax per unit of time and can be added to interest rates. The second is exempt from the tax. Alternatively, we can interpret the taxed sector as the set of taxed transactions.

We define the following variables:

$$D^t(i^{td}, i^{ed}, X^t) = \text{taxed group's demand for credit,}$$
$$D^e(i^{ed}, i^{td}, X^e) = \text{exempt group's demand for credit,}$$

where i^{td} = interest rate charged to the taxed group, in domestic currency; i^{ed} = interest rate charged to the exempt group, in domestic currency; X^t = vector of other explanatory variables for D^t; and X^e = vector of other explanatory variables for D^e.

These are stock demands, in the tradition of portfolio models. Partial adjustment can be added to account for flows. The demand for credit from each group falls when its "own" interest rate increases, so $D_1^t < 0$ and $D_1^e < 0$, where the subscript indicates the argument with respect to which the derivative is taken. In addition, we assume that one group's demand for credit increases in response to an increase in the interest rate charged to the other group, so $D_2^t \geq 0$ and $D_2^e \geq 0$. This may be justified with reference to competition on local credit markets between the taxed and exempt groups. For example, if the taxed group includes the local banks, there may be disintermediation in the cross-border credit market by exempt firms, who stop borrowing from local banks and borrow directly from abroad both for their own needs and to relend to their local clients or suppliers on better terms than the local banks.

The supply of nonresident credit to each group of agents is as follows:

$$S^t(i^{ts}, Z^t) = \text{credit supplied by nonresidents to the taxed group,}$$
$$S^e(i^{es}, Z^e) = \text{credit supplied by nonresidents to the exempt group,}$$

where interest rates are those charged by suppliers – hence the superscript s – and Z^t and Z^e are vectors of other factors that influence credit availability to each sector. Assuming that there is a uniform interest rate within each sector, nonresident supply can also be represented through supply price functions:

$$i^{ts} = i^* + E\{dlnE/dt\} + r^t(S^t, Z^t),\tag{4.1a}$$

$$i^{es} = i^* + E\{dlnE/dt\} + r^e(S^e, Z^e),\tag{4.1b}$$

where i^* is the foreign interest rate for the given term, $E\{dlnE/dt\}$ is the expected rate of devaluation for the period, and r is the uniform risk premium charged by international lenders to each sector in that period. The risk premium represents the supply price of funds. In general, both $r^t < r^e$ and $r^t > r^e$ are possible.

A special case exists where the supply of foreign credit is completely elastic, or equivalently, where the risk premium for each sector is independent of the amount of credit:

$$S_1^t = \infty \quad \text{when} \quad i^{ts} = i^* + E\{dlnE/dt\} + (r^t)_{\text{const}},\tag{4.2a}$$

$$S_1^e = \infty \quad \text{when} \quad i^{es} = i^* + E\{dlnE/dt\} + (r^e)_{\text{const}},\tag{4.2b}$$

where the "const" subscripts indicate that these variables are constants.

The supply of credit by residents (such as domestic pension funds, domestic firms, and wealthy individuals) is special, because residents are always exempt from capital controls when lending to the taxed sector. This might render the capital control irrelevant if resident investors manage a sufficiently large number of funds and the liabilities of all borrowers (domestic and foreign) are perfect substitutes. This is because they might finance the taxed sector by themselves. Dooley and Chinn (1995) make this assumption, an extreme one because, as shown below, it implicitly imposes irrelevance.

We analyze the general case in which resident investors consider the liabilities of domestic borrowers (both taxed and exempt) and foreign borrowers as imperfect substitutes. Thus $S_{res}^t(i^t, i^e, i^* + E\{dlnE/dt\})$ and $S_{res}^e(i^t, i^e, i^* + E\{dlnE/dt\})$ are residents' supplies of funds to the taxed and exempt sectors. This allows us to interpret the demands D^t and D^e as the net demands for foreign funds, that is, as the excess demands after subtracting the domestic supply functions.

This interpretation reflects a modification relative to the conventional approach, because there is a new argument in the net demand functions, namely, the interest rate earned by resident investors when investing abroad ($i^* + E\{dlnE/dt\}$). This new argument is not included in the vectors X^t and X^e. The impact of this new argument on net demand is given by the derivatives D_3^t and D_3^e, both of which are positive. When the return on investing abroad rises for domestic investors, they react by reducing their supply of funds to both types of domestic borrowers, increasing those borrowers' net demands for foreign funds.

This formulation allows for imperfect substitution in the net demand for credit between the taxed and exempt sectors. To keep the presentation simple, foreign supply is assumed to be perfectly elastic. This is a strong assumption, which the econometric work below shows does not hold for Chile.

4.2.2   Irrelevance and ineffectiveness

The presence of a selective capital control falling on the taxed sector is represented by a tax, θ defined for the term during which flows are occurring. We now define three concepts. First, we say that a capital control is "irrelevant" when a control of infinitesimal size $d\theta$ is introduced and has the following effects:

$$\partial D^t / \partial \theta = -\infty \quad \text{when} \quad \theta = 0, \tag{4.3a}$$

$$\partial D^e / \partial \theta = \infty \quad \text{when} \quad \theta = 0, \tag{4.3b}$$

and

$$\partial (D^t + D^e) / \partial \theta = 0 \quad \text{when} \quad \theta = 0. \tag{4.3c}$$

If irrelevance applies, the imposition of tax $d\theta$ leads to the disappearance of demand from the taxed sector, or equivalently, disappearance of the taxed transactions. That demand is fully taken up by the exempt sector (or exempt transactions) and total flows are unchanged. This is what we have in mind when we say that a capital control is fully avoided. Note that the revenue from this tax is zero. The 100% URR imposed by Spain on incremental peseta bank loans to non-residents in October 1992, as described by Garber and Taylor (1995), seems to have been irrelevant for its 3-month term, since the domestic–offshore interest rate differential was raised by only a few basis points for 3-month swaps.

Second, we define a capital control as "ineffective in influencing capital flows" if:

$$\partial D^t / \partial \theta < 0, \tag{4.4a}$$

$$\partial D^e / \partial \theta > 0, \tag{4.4b}$$

but

$$\partial (D^t + D^e) / \partial \theta = 0. \tag{4.4c}$$

If this condition holds, the volume of funds reaching the taxed sector falls. However, the total inflow to the two sectors taken together is unaffected, because the flows that reach the exempt sector increase sufficiently to compensate fully for the reduction in those going to the taxed sector. Having an effective capital control can mean only that it can be used to counteract a surge in capital inflows. Note that in this case revenue from the tax is expected to be positive and may even be substantial.

We define a capital control as "counterproductive" if equations (4.4a) and (4.4b) are met, but $\partial(D^t + D^e)/\partial\theta > 0$. This might happen if the capital control is interpreted by market participants as a signal of a future policy that makes it profitable to increase total flows now.

Third, we define "full effectiveness" for a capital control as a case where a tax rate θ^* exists that eliminates the interest-sensitive component of taxed inflows, without increasing exempt inflows at all:

$$D^t(\theta^*) = K(X^t) < D^t(0) \text{ for all } \theta > \theta^*, \tag{4.5a}$$

and

$$D^e(\theta^*) = D^e(0) \text{ for all } \theta > \theta^*, \tag{4.5b}$$

where $K(X^t)$ is the autonomous component of the capital flows to the taxed sector. This extreme result can be obtained only when there is no further substitution of the taxed flows by other flows during the given period.

Note that in this case tax revenue will be zero, just as with irrelevance, when $K(X^t)$ is zero. It would be unusual for the authorities to impose selective capital controls just to increase tax revenue. Thus, receiving zero revenue from the tax would not contradict the notion of effectiveness from a macroeconomic standpoint.

We define effectiveness from a macroeconomic perspective, because the macro-economy is influenced by the total amount of flows regardless of their sectoral composition. Of course, there is no suggestion that the yields on financial instruments are unaffected by taxation. Effectiveness as applied here refers to the ability to influence total flows, without any implications for the effectiveness of monetary policy.

4.2.3 Why is there an exempt sector?

The question arises as to why there is a set of agents exempt from the tax. It may appear that, in order to achieve total effectiveness, the authorities merely need to avoid granting exemptions. In practice, achieving full coverage for a selective capital control is difficult. One elementary problem is the absence of the administrative capacity required for enforcement. This is a substantial problem in markets for foreign exchange, where local banks are not the only admissible dealers, or where such banks are not tightly regulated, as in many emerging markets. Furthermore, in a market with loosely regulated nonbank dealers, cross-border transactions can go unrecorded at little cost to participants in those transactions.

There is also the problem of the relabeling of taxed flows. For example, if short-term credits are taxed, then an arbitrageur might avoid the tax by arranging a long-term credit with a prepayment option or by contracting two equal and opposite long-term loans with slightly different maturities. If only loans are taxed, an arbitrageur might arrange for an equity investment to be held in domestic short-term deposits to avoid the tax. An arbitrageur might also ask a foreign direct investor with profits to repatriate to lend him/her the funds domestically, while in exchange he/she lends to the investor abroad.

The Chilean authorities have improved the design of the tax substantially over time, closing new evasion routes. The same learning path has been followed by academic proposals. The initial proposal by Eichengreen and Wyplosz (1993) would tax only the net foreign exchange positions of "banks and other institutions dealing on their own accounts". Further discussion recognized that net positions at the end of each trading day could be shifted to offshore financial centers.

A subsequent proposal by Eichengreen *et al.* (1995) would tax "all bank loans to or from all nonresidents", but on a transitory basis. However, the Chilean tax has been adopted on a permanent basis; the possibilities for term arbitrage under such a capital control are not yet fully understood.

A further problem is that banks and other financial institutions can be disintermediated by exempt corporations, such as those involved in international trade. Disintermediation is problematic on efficiency grounds and also because the financial sector is politically powerful in most countries. Options include limiting the duration of the capital control policy, or extending it to nonbank corporations. When confronting disintermediation, Eichengreen *et al.* (1995) recommend that capital controls within the European Union be imposed for a period limited to 2 years (namely, the last two in the transition to the European Monetary Union). The Chilean authorities have taken the opposite approach, in 1992 extending the tax to most loans from nonresidents – including many of those received by corporations – on a permanent basis.

One problem with the Chilean approach is that in countries where exports are considered the engine of national growth, there are strong political objections to permanent taxes on trade credits taken out by exporters. For this reason, the Chilean Central Bank was forced to exempt trade credit. When exporters and importers are exempt from a selective capital control, its macroeconomic effectiveness is obviously impaired.

The greatest problem of all is that a "selective" capital control presumes there are exempt flows, that is, ones that must be exempt for economic or political reasons. But if all exemptions are eliminated to prevent avoidance, then the capital control is no longer selective.

4.3 Selective Capital Controls and the Exchange Rate Regime

In open economies, the monetary authorities have only one policy tool but two policy targets: interest rates and exchange rates. However, imposing a capital control provides them with two policy tools, and in theory they may use these two tools to reach both targets simultaneously. This section investigates whether this is correct. We assume perfect capital mobility (i.e., constant risk premia in foreign supply), that domestic banks are part of the taxed sector, and that capital controls apply to all bank transactions. The last two assumptions imply that the capital control is relevant.

4.3.1 Effectiveness under a fixed exchange rate

First consider a managed or predetermined exchange rate regime, where $dlnE/dt$ is set by the authorities. The effects of the control in this case are summarized in *Table 4.1*. In this regime the monetary policy dilemma is that short-term capital flows completely undermine any attempt to vary i^d through open market operations. The exchange rate target is the only one that can be met.

To simplify the notation we define

$$i^* + \{dlnE/dt\}_{\text{auth}} + r^t \equiv i^{*t}, \tag{4.6}$$

where $\{dlnE/dt\}_{\text{auth}}$ is the rate of devaluation set by the authorities and i^{*t} is the foreign interest rate perceived by the taxed sector.

Market equilibrium requires that:

$$i^{td} = i^{*t} + \theta, \tag{4.7a}$$

$$i^{ed} = i^{*t} + [r^e - r^t], \tag{4.7b}$$

$$S^t = D^t(i^{*t} + \theta, i^{*t} + [r^e - r^t], i^{*t} - r^t, X^t), \tag{4.7c}$$

$$S^e = D^e(i^{*t} + [r^e - r^t], i^{*t} + \theta, i^{*t} - r^t, X^e). \tag{4.7d}$$

Table 4.1. Impact of a selective capital control under elastic supply of funds to both sectors.

	Impact of an increase in capital control tax rate θ on		
I. Fixed exchange rate[a]			
Case	Balance of payments & sterilization costs	i^t	i^e
Irrelevance	0	Taxed sector disappears	0
Sign of $\partial(D^t + D^e)/\partial\theta$			
Ineffective	0	+	0
Fully effective			
Total effect of θ	–	0	0
Effect of θ at the margin	0	0	0
II. Freely floating exchange rate[b]			
Case	$dlnE/dt^d$	i^e	Net credit flows
Irrelevance[c]	Taxed sector disappears	0	0
Sign of $\theta(D^t + D^e)/\partial\theta$			
Ineffective	–	–	0
Fully effective			
Total effect of θ	0	0	?
Effect of θ at the margin	0	0	0

[a]Exchange rate (E) set separately.
[b]Interest rate (it^d) set separately.
[c]Forex market dominated by exempt sector.
[d]Under a free-floating exchange rate regime, sterilization costs are always zero.

Given the fixed exchange rate and relevance, the capital control is able to raise the domestic interest rate for the taxed sector, as shown in equation (4.7a). The interest rate in the exempt sector is not affected by the capital control under fixed exchange rates, as shown in equation (4.7b). Thus, under a fixed exchange rate, the capital control allows the simultaneous achievement of both the exchange rate target and the interest rate target for the taxed sector. However, the authorities cannot influence interest rates in the exempt sector, so that the capital control is insufficient to give full policy autonomy to the central bank.

Beside the exchange rate and the interest rate targets, there is an implicit third policy objective, namely, minimizing the quasi-fiscal losses due to sterilization of the monetary effects of purchases of international reserves. Does the capital control help with this third policy objective? Consider a scenario where there is an exogenous increase in capital inflows, so the overall balance of payments is in surplus because the central bank must buy international reserves to prevent an appreciation. This may fuel domestic inflation or, if sterilized, create a growing quasi-fiscal deficit. Now consider an increase in the capital control θ to prevent this. To find the impact of the capital control on the balance of payments, we employ equations (4.7c) and (4.7d) to obtain:

$$\partial(D^t + D^e)/\partial\theta|_{\text{fixed exchange rates}} = D_1^t + D_2^e. \tag{4.8}$$

The left-hand side of equation (4.8) is the degree of effectiveness [see definition (4.4c)]. The first term on the right-hand side is positive, and the second negative, so the total may take either sign. If the sensitivity of the taxed sector to the interest rate charged in it is similar in size to the cross sensitivity of the exempt sector to the interest rate charged in the taxed sector, the capital control might not help the central bank to reduce its purchases of international reserves.

What happens if the tax rate θ is raised so much that interest-sensitive, short-term flows to the taxed sector are eliminated? This happens for flows that are very short term, when an unremunerated reserve requirement such as the Chilean one is imposed, because the tax rate per unit of time for those flows can be very large. In this case, the capital control is fully effective for the relevant term, so equation (4.7a) becomes an inequality $(i^{td} < i^{*t} + \theta)$ and θ ceases to influence market equilibrium for flows within that period. Instead, domestic monetary policy, i^{td}, during that period sets equilibrium, even though the exchange rate is predetermined. In this case, the authorities "solve" their policy dilemma for flows, in that they can set both the domestic interest rate and the exchange rate directly during that period. Such a policy may discriminate dramatically, of course, between the exempt and taxed sectors, and between flows of different terms.

4.3.2 Effectiveness under a freely floating exchange rate

Now consider a freely floating exchange rate regime under perfect capital mobility (with constant risk premia in foreign supply). In this regime, the authorities set the interest rate in the domestic money market, so their policy aims in this area can be reached directly. In addition, there are no quasi-fiscal deficits from sterilizing purchases of international reserves, because the authorities do not make such purchases. However, there is a policy dilemma under this regime, which stems from the fact that every time the authorities tighten monetary policy, the exchange rate appreciates on impact and interest groups tied to the tradable goods sector complain because it loses competitiveness. The presence of a second policy tool, the capital control, raises the question of whether this dilemma can be avoided.

To see whether this is the case, consider a situation in which the authorities tighten monetary policy (raise i^{td}) and at the same time increase θ, the rate of the capital control. We assume that domestic banks are part of the taxed sector, so the authorities can set i^{td} even if the absolute amount of net inflows to the taxed sector is negative. It turns out that in any one term for credit flows, there are two possible outcomes from this combination of policies.

If the exchange rate is determined in the taxed sector, the uncovered interest parity condition in the sector alone sets the expected rate of devaluation as a function of domestic monetary policy:

$$E\{dlnE/dt\} = (i^{td})_{\text{auth}} - (i^* + r^t) - \theta. \tag{4.9a}$$

The only assumption required for this result is that the foreign exchange market is unified for credit flows of the given term, in that both the taxed and exempt sectors can purchase and sell foreign exchange at the same prices for this term. According to equation (4.9a), when the authorities tighten monetary policy alone, the rate of subsequent devaluation must increase. Thus, the level of the exchange rate must appreciate on impact to allow the exchange rate to converge to its long-run equilibrium value. This is true regardless of the level of θ.

Alternatively, equation (4.9a) also shows that if the authorities vary monetary policy $[(i^{td})_{\text{auth}}]$ together with θ in order to keep the right hand side of equation (4.9a) constant, the exchange rate's path is unaffected. This proves that a relevant capital control allows authorities committed to a freely floating exchange rate regime to reach both policy objectives simultaneously, that is, it allows them to set both the interest rate and the exchange rate simultaneously for a given term. This is done without incurring a quasi-fiscal deficit. The conditions for this result are that a freely floating regime is adopted and that the capital control is moved together with monetary policy. Of course, the application of such a policy requires the continuous monitoring of changes in the risk premia r^t and r^e in dozens of credit markets. The single tax rate would have to be adjusted on a weekly basis in response to some measure of the average change in the risk premia. Such a process may generate uncertainty and inefficiency.

We consider next the effects on the exempt market. Uncovered interest parity in this market is given by equation (4.1b). When $E\{dlnE/dt\}$ is eliminated using equation (4.9a), we obtain

$$i^{ed} = (i^{td})_{\text{auth}} - \theta + [r^e - r^t]. \tag{4.9b}$$

This equation shows that the domestic interest rate in the exempt market is not governed by domestic monetary policy (i^{td}) when the capital control θ is varied simultaneously to cancel out the changes in i^{td}. In such a setting, monetary policy does not affect the exempt market, just as in the fixed exchange rate regime. Another implication of equation (4.9b) is that the interest rate in the exempt market after risk adjustment is θ percent below the rate in the taxed market. Thus, the capital control continues to misallocate resources between the taxed and exempt sectors.

What is the impact of the control on capital flows? Market equilibrium requires that:

$$S^t = D^t((i^{td})_{\text{auth}}, (i^{td})_{\text{auth}} - \theta + r^e - r^t, (i^{td})_{\text{auth}} - \theta - r^t, X^t), \qquad (4.9c)$$

$$S^e = D^e((i^{td})_{\text{auth}} - \theta + r^e - r^t, (i^{td})_{\text{auth}}, (i^{td})_{\text{auth}} - \theta - r^t, X^e). \qquad (4.9d)$$

The third argument in the net demand functions shows the reaction of domestic investors to an increase in θ: an increase in the capital control reduces the rate of change of the exchange rate as required by interest arbitrage in the taxed sector. This reduces domestic investors' return on investing abroad, and they react by bringing funds back home and increasing their supply of funds to domestic users, reducing the net demand for foreign funds.[4] Equations (4.9a) and (4.9b) show that if the central bank tightens monetary policy and simultaneously raises the capital control rate, the flows to both markets are unaffected.

Another question is whether the application of the capital control alone can influence total domestic credit. This can be calculated from equations (4.9c) and (4.9d):

$$\partial D^t + D^e)/\partial\theta|_{\text{floating exchange rate}} = (-1) \cdot \{D_2^t + D_3^t + D_1^e + D_3^e\}. \qquad (4.10)$$

When the capital control alone is increased, the expected rate of depreciation of the exchange rate falls, as required by equation (4.9a), forcing the exchange rate to depreciate on impact. Alternatively, if the authorities want a double impact on the appreciation of the exchange rate, they can raise domestic interest rates and simultaneously reduce the capital control θ.

However, the sign of the effect of θ alone on total domestic credit is ambiguous. When only the capital control is increased, the interest rate in the exempt sector falls, as shown by equation (4.9b), inducing higher inflows to the exempt sector (D_1^e is positive), reducing inflows to the taxed sector (D_2^t is negative), and inducing domestic savers to move abroad (D_3^t and D_3^e are negative).

What is the significance of the fact that equation (4.10) is different from zero? Recall that this is a partial equilibrium model explaining only credit flows. If the capital control turns out not to influence total credit flows [i.e., $\partial(D^t + D^e)/\partial\theta = 0$], other foreign exchange flows can remain at their original levels, even if θ increases. Conversely, if the capital control influences total credit flows, other foreign exchange flows, such as current account transactions or direct foreign investment, must go through further adjustments to keep the balance of payments in equilibrium as required by the freely floating exchange rate regime. Thus, equation (4.10) shows the impact of the capital control on credit flows alone, not on the overall balance of payments, which is zero under free floating.[5]

The fact that equations (4.8) and (4.10) are not identical shows that the influence of a given capital control is a function of the intervention regime in the foreign exchange market.

If the tax rate θ is raised so much that interest-sensitive, short-term flows to the taxed sector are eliminated (full effectiveness), then marginal flows to the taxed sector do not control the level of the foreign exchange rate and equation (4.9a) is not met. When a URR such as the Chilean one is imposed, this happens for flows that are very short term, because for these flows the tax rate per unit of time is very large. For flows of these terms, the capital control rate θ does not influence equilibrium. The authorities "solve" their policy dilemma, in that although they set domestic interest rates in the taxed sector (i^{td}), they are free to use exchange rate policy to control the interest rate in the exempt sector. In this case, equation (4.9b) is replaced by $i^{ed} = E\{d\ln E/dt\}_{\text{auth}} + i^* + r^e$. Again, the policy chosen by the authorities may discriminate dramatically between the exempt and the taxed sectors, and between credit flows of different terms.

4.3.3 Empirical implications

The framework developed above suggests that looking at the volume of tax revenue is a simple method of ascertaining whether relevance applies in the case of a given country. If the volume of tax revenue is very small, then either irrelevance or full effectiveness must have been obtained. If tax revenue is substantial, neither of these scenarios can have applied.

Relevance can also be ascertained in the case of a fixed or predetermined exchange rate regime, in this case by looking at the spread between domestic interest rates in the taxed sector and foreign interest rates, for credit flows of a given term. If the capital control is relevant then this interest rate differential should evolve over time following θ [see equation (4.7a)].

However, the main point is that this differential is uninformative regarding effectiveness under fixed exchange rates. Uncovered interest parity, as expressed in equations (4.7a) and (4.7b), is compatible with any degree of effectiveness as long as the capital control is relevant. Empirical work is needed to estimate the degree of effectiveness of the capital control, that is, the value of $\partial(D^t + D^e)/\partial\theta$. Because effectiveness may be different for credit flows of different terms, and data on flows classified by term is usually unavailable, only an average can be measured.

Under a freely floating regime, relevance implies that the spread between the interest rates in the taxed and exempt sector ($i^{td} - i^{ed}$) should also evolve over time following θ, abstracting from changes in $r^t - r^e$ [see equation (4.9b)]. Fortunately, a measurement of effectiveness is unnecessary under such a regime, as it always obtains for credit flows at terms for which transactions in the taxed sector determine the exchange rate. At shorter terms, where interest-sensitive credit flows have been eliminated, effectiveness is also obvious.

4.4   A Case Study: The Chilean Capital Control

The next sections apply the framework developed above to the Chilean URR in the 1987–1996 period. In June 1991, the central bank imposed a URR of 20% on foreign credits, covering most of those received by both resident banks and nonbanks. In May 1992, the URR was raised to 30%, where it has since remained. This section describes the reasons provided by the Chilean authorities for imposing a URR on capital inflows on a permanent basis and then describes the microeconomic details and results.

4.4.1   Improving tradeoff between monetary independence and real exchange rate targets

It may appear surprising that Chile introduced a URR on capital inflows, given that it has been moving toward market-based resource allocation since 1974. However, the country has a long tradition of regulating the transactions of private agents participating in capital flows.[6] Indeed, for many years, Chilean economists have considered the private international financial market to be unreliable. Since 1991, a number of specific arguments have been offered by the Chilean authorities to justify the imposition of permanent URRs on inflows.

The Central Bank of Chile has eschewed the use of a fixed nominal exchange rate as a means to control inflation. Accordingly, it has allowed the nominal exchange rate to float within a relatively wide band[7] and has managed aggregate demand through interest rate policy. When it wants to reduce inflation, it increases domestic interest rates. This dampens aggregate demand directly, but also attracts capital inflows that spur an appreciation of the currency and reduce the inflation rate for traded goods. If allowed to work, both measures contribute to achieving the desired reduction in domestic inflation.

The Chilean authorities are, however, also concerned with the real exchange rate (RER), which affects the competitiveness of Chilean exporters. Export growth is a national goal with widespread political support. The dilemma for the authorities stems from the fact that a tightening of monetary policy is more effective in reducing inflation when it is helped by a nominal appreciation (and the RER target is sacrificed in the short term).

One tool used by the Chilean authorities to deal with this dilemma has been massive sterilized intervention. The central bank has tried to prevent an appreciation of the currency by supporting the current exchange rate, financing these purchases by issuing costly domestic debt. The heavy use of this tool in Chile implies that the actual exchange rate regime has been very close to a predetermined or fixed exchange rate regime, except in episodes of discrete appreciations. This outcome illustrates the extent to which the authorities have been concerned with preventing an appreciation of the RER.

The URR is the other tool used by the authorities to deal with this dilemma. The URR was expected to widen interest rate differentials in such a way as to avoid provoking large capital inflows. If the URR reduces arbitrage, then the central bank can increase domestic interest rates without inducing a nominal appreciation (under a freely floating regime) or without engaging in costly sterilized intervention (under a fixed regime). Because the need to improve upon monetary policy tradeoffs is permanent, so is the URR tax.

4.4.2 Improving the mixture of foreign financing for the private sector

Certain types of capital flows are more desirable than others. In particular, long-term finance is deemed preferable to short-term debt finance. The latter entails a liquidity risk for the debtor country, as volatility and the probability of flow reversals is thought to be smaller for long-term finance. Among forms of longer-term finance, equity flows such as foreign direct investment (FDI) are seen as preferable to long-term debt, because FDI provides a means to share risks with entities outside the domestic economy. As this ordering is permanent, URRs should also be permanent. Although this line of reasoning has been hotly debated, we test below whether a URR is an effective tool to shift the composition of foreign finance by reducing the amount of total short-term credit as a proportion of GDP.[8]

4.4.3 Microeconomic description

The Chilean URR may be described as an "asymmetric Tobin tax". It is similar to a Tobin tax (Tobin, 1978) in that it is permanent and because the amount of the tax is a constant percentage of the size of the credit, regardless of its maturity.[9] This implies that the tax rate per unit of time is higher for credits of shorter maturities. It is asymmetric because it is levied only on inflows of credit, not on outflows. However, the URR is different from a Tobin tax because it is not levied on all foreign exchange transactions, but only on foreign credits, and is not levied by all countries, but only by the receiving country. The tax rate per unit time implicit in a URR is:

θ = [lost interest ($)/amount of funds left to lend ($)]/days to maturity,   (4.11)

which leads to:

$$\theta\left[\frac{(i^*+s)\cdot r}{1-r}\right] \cdot \frac{\text{Holding period}}{\text{Maturity}} \text{ for inflows and 0 for outflows,[10]} \qquad (4.12)$$

where θ = tax rate per unit time, as a percentage of funds available to lend. When $(i^* + s)$ is the interest cost of marginal funds, θ is a marginal rate as well; r = rate of reserve requirement;[11] i^* = interbank nominal interest rate in foreign currency; s = spread over the interbank rate charged to arbitrageurs;[12] Holding period (HP) = minimum holding period of the reserves, set by the capital control. The HP was raised to 1 year in May 1992, but during a brief period before then the HP was more complex.

If the HP is fixed, the effective tax rate per unit of time is a function of the maturity of the credit. This justifies referring to URR as a "selective" capital control, as it taxes longer-term foreign credits at a much lower rate per period. For example, at the initial reserve requirement rate (20%), with an HP of 1 year and a 5% foreign interest rate, a 10-year international bond paid a modest effective annual surcharge of $(0.2/0.8)(1/10)(5\%) = 0.125\%$.

From virtually the beginning of the URR's existence, the central bank has offered arbitrageurs the opportunity to pay an up-front fee instead of holding reserves without remuneration. The up-front fee has been defined as the dollar LIBOR (London Inter-Bank Offered Rate) plus a surcharge, applied over the appropriate holding period. The resulting tax rate per unit of time on inflows is

$$\theta' = r \cdot (i_{\text{dollar}} + \text{surcharge}) \cdot (\text{HP/Maturity}), \qquad (4.13)$$

where i_{dollar} is the dollar LIBOR. Note that $(1 - r)$ does not appear in equation (4.13). In practice, the surcharge has been adjusted over time so that θ' is almost the same as θ.

One of the drawbacks of the Chilean URR is that it does not allow the effective tax rate to be fully controlled by the local authorities, unless the reserve rate (r) is adjusted on a weekly (or even daily) basis in response to changes in foreign interest rates. Moreover, for the URR tax to respond automatically to the domestic interest rate, it would have to be maintained in the local currency (pesos).

4.4.4 Estimates of θ for Chile

Table 4.2 presents our estimates of θ for a 180-day foreign credit to Chilean residents. The first point to be made from *Table 4.2* is that the Chilean authorities have

Table 4.2. Implicit annual tax on inflows of new 180-day credits in Chile.

Quarter	Tax rate (% per year)	Quarter	Tax rate (% per year)
		1994:1	3.3
Until 1991:2	0	1994:2	3.3
1991:3	1.6	1994:3	3.3
1991:4	1.4	1994:4	3.6
1992:1	1.3	1995:1	6.7
1992:2	1.8	1995:2	6.3
1992:3	3.2	1995:3	5.7
1992:4	3.9	1995:4	5.8
1993:1	3.4	1996:1	5.5
1993:2	3.5	1996:2	5.7
1993:3	4.1	1996:3	5.7
1993:4	3.5	1996:4	5.6

Notes: The tax rates presented here differ from those in Soto (1995) because: (i) our figures for 1992:2, 1992:3, and 1994:4 take into account the fact that the tax rate changed in mid-quarter; and (ii) our figures also take the spread into account. The tax rates in this table apply to flows of new credit; the rates for increases in the stock of credit lines for international trade credit are slightly different in some quarters.

managed the URR in such a way as to increase θ substantially over time, but have not changed it on a monthly basis. They have done this mostly without varying the reserve rate r, which they changed only in 1992. Instead, they have increased the holding period (in 1992) and restricted the right of arbitrageurs to choose the currency in which the reserves can be held. Elsewhere, we show that optimization by an arbitrageur leads him or her to select the currency in which the nominal interest rate is minimal, which since 1993 has been the Japanese yen (Valdés-Prieto and Soto, 1996). The estimates in *Table 4.2* take into account this optimization. Thus, when the authorities changed policy and forced arbitrageurs to hold their reserves in US dollars (in December 1994), the value of θ almost doubled. This regulatory change coincided with the Mexican crisis, a fact that will raise some problems of interpretation discussed below.

The second point from *Table 4.2* is that the tax rates in Chile on 180-day credits (in the 3–6% range) have been substantially smaller than the gains that could have been obtained by predicting the timing of the maxi appreciations that occurred in the sample period. The order of magnitude of those gains can be gauged by the standard deviation of the change in the RER over 1987–1996, which was 3.1% per quarter, or 13% per year (i.e., much larger than 3–6%). However, predicting exchange rate movements 180 days ahead is difficult.

Next consider whether a URR can prevent a speculative attack. Take as an example a 5% appreciation predicted 1 month ahead with a high degree of certainty. This provides a profit per unit of time of 80% on an annual basis. If we take, however, a URR tax like the one reported for 1996 in *Table 4.2*, such as 6%, it must be multiplied by 6 in the case of a 30-day credit, which is only 36%. As this is much less than 80%, the arbitrageur is not deterred by a URR at the Chilean level with a constant reserve rate (r) and holding period. This implies that a Chilean-style URR cannot protect a central bank from a speculative surge in inflows (or outflows). Recall that reducing the size of volatile short-term foreign credits in relation to the economy, in order to prevent domestic repercussions if these flows reverse suddenly, was one of the policy objectives mentioned in the introduction. A Chilean-style URR can influence only the permanent component of capital flows.

This points to a flaw in the proposal by Eichengreen *et al.* (1995) to use URRs to prevent speculative attacks on European currencies en route to the EMU. This tool is ineffective unless reserve rates are raised to levels such as 50% or holding periods raised to two years. However, even then speculative attacks with a horizon of only 1 week would still earn a profit. Accordingly, it remains to be seen whether a URR-based capital control can prevent speculative attacks.

4.4.5 Proof of relevance of Chilean URR

As explained in Section 4.3, the volume of tax revenue is a simple but telling indicator of the effectiveness of a selective capital control. Such revenue should be zero if the capital control is irrelevant. If there is total effectiveness at the margin, the tax revenue could still be positive if the interest-insensitive capital flow to the taxed sector is positive.

Based on central bank data, we have estimated the tax revenue earned by URR over 1991–1996. This revenue is defined as the nominal interest earned by the central bank on such reserves, plus the up-front fees paid on those flows whose recipients chose that mechanism. The revenue observed in Chile is reported in *Table 4.3*.

Revenue of 0.11% of gross domestic product (GDP) is certainly significant, so the Chilean URR could not have been irrelevant in the sample period. A significant number of market participants, including domestic banks, were unable to substitute exempt inflows for the taxed inflows. Moreover, those market participants were not fully deterred by the URR from intermediating some inflows, because in that case tax revenue would have been zero. Thus, the URR exhibits at least an intermediate degree of effectiveness in Chile.

This contrasts with the experience of Spain in late 1992, where the capital control quickly became irrelevant according to De Gregorio (1995) and Garber and

Table 4.3. Revenue from the Chilean unremunerated reserve requirement.[a]

Year	US$ (million)	% of GDP
1991	6.3	0.02
1992	27.2	0.06
1993	40.6	0.09
1994	63.0	0.12
1995	73.8	0.11
1996	82.2	0.11

[a]Revenue is calculated as $R = i * \cdot$ (reserves held against stock of bank short-term credit) + $(i * t + \theta) \cdot$ (amount of credits that chose to pay up-front fees). These figures exclude the revenue from the URR imposed on domestic deposits expressed in foreign currency, which was almost $20 million in 1996, bringing total URR revenue to 0.13% of GDP that year. This series differs from the one reported by Soto (1995:14), who was forced by a limited data set to rely on assumptions that greatly simplified reality.

Taylor (1995). One possible explanation for this difference with respect to Spain is that the Chilean authorities have sought to close loopholes and to increase the tax base and the tax rate on an ongoing basis. In contrast, in Spain the capital controls were abandoned after 60 days of application because their original purpose, to provide some breathing space, had been fulfilled.

4.5   Degree of Effectiveness of Chilean URR

The data on tax revenue show that the URR has exhibited at least an intermediate degree of effectiveness in Chile. This section seeks to determine the magnitude of such effectiveness. To do this we investigate the impact of the URR tax on the volume of total short-term, cross-border credit flows, considering both taxed and exempt flows, as reported in the balance of payments.

This choice implies that we will be unable to consider tax avoidance methods that substitute taxed short-term flows for exempt flows that are not classified as short-term in Chilean statistics, such as portfolio investment, medium-term debt with prepayment options, and over-reporting of profits earned abroad. Thus, the work in this section may find that the tax reduces short-term credit flows, even though it does not reduce total short-term flows, more broadly defined. We also study quarterly data on total short-term credit inflows to the private sector. The URR tax began in June 1991, which was positive in 27 of the 40 quarters under investigation.[13]

Measurement of the impact of the URR tax on short-term credit flows requires keeping "everything else" constant, which necessitates building a consistent econometric model of those flows, which we now present.

4.5.1   Economic discussion of econometric model

The net short-term credits being observed should be the outcome of at least three types of decisions: (i) portfolio balance considerations; (ii) changes in the volume of trade credit; and (iii) deliberate policy.

Regarding portfolio balance considerations, the interest rate differential between Chile and abroad should affect the net inflow. Thus, foreign interest rates, domestic interest rates, and the tax rate θ implicit in the URR (taken from *Table 4.2*) should be part of the explanatory variables. In addition, we need an estimate of the expected depreciation of the peso. Because there are no data on this variable, we project the expected depreciation with a supplementary model, described below. Portfolio balance should also be influenced by supply-side factors such as the country's risk rating, as well as phenomena such as the Mexican crisis and, more generally, by variations in the total capital flows going to emerging markets.

As for the volume of trade credit, it is proportional to the volume of international trade. In Chile, both exports and imports are financed abroad, although to different extents.

Deliberate macroeconomic policy determines domestic interest rates, as already mentioned, but in addition sterilized foreign exchange intervention may have another influence. If capital mobility is imperfect, the authorities may engage in such intervention so as to allow the observed interest rate differential to diverge from its equilibrium value. Foreign exchange purchases should increase short-term inflows to the private sector. Policies regarding the taxation of other capital flows, such as FDI and portfolio investment, may have secondary effects on short-term credits, but we cannot incorporate them in the model due to the lack of data available.

On this basis, we postulate behavioral equation (4.14). The expected signs of the coefficients are shown below each variable.

$$\text{STCERR} = h(\text{PRBC}; \text{I}^*; \text{E}\{\partial \ln (\text{RER})/\partial t\}; \text{TAX}; \text{RATING}; \text{MA}; \text{IMP}; \text{EXP}; \text{FOP}), (4.14)$$
$$\quad\quad (+)\quad (-)\quad\quad\quad (-)\quad\quad\quad (-)\quad\quad (+)\quad\quad (+)\ (+\text{ or }0)\ (+\text{ or }0)\ (+)$$

where STCERR = total short-term credits to the private sector, net of amortizations and other debt movements, from the quarterly balance of payments, as a share of quarterly Chilean GDP in dollars. The increase in unremunerated reserves is included in published credit figures, therefore this value was subtracted. Those funds never enter the currency market, because they are foreign currency deposits in the central bank; the central bank invests them abroad, as part of international reserves. If this values is not subtracted, an increase in the reserve rate could increase STCERR even if STCERR net of reserves falls. We added errors and omissions from the balance of payments because we found that doing so raises the adjusted R^2 and makes the coefficient estimates more significant. PRBC = interest rate used by the authorities to set monetary policy. In Chile, this is the rate paid on CPI-indexed, short-term paper, so it is a "real" rate. I^* = foreign real interest rates, as measured by the dollar LIBOR minus the rate of change of the US wholesale price index. $E\{\partial \ln(RER)/\partial t\}$ = expected real rate of depreciation of the currency, not observable but estimated via a separate model. TAX = tax rate on short-term capital inflows associated with the URR (from *Table 4.2*). The URR tax rate appears separately because its coverage is not universal. Its effectiveness cannot be tested if we impose the restriction that only $(I^* + TAX)$ influences flows. RATING = rating of the country's debt by Standard and Poor's. This variable proxies shifts in the supply curve of foreign funds to Chile. After some experimentation, we set this variable at unity for periods in which government foreign debt has been rated as BBB+ or above and 0 otherwise. MA = aggregate capital account balance of Latin American countries, in dollars, expressed as a ratio to Chilean GDP. This variable proxies other shifts in the supply curve of foreign funds to Chile (it is measured on an annual basis). IMP = imports of goods as a fraction of GDP. EXP = exports of goods as a fraction of GDP. FOP = net foreign exchange purchases by the central bank as a share of GDP.

The purpose of the econometric model is to measure the value of $\partial(D^t + D^e)/\partial\theta$, which in this case is $\partial STCERR/\partial TAX$. In other words, we are primarily interested in the coefficient on TAX in equation (4.14).

There is a lack of data suitable for measuring the expected depreciation term in equation (4.14). We deal with this problem by replacing $E\{\partial \ln(RER)/\partial t\}$ with the projected value obtained from the following 3-step procedure. First, we estimate a model in which the RER is explained by a time trend, the share of government expenditure in GDP, the terms of trade, and the risk rating of the country's debt (which improved substantially during the period). Second, we estimate a model in which the rate of change of the real exchange rate (ΔRER) is regressed on the lagged change in the nominal exchange rate, foreign currency purchases by the central bank, nominal interest rates, the tax rate of the URR, and two lagged residuals from the first equation. The combination of the two steps is similar to an error–correction approach, but it differs from the one reported in Valdés-Prieto and Soto (1996) due to data revisions, a longer sample, and changes in the specification. The third step smoothes the rate of devaluation predicted in the second step, using a standard software package that employs a weighted average of the current and last values, where the weights are optimized.[14]

An advantage of basing the analysis on the real exchange rate, rather than the nominal one, is that doing so allows us to deal with the complexities of the intervention regime followed in Chile in the sample period. In some subperiods the exchange rate was allowed to float, mostly in a dirty fashion, but in other periods the exchange rate was fixed at the "floor" of a band that was first honored and then abandoned when the reserve buildup was deemed excessive.

Because a shock to capital inflows may induce the authorities to change policy, the policy variables in equation (4.14) are potentially endogenous. The three policy variables are PRBC, TAX, and FOP. As equation (4.14) contains only 10 variables, we can deal with potential simultaneity by employing instrumental variable techniques. In particular, we replace PRBC and TAX by their predicted values, as obtained from regressions run on a set of instruments. FOP should receive the same treatment, since the authorities can increase the use of sterilization in reaction to an increase in short-term inflows. However, it was impossible to find a set of instruments for FOP with a suitably high R^2. In any case, the direction in which the endogeneity of FOP would bias the coefficient on TAX – the estimate of primary interest – is unclear.

Table 4.4 presents the results of estimating equation (4.14) with TAX and PRBC replaced by their instrumental variables, TAX' and PRBC', respectively. The estimated standard errors are constructed from the relevant predicted values based on the actual values of PRBC and TAX. The coefficients on RATING, MA, and EXP are not significant, and neither is the instrument for PRBC, but the signs of the other coefficients are as expected.

4.5.2   Effectiveness of a permanent URR

Table 4.4 presents the results of running four regressions. The first is the best regression for the sample period 1987:1 to 1994:4, which excludes the period after the Mexican crisis of December 1994. The results replicate previous results by the authors, showing that the rate of URR tax (applied on a permanent basis) did not reduce short-term credits to Chile at all. On the contrary, the URR was counterproductive, in that a higher permanent TAX stimulated further credit inflows, maybe because a higher TAX announced higher domestic interest rates.

The second regression in *Table 4.4* expands the sample to include 1995 (the year the "Tequila effect" was felt in many Latin American countries) and 1996. A problem with doing so is that the tax rate doubled between 1994 and 1995, because the central bank changed its regulations and required arbitrageurs to hold their reserves in dollars rather than yen, which paid a much lower nominal interest rate. This dramatic change in TAX raises the possibility that the URR became effective at these much higher tax rates, even though it was ineffective at lower rates. To take this possibility into account, we split TAX in two variables, as follows:[15]

$$\text{TAX1} = \min\{\text{TAX}; 0.045\}; \text{TAX2} = \max\{\text{TAX} - 0.045; 0\}. \qquad (4.15)$$

Table 4.4. Effectiveness of Chilean unremunerated reserve requirement: Regression results.[a] Dependent variable: Net short-term credit inflows to the private sector plus errors and omissions (STCERR).

Regression no.	1	2	3	4
	1987:4	1987:4	1989:4	1987:4
Sample period:	to 1994:4	to 1996:4	to 1996:4	to 1996:4
Constant	−0.43	−0.39	−0.24	−0.47
	(−4.64)	(−3.88)	(−1.66)	(−3.57)
IMP	1.74	1.61	1.26	1.77
	(4.37)	(3.68)	(2.39)	(3.47)
PRBC[a]	−0.34	−0.24	−0.57	−0.043
	(−0.97)	(−0.59)	(−1.11)	(−0.07)
PRBC × TAX1	−	−	−	20.2
				(0.13)
PRBC × TAX2	−	−	−	−418.6
				(−0.86)
I*	0.01	−0.38	−0.68	−0.004
	(0.02)	(−0.78)	(−1.08)	(−0.004)
Expected real devaluation	−0.45	−0.61	−0.35	−0.52
	(−2.51)	(−3.16)	(−0.91)	(−1.13)
TAX[b]	1.09	−	−	−
	(1.45)			
TAX1[b]	−	0.33	−0.21	−0.05
		(0.40)	(−0.22)	(−0.004)
TAX2[b]	−	−2.38	−1.81	23.05
		(−1.60)	(−1.06)	(0.74)
FOP	0.68	0.69	0.49	0.82
	(3.93)	(3.48)	(1.85)	(3.41)
Lagged dependent variable	−0.18	−0.27	−0.31	−0.30
	(−1.28)	(−2.13)	(−2.02)	(−1.97)
Adjusted R^2:	0.56	0.51	0.43	0.36
Durbin's h:	−1.41	−0.88	0.36	−1.53
Number of observations:	29	37	32	37

[a] See text for definitions of variables. Standard errors are in parentheses. They are based on the residuals obtained from the actual values of the explanatory variables and the estimated coefficients.
[b] Instrumental variable; see text for discussion.

The coefficients on TAX1 and TAX2 in *Table 4.4* are consistent with the hypothesis that there is a threshold above which these taxes reduce the volume of short-term credits. The coefficient of TAX1 is almost zero, showing that in the expanded sample low tax rates are ineffective but not counterproductive. The coefficient of TAX2 is negative, suggesting that a threshold effect is present. However, its coefficient is insignificantly different from zero (the t-statistic is equal to −1.60), so the existence of a threshold effect has not been established. Conversely, TAX2 behaves essentially as a dummy variable for 1995–1996, so these results may simply show that other factors shifted the supply curve of foreign funds to Chile and the URR tax continued to be ineffective.

In addition, these results do not take into account the effect of tax avoidance methods that substitute exempt flows for taxed short-term flows that are not classified as short-term credit in Chilean statistics. Indeed, during 1995 the central bank found that there had been a substantial increase in "secondary American Depository Receipt" operations. Such operations entail an arbitrageur taking a position in Chilean equities traded on the New York stock exchange and simultaneously hedging it by taking the opposite position on the Santiago stock exchange. After the URR tax on credits was doubled in early 1995, the central bank realized that the hedging float had grown enormously because it was exempt from the URR tax. The authorities reacted by applying the URR tax to all hedging operations, which, of course, allowed individual share prices to diverge between Santiago and New York. This introduced a new reason for domestic investors to do their trading in Chilean equities on the New York stock exchange, disintermediating the Santiago exchange. The hedging float is not included in our short-term credit figures, therefore our regression cannot measure the overall effectiveness of the URR tax.

Once this loophole was closed, new ones were sought by investors. In early 1996, Credit Suisse invested $700 million in the equity of a custom-made investment company devoted to holding Chilean short-term debt. According to the rules, after one year it could repatriate the original investment. Other banks followed suit. The central bank moved to close this loophole, but it did so in an arbitrary manner, introducing case-by-case qualification of equity investments, determining whether they were exempt from the URR tax. Thus, even if the work in this section finds that the URR tax reduces short-term credit flows, it remains to be seen if it does the same for the more broadly defined total short-term flows.

The third regression in *Table 4.4* considers in particular the subsample 1989:1 to 1996:4, due to concerns that the earlier period (1987 and 1988) may have been structurally different, owing to Chile's much more limited access to international capital markets at that time. This regression includes the split TAX variables. The results are weaker than for the full period, but the main fact is that the URR tax became effective only for high tax rates stands.

4.5.3   Selective capital controls and monetary independence

The ability of the URR tax to decrease the elasticity of capital flows to the domestic interest rate set by the monetary authorities (PRBC) was also looked at. We did so by adding an interaction term to equation (4.14), which was the product of PRBC and TAX'. Because TAX is split into two variables, we also split the interaction term. The results of running regression 4 in *Table 4.4* show that the coefficient on the interaction term is essentially zero for low URR taxes. Thus, under a regime in which the URR tax does not affect short-term credits, domestic interest rates do not affect such credits either.

For high URR taxes, the point estimate of the coefficient on the interaction term is imprecise, because this term seems to be highly correlated with TAX2, whose coefficient changes sign and is of an implausibly large magnitude. Thus, this regression does not provide useful information for high URR tax levels.

4.5.4   "Emergency" versus permanent capital controls

Eichengreen *et al.* (1995) recommend using a URR for periods not exceeding 6 months. This advice is based on the Spanish experience, where URRs were used to gain breathing space during the speculative attacks of late 1992. Later, the advice was followed by Malaysia, which imposed capital controls in early 1994 and removed them after 6 months.

Although the Chilean data set offers the advantage of a very extended sample (10 years), as it is available only on a quarterly basis it cannot be used to test this policy recommendation directly. However, we can report that the lags of TAX and the lags of the dependent variables do not have significant coefficients in equation (4.14), when tested on our sample. This result implies that the adjustment process for total short-term credits plus errors and omissions occurs entirely within a single quarter, suggesting that the 6-month limit is an upper bound. A more realistic one might be 3 months.

4.5.5   Related results

Valdés-Prieto and Soto (1996) find that during the same sample period used here an increase in TAX has an insignificant impact on the path of the equilibrium real exchange rate. They also find that the URR tax does not lead to a depreciation of the real exchange rate in the short term, as estimated by a short-run equation of an error correction model. Soto (1995:38–49) also finds the same sign for this coefficient in his econometric model for trade-related credit lines intermediated by domestic banks. Chumacero *et al.* (1996) build a different econometric model for capital flows to Chile and apply it to a similar sample period. They find that an increase in the URR tax increases short-term capital flows in the first two quarters, but that it has a small negative long-term effect.

4.6   Policy Evaluation of Selective Capital Controls

It has been claimed that selective capital controls are beneficial because they can help resolve a dilemma faced by a country's monetary authorities. Those authorities face a dilemma when they confront international capital mobility: they cannot set domestic interest rates and the exchange rate independently. If selective capital controls can help resolve this dilemma, they will be welcome. For example, in a floating exchange rate regime, capital controls may be used to deal with the implications for competitiveness of lowering domestic interest rates to permit higher investment and growth, or of raising domestic interest rates to curb inflation.

The theoretical part of this chapter found that capital controls may help to resolve this dilemma in two very different ways. In the first case, capital controls are so tight that interest-sensitive flows to the taxed sector disappear completely. This case will be discussed at the end of this section. In the second case, interest sensitive flows and overall market equilibrium are influenced by the capital control's tax rate. In this case, the tax rate θ can be changed continuously to guide the economy. We have found that this can be done only under a freely floating exchange rate regime. In a free float, a relevant capital control always leads to the depreciation of the currency on impact, compensating for the appreciation caused by tighter monetary policy. Thus, in this case a selective capital control does away with the policy dilemma and provides concrete benefits.

Under a fixed or predetermined exchange rate regime, the situation is ambiguous. A selective capital control raises the interest rate in the taxed sector, but substitution may mean that the measure's impact on total credit flows is small. When this is the case, the capital control does not help reduce the quasi-fiscal deficit associated with sterilization, so the policy dilemma remains. Thus, the issue of the effectiveness of a selective capital control is critical for countries such as Chile, which follow a fixed or predetermined exchange rate regime.

Our econometric evidence for Chile demonstrates that the URR was ineffective during the period 1991–1994. Our regressions also suggest that the doubling of the rate of the URR tax in 1995–1996 may have achieved a threshold at which the Chilean capital control became effective, but this result is not statistically strong. In any case, the threshold result can also be interpreted in other ways. For example, in 1995–1996 arbitrageurs were driven by the higher tax rates to find new methods to evade the controls, using routes not classified as short-term credits in the Chilean balance of payments. It remains an open question whether, using a wider definition of short-term flows, the Chilean capital control would still be found to have been effective over 1995–1996. Another interpretation that questions the URR tax's effectiveness is that the increase in URR tax rates behaved as a dummy variable for 1995–1996. In that case, our results would show that other factors shifted the supply curve of foreign funds to Chile, and the URR tax remained ineffective.

Permanent URRs with a constant implicit tax rate, such as the one used in Chile, have not been espoused in the academic literature. On the contrary, Eichengreen *et al.* (1995) propose the use of URRs on a temporary basis, limited to 6 months, and only to confront surges in capital flows or speculative attacks. Why have the Chilean authorities adopted high implicit tax rates on a permanent basis? One interpretation is that the monetary authorities are seeking to eliminate interest-sensitive short-term flows. If they managed to accomplish this, they would resolve their policy dilemma, in that they could set both the interest rate and the exchange rate directly.

This possibility raises the question of whether selective capital controls are harmless. At one extreme, when selective capital controls are ineffective, that is, when they do not help the monetary authorities solve their policy dilemma, there might be little harm in having them. At the other extreme, when selective capital controls are raised to such high levels that all interest-sensitive flows to the taxed sector are eliminated at the margin, harm may be substantial. The costs of capital controls merit an analysis, so that they can be compared with their alleged benefits.

One political problem with selective capital controls is that they allow the authorities to discriminate in a massive way between the taxed and exempt sectors, should they wish to do so. In Chile, only large corporations are able to obtain direct credit from their foreign counterparts, a practice exempt from the URR tax, leaving smaller exporters to bear the tax burden. Within the taxed sector, some inframarginal flows can earn large rents. More critically, the difference in interest rates between the sectors leads to a large difference in the willingness to pay for assets. This differential appears to have generated large redistributions of wealth and an increase in economic concentration in Chile, as exempt sector firms have purchased taxed-sector firms at what, for them, are bargain prices.

The theoretical literature argues that selective capital controls create resource allocation problems. First, selective capital controls are seen as a direct tax on the use of an input employed in many sectors, namely, short-term cross-border credit. Some sectors, including exporters, use this input more intensively and are thus taxed relative to other sectors. A second problem is that the controls impair the competitiveness of domestic banks and other domestic intermediaries in cross-border financial markets. A third problem is that the resources spent bypassing and avoiding the controls are wasted from a social point of view.

From a policy perspective, capital controls are accused of reducing the quality of policy-making. From the perspective of macroeconomic policy, ineffective selective capital controls may lull the authorities into believing that they have more control than what they actually have. This can delay for years the hard job of using fiscal policy to manage the transition to lower interest rate differentials.[16]

Alternatively, the quest for effective capital controls may encourage a drift toward more centralized resource allocation. When the effectiveness of the URR was questioned in the Chilean policy debate in 1995, and again in 1997, influential politicians proposed a shift to global quotas on all inflows, including FDI.[17] In March 1994, the Chilean Congress approved a law allowing the central bank to impose quotas on monthly changes in the level of foreign assets held by the main institutional investors, including commercial banks, pension funds, mutual funds, and insurance companies. This power has not been used up to now, but the trend raises questions. Thus, the evidence indicates that selective capital controls imposed on a permanent basis may be politically unstable, in the sense that they either disappear or grow ceaselessly.

Finally, it has been suggested in the policy literature that a benefit of selective capital controls is that they can act as a substitute for mediocre prudential supervision of domestic banks. Although this may hold for some institutional environments, it turns out that sound banking supervision and selective capital controls are complementary in a large number of cases. If prudential banking supervision is mediocre or nonexistent, foreign exchange transactions by domestic banks can be easily substituted with equivalent transactions made by domestic corporations backed by credits and guarantees issued by domestic banks. As in the Chilean experience of 1978–1982, short-term foreign credit to domestic corporations – which was more than half of the total – may be based on guarantees by domestic banks (Valdés-Prieto, 1994). Foreign exchange rate risk for domestic banks may simply be transformed into credit risk. Accordingly, sound prudential supervision is the first requirement for effective capital controls.

A second requirement for the effectiveness of a URR is that only regulated banking corporations are allowed to engage in banking activity. If this is not the case, then nonbanks are likely to disintermediate taxed banks and render the capital control irrelevant. A third requirement is tight control on the part of the tax authorities over the firms engaged in international trade. The requirement that nonbanks keep tax records offers a basis for controlling compliance with capital controls among such entities. If these three requirements are not met in a given country, selective capital controls are likely to fail to provide benefits.

Acknowledgments

We appreciate the comments of various participants in the workshop at IIASA in May 1997, including Mark Allen, Santiago Fernández de Lis, and Robert Holzmann. This paper is a continuation of the one presented at the workshop held at the World Bank on 22 September 1995, and at the Second Annual Seminar on Macroeconomics held at Alto Jahuel, Chile, on 10 November 1995. We are grateful for the comments at those meetings of A. Battarcharya, V. Carril, A. Fernández, S. Fischer, M. Guitián, Leonardo Hernández, L. O. Herrera, L.F. Lagos, F. Lefort, F. Ossa, F. Rosende, M. Schiff, K. Schmidt-Hebbel, A. Velasco, and J. Vial. Any remaining mistakes are the authors' responsibility.

Notes

[1] As reported in the newspaper *El Mercurio*, Santiago, 5 September 1995, page A1.

[2] As reported in *El Mercurio*, Santiago, 26 November 1996, page A13.

[3] Although 40 observations may seem insufficient for conventional empirical work, 10 years is almost a lifetime in the fast-moving world of capital flows and exchange rates. The sample period includes events such as the Gulf War, the end of the Latin American debt crisis, and the aftermath of the Mexican crisis of 1994.

[4] Such behavior has been reported for Chile.

[5] We owe this observation to Patricio Arrau.

[6] In the late 1970s, the same authorities that liberalized domestic interest rates and international trade imposed draconian URRs on certain capital inflows. On financial liberalization in Chile, see Valdés-Prieto (1994).

[7] Minor interventions in the foreign exchange market are not inconsistent with this broad policy.

[8] In theory, an alternative is to test whether URRs reduce the share of short-term credit in total foreign finance. In practice, the share of net short-term credit fluctuates widely between –50% and 100% in the sample period; in some quarters, the denominator is negative. Accordingly, it would be impractical to test this alternative hypothesis.

[9] The Chilean URR was not always a Tobin-type tax. During June 1991–May 1992, the authorities made the holding period (HP) of a deposit a function of the maturity of the credit. If the maturity was below 90 days, the HP was fixed at 90 days. If the maturity was above 360 days, the HP was fixed at 1 year. If the maturity was between 90 and 360 days, the HP was set equal to that maturity.

[10] Labán and Larraín (1994) constructed an alternative measure of the effective tax on capital inflows; however, it can be criticized because it subsumes under this heading separate factors such as the size of the foreign exchange intervention band and the composition of the basket of currencies used to define the band's central rate.

[11] There is a legal limit on r, but it is not binding. The central bank law states that the average of all reserve requirements, including those on domestic deposits, may not exceed 40%.

[12] Conceptually, s is not a flat amount, but a function of the relative sizes of the collateral acceptable to foreign lenders and the loan (including reserves). In practice, the spread is obtained from published monthly data on the average spread.

[13] Monthly data are not available.

[14] The results of running these regressions are available from the authors upon request.

[15] The level at which we make the split, 4.5%, was set arbitrarily, but changing it did not alter the results.

[16] Several Chilean analysts think that during 1992–1994 the central bank became over-confident about using interest rate policy, among other measures, due to the presence of the URR.

[17] The President of the Christian Democratic Party, the main party of the governing coalition, declared that "a global restriction on capital inflows may be necessary" (*El Diario*, 5 July 1995, Santiago). Senator Carlos Ominami recently proposed establishing a special tax on FDI in the mining sector in order to reduce inflows and alleviate the appreciation of the RER (*El Mercurio*, 27 August 1997, p. B6).

References

Chumacero, R., Labán, R., and Larraín, F., 1996, What determines capital inflows? An empirical analysis for Chile, paper presented at conference organized by Instituto de Economía, Universidad Católica de Chile, Santiago, Chile, July.

De Gregorio, J., 1995, Financial opening and capital controls: The experience of Spain, in R. Dornbusch and Y.C. Park, eds., *Financial Opening: Policy Lessons for Korea*, Korea Institute of Finance, Seoul, Korea.

Dooley, M., and Chinn, M., 1995, Financial Repression and Capital Mobility: Why Capital Flows and Covered Interest Rate Differentials Fail to Measure Capital Market Integration, National Bureau of Economic Research Working Paper No. 5347, Cambridge, MA, USA.

Eichengreen, B., and Wyplosz, C., 1993, The unstable EMS, *Brookings Papers on Economic Activity*, **2**:51–143.

Eichengreen, B., Tobin, J., and Wyplosz, C., 1995, Two cases for sand in the wheels of international finance, *Economic Journal*, **105**(January):162–172.

Garber, P., and Taylor, M., 1995, Sand in the wheels of foreign exchange markets: A sceptical note, *Economic Journal*, **105**(January):173–180.

Gravelle, J., 1991, Do IRAs increase savings? *Journal of Economic Perspectives*, **5**(2):133–148.

Labán, R., and Larraín, F., 1994, What Drives Capital Inflows? Lessons From the Recent Chilean Experience, Working Paper No. 168, Instituto de Economía, Universidad Católica de Chile, Santiago, Chile.

Soto, M., 1995, Encaje a los Créditos Externos: La Evidencia Empírica en Chile, Master's Thesis in Economics, Instituto de Economía, Universidad Católica de Chile, Santiago, Chile.

Tobin, J., 1978, A proposal for international monetary reform, *Eastern Economic Journal*, **4**:153–159.

Valdés-Prieto, S., 1994, Financial liberalization and the capital account: Chile 1974–84, in G. Caprio, I. Atiyas, and J. Hanson, eds., *Financial Reform: Theory and Experience*, Cambridge University Press, Cambridge, UK.

Valdés-Prieto, S., and Soto, M., 1996, ¿Es el control selectivo de capitales efectivo en Chile? Su efecto sobre el tipo de cambio real, *Cuadernos de Economía*, **98**(April):77–104.

Part II

Recent Experience in More Advanced Transition Countries

Chapter 5

Capital Inflows to Hungary and Accompanying Policy Responses, 1995–1996

Gábor Oblath

5.1   Introduction

Hungary has had a long history of drawing on foreign capital to finance current account deficits. However, its experience with significant capital inflows accompanied by significant strengthening of the current account is rather recent. This chapter attempts to analyze and explain this experience.

By 1990, as a result of heavy foreign borrowing [mainly by the National Bank of Hungary (NBH)] during the 1970s and 1980s, the country had accumulated a stock of gross foreign debt amounting to 64% of gross domestic product (GDP); the net foreign debt had reached 48% thereof. During 1991 and 1992, the gross foreign debt stabilized, while its net equivalent even declined. The next 2 years saw a fundamental reversal of these developments, as the country's net foreign debt increased by more than $5.5 billion. By early 1995, it had become evident that Hungary was headed toward a balance of payments (BOP) crisis. In the absence of corrective policy measures, financing the country's external imbalances would have been impossible.

An earlier version of this chapter was published in *Empirica*, Volume 25, Number 1, 1998, Kluwer Academic Publishers.

A stabilization package was implemented in March 1995, with rapid effects. Economic growth decelerated, the rate of inflation increased significantly, and real wages decreased substantially. The current account deficit also began to decline and large amounts of private foreign capital began to flow into the country.

A steady inflow of private foreign capital and an accompanying improvement in the current account – the two main features of Hungarian BOP developments since March 1995 – are the major topics of this chapter. We focus on developments in the period 1995–1996, and review the composition and characteristics of, as well as the policy responses to, net capital flows into the country. The earlier history of capital flows (i.e., the accumulation of foreign public debt during the socialist era), is not covered in this chapter[1] and developments in the period 1990–1994 are discussed only briefly.

In order to clarify the nature, implications, and monetary impact of recent capital flows to and from Hungary, we present a framework that focuses on the distinction between capital flows to or from the private sector on the one hand, and those to and from the public sector [the government and central bank (CB)] on the other. The importance of this distinction relates to certain peculiarities in Hungary in the period under review (i.e., 1995–1996). These are as follows: (i) a large inherited foreign public debt, entailing heavy debt service obligations; (ii) certain institutional features, such as the fact that foreign debt was held by the CB and that the government's foreign transactions bypassed the foreign exchange market; (iii) specific policy objectives, such as an attempt to avoid both a deterioration in the current account and an excessive accumulation of foreign exchange reserves in the face of capital inflows; and (iv) some special characteristics of the capital inflows, in particular the large size and share of "foreign direct investment" (FDI) flows to the government, which in fact consisted of privatization revenues. Because of these features, indicators of total net capital inflows to the country may be misleading, especially when figures for 1995 and 1996 are compared.[2]

Hungary recorded an immense total net capital inflow in 1995 (17% of GDP), but in 1996 the corresponding figure was practically nil. This appears to indicate a radical turnaround in the direction of capital flows. However, throughout 1996 (in fact, beginning in the second quarter of 1995), the NBH was more or less continuously engaged in sterilizing huge capital inflows. But how can nonexistent net capital inflows be sterilized? The separation of the private and government sectors with regard to net capital inflows helps in resolving this apparent contradiction: in 1996, the private sector was a net recipient of foreign capital, while the government sector was involved in repaying foreign public debt. Although the two items, which carry opposite signs, may cancel each other out in the BOP – resulting in a nearly zero net capital inflow into the country – the monetary effects of the two flows are not necessarily offsetting.

This indicates the major reason why it is essential to distinguish between net capital flows to or from both the private and public sectors. The domestic monetary impact of net capital flows – at least in the Hungarian institutional and policy context – crucially depended on which of the two sectors was the "recipient" or "source" of the flows.

Another feature of Hungary's recent experience with capital flows is that both foreigners (nonresidents) and the domestic (resident) private sector are sources of "capital inflows". Two distinct issues are involved here. First, part of observed capital inflows may be due to a reversal of former unrecorded capital outflows, and part of the recorded improvement in the current account may result from the return of flight capital. Second, and more important, a special kind of "capital inflow" may originate from the domestic economy in the form of the conversion of domestic foreign exchange deposits into home currency. This transaction may be motivated by similar factors and may have similar effects as its counterparts for conventional capital inflows. Indeed, the monetary authorities do not distinguish between "domestic" and conventional capital inflows. Both resulted in NBH intervention on the domestic foreign exchange market, and the bank's decisions concerning sterilization did not depend on whether its intervention was due to domestic conversion or conventional capital inflows.

A final empirical difficulty in interpreting the monetary effects of net capital inflows in Hungary in 1996 relates to the fact that, while the overall private sector was a recipient of net capital inflows, the commercial banking sector (a subsector thereof) was a net capital exporter. The monetary consequences of this capital outflow may depend on whether the characteristics and effects of this subsector's net capital exports are more similar to those of the private sector than to those of the government sector.

This chapter focuses on the sectoral decomposition of net capital inflows and their implications for CB intervention, as well as on the policies aimed at dealing with the consequences of that intervention (sterilization), irrespective of whether the relevant transactions involved conventional or "domestic" capital inflows. Our approach does not permit the direct analysis of behavioral relationships, as our framework attempts to explain why and how the effects of net capital flows to and from various sectors differ. Moreover, we only briefly touch upon the real effects of capital inflows (e.g., on capital accumulation). We also neglect several important questions regarding the relationship between capital inflows and the policy responses to them; some of these (e.g., the effects of sterilization on inflows) are addressed by other authors (see, e.g., Árvai, 1997).[3] We make no attempt to review the extensive international literature on capital inflows,[4] or to make direct comparisons between Hungary and other countries experiencing surges in net capital inflows. However, there is an implicit comparison in our treatment of the topic: our approach is meant to reveal the unconventional features of recent capital inflows (and related problems) in Hungary.

The next section provides background for the discussion of the remainder of the chapter: we discuss foreign capital flows to and from Hungary over 1990–1994, and present the main features and implications of the March 1995 stabilization package. This is followed by a brief presentation of a conceptual framework for analyzing developments related to capital inflows and separating out their sectoral components. Section 5.4 applies this framework to recent capital inflows to Hungary; it also contains a discussion of some relevant problems in interpreting official statistics. Section 5.5 reviews Hungary's experience with sterilized intervention and the costs and effectiveness of sterilization. Finally, in Section 5.6 we review some other policy responses to foreign and domestic capital inflows, touch upon the situation in 1997, and draw some conclusions.

5.2   Capital Flows Before and After the Stabilization Package of March 1995: An Overview

5.2.1   Developments in the early 1990s

By 1990, the start of the political transformation, Hungary had accumulated an excessively large foreign debt. The new government that took office after the first democratic elections decided that the political and economic costs of adopting a "new debt strategy", that is, of starting negotiations for rescheduling and/or reducing the debt, would be higher than if following the policy of its predecessors. Therefore, it continued to fully service the inherited debt – which at the time consisted almost entirely of public debt – in order to maintain the country's creditworthiness. The new government's major short-term goals were stabilizing the level of the gross debt and increasing the foreign exchange reserves; the latter had been run down before the elections as a result of uncertainties surrounding the country's future debt strategy.

Consequently, in the early years of the transition, net capital inflows related to public borrowing were negligible or even negative; in 1990 the country experienced a net capital outflow of about 2% of GDP. By remaining creditworthy, Hungary managed to avoid the economic disruptions often associated with international insolvency. Moreover, the retention of creditworthiness very likely contributed to the subsequent sizable inflows of FDI: the country has received the largest FDI inflows among the transition economies during the 1990s.[5]

Between 1990 and 1992, the current account was in modest surplus (between 0.4% and 0.9% of GDP), while net interest payments on external debt amounted to 4% of GDP, which indicates the darker side of the debt strategy. Thus, the

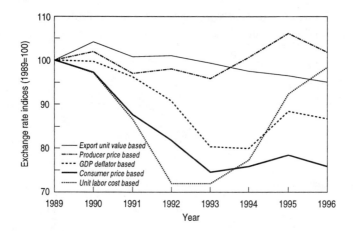

Figure 5.1. Real exchange rate indices for Hungary (1989 = 100).

surplus on the primary (noninterest) current account was significant in these years, averaging around 4.6% of GDP. Such primary surpluses enabled the government to avoid increasing the gross foreign debt and to reduce the net debt.

In these years, net capital inflows on average represented 2.2% of GDP. Their structure in 1991–1992 was characterized by substantial FDI inflows and a moderate amount of foreign credits taken by the nonpublic (in particular, the corporate) sector, while the public sector, as indicated, decreased its net foreign debt (see *Tables 5.1a,b* and *5.2*).

The modest current account surpluses observed between 1990 and 1992 turned into huge deficits in the next 2 years, reaching –9% and –9.4% of GDP in 1993 and 1994, respectively. The major factor behind the deterioration of the current account was the turnaround in the trade balance due to a collapse of exports and a massive increase in imports. These changes occurred partly because several temporary factors that had contributed to the improvement in the trade balance at the start of the transition ceased to exert a favorable impact on the country's exports to the West. However, serious policy mistakes, involving the combination of a massive real appreciation of the domestic currency at a time of large-scale import liberalization and unduly lax monetary policy (in 1993), also played an important role in the drastic deterioration of the current account.[6] For the development of real exchange rates in Hungary, see *Figure 5.1*.

The 2 years of large and growing current account imbalances were, by definition, accompanied by significant net capital inflows to the country (15.8% and 7.8% of GDP in 1993 and 1994, respectively). The bulk of these flows was debt-creating: the country's net foreign debt increased by $5.7 billion, from 35.7% of GDP in 1992 to 45.5% in 1994. This time, however, the major component of the

Table 5.1a. Hungary's gross and net foreign debt in convertible currencies, 1990–1996 (end of period, billion US$).

	1990	1991	1992	1993	1994	1995	1996
Gross							
1. Public debt (NBH+govt.)	18.21	19.43	17.77	20.36	22.45	23.22	18.47
1.1. Goverment	0.47	1.51	1.65	2.01	2.26	2.03	2.07
1.2. NBH	17.74	17.92	16.12	18.35	20.20	21.19	16.40
2. Private	3.06	3.23	3.68	4.20	6.07	8.44	9.18
2.1. Commercial banks	1.83	1.99	1.81	1.78	2.38	2.88	3.09
2.2. Enterprises	1.23	1.24	1.87	2.42	3.69	5.56	6.09
Total (1+2)	21.27	22.66	21.44	24.56	28.52	31.66	27.65
Net							
1. Public debt (NBH+govt.)	16.57	15.06	13.13	13.39	15.22	11.03	7.91
1.1. Goverment	0.25	1.30	1.47	1.84	2.09	1.87	1.30
1.2. NBH	16.32	13.76	11.66	11.55	13.13	9.16	6.61
2. Private	−0.64	−0.51	0.15	1.53	3.71	5.79	6.35
2.1. Commercial banks	0.67	0.59	0.31	0.45	1.35	1.96	1.41
2.2. Enterprises	−1.31	−1.10	−0.16	1.08	2.36	3.83	4.94
Total (1+2)	15.93	14.55	13.28	14.92	18.93	16.82	14.26
Assets							
1. Public sector (NBH+govt.)	1.64	4.37	4.64	6.97	7.23	12.19	10.56
1.1. Goverment	0.22	0.21	0.18	0.17	0.17	0.16	0.77
1.2. NBH	1.42	4.16	4.46	6.80	7.07	12.03	9.79
2. Private	3.70	3.74	3.53	2.67	2.36	2.65	2.83
2.1. Commercial banks	1.16	1.40	1.50	1.33	1.03	0.92	1.68
2.2. Enterprises	2.54	2.34	2.03	1.34	1.33	1.73	1.15
Total (1+2)	5.34	8.11	8.16	9.64	9.59	14.84	13.39

Note: Discrepancies due to rounding may exist. Source: NBH.

Table 5.1b. Sectoral shares of Hungary's gross and net foreign debt, 1990–1996 (in %).

	1990	1991	1992	1993	1994	1995	1996
Gross							
1. Public debt (NBH+govt.)	85.6	85.7	82.9	82.9	78.7	73.3	66.8
1.1. Goverment	2.2	6.7	7.7	8.2	7.9	6.4	7.5
1.2. NBH	83.4	79.1	75.2	74.7	70.8	66.9	59.3
2. Private	14.4	14.3	17.2	17.1	21.3	26.7	33.2
2.1. Commercial banks	8.6	8.8	8.4	7.2	8.3	9.1	11.2
2.2. Enterprises	5.8	5.5	8.7	9.9	12.9	17.6	22.0
Total (1+2)	100	100	100	100	100	100	100
Net							
1. Public debt (NBH+govt.)	104.0	103.5	98.9	89.7	80.4	65.6	55.5
1.1. Goverment	1.6	8.9	11.1	12.3	11.0	11.1	9.1
1.2. NBH	102.4	94.6	87.8	77.4	69.4	54.5	46.4
2. Private	−4.0	−3.5	1.1	10.3	19.6	34.4	44.5
2.1. Commercial banks	4.2	4.1	2.3	3.0	7.1	11.7	9.9
2.2. Enterprises	−8.2	−7.6	−1.2	7.2	12.5	22.8	34.6
Total (1+2)	100	100	100	100	100	100	100

Note: Discrepancies due to rounding may exist. Source: NBH.

Table 5.2. Capital inflows to Hungary, 1990–1996.

	1990	1991	1992	1993	1994	1995	1996
Current account							
In million US$	127	267	324	–3455	–3911	–2480	–1678
As % of GDP	0.4	0.8	0.9	–9.0	–9.4	–5.7	–3.9
Investment income (net)							
In million US$	–1438	–1363	–1261	–1186	–1403	–1793	–1434
As % of GDP	–4.35	–4.08	–3.39	–3.08	–3.37	–4.10	–3.30
Primary balance							
In million US$	1565	1630	1585	–2269	–2508	–687	–244
As % of GDP	4.7	4.9	4.3	–5.9	–6.0	–1.6	–0.6
Capital flows, medium- and long-term (million $)							
Capital (net)	204	3070	432	5632	2295	5601	–726
Of which							
FDI (incl. privatization revenue)	311	1459	1471	2339	1146	4453	1987
Portfolio and other (net)	–107	1611	–1039	3293	1149	1148	–2713
Capital transfers	–	–	–	–	–	–	156
Short-term capital (net), including NEO	–893	–617	5	459	960	1411	790
Total capital inflows (net)							
In million US$	–689	2453	437	6091	3255	7012	220
As % of GDP	–2.1	7.3	1.2	15.8	7.8	16.0	0.5
Overall balance (increase in reserves)							
In million US$	–562	2720	761	2635	–656	4532	–1458
As % of GDP	–1.7	8.1	2.0	6.8	–1.6	10.4	–3.4

Abbreviation: NEO, net errors and omissions.
Source: NBH.

increment came from foreign credits taken by the private sector. Nondebt-creating net capital inflows represented $3.5 billion, less than 40% of total inflows. Of these, privatization revenues amounted to $1.3 billion (most of it realized in 1993), with the rest accounted for by FDI in the narrower sense (i.e., conventional direct investment).[7]

Capital inflows to the private sector and the privatization revenues of the public sector, taken together, nearly covered the current account deficit during the 2 years in question; the remaining portion of net inflows corresponded to the increase in foreign exchange reserves. Moreover, after three years of large declines in gross capital formation, 1993 and 1994 saw marked upturns in investment activity.

While these developments may suggest that there was nothing inherently un-desirable about the large current account imbalances in those years, such an in-terpretation would be mistaken. There are three reasons for this. First, because Hungary inherited an extremely large foreign debt stock from the pre-democratic era, foreign investors and international organizations focused on the rapid increase in indebtedness, rather than on the change in its distribution between private and public debt. Second, by 1994, the current account deficit was no longer fully cov-ered by capital inflows, but by the use of previously accumulated reserves. Third, the deterioration in the trade and current account balances clearly accelerated in late 1994 and early 1995, during the time of the Mexican crisis. Investors were looking for the "next candidate", and there were obvious signs of massive capital flight from the country.[8] It was evident that something had to be done to avoid financial collapse.

5.2.2   Developments after March 1995

The government belatedly decided to introduce a stabilization package in March 1995. That package consisted of a 9% step devaluation of the forint, combined with the introduction of a crawling peg (more precisely a crawling band, initially involving a monthly 1.9% devaluation), an 8% surcharge on imports, a reduction in fiscal expenditures, a restrictive monetary policy, and a strict incomes policy in the public sector. By the second half of 1995, the policy package had resulted in a substantial improvement in both the external and the fiscal balances; eventually, it led to large private foreign capital inflows as well.

The new exchange rate regime meant a switch from a "fixed, but adjustable peg" to a crawling peg (with a band of 2.25%). The earlier adjustable peg sys-tem had created serious uncertainties for exporters and importers and offered wide possibilities for speculation against the domestic currency. As the inflation rate in Hungary was significantly higher than those of its major trading partners, and the growing current account deficit was considered a clear sign of the overvaluation of the forint, expectations of a major devaluation – despite small periodic ones – became more or less permanent. Speculative attacks became increasingly frequent and aggressive from the second half of 1994 onward. Speculation against the forint, however, ceased after the introduction of the crawling band regime, which provided for a significant initial degree of automatic adjustment. As the new exchange rate regime proved sustainable and credible, even after the reduction of the monthly crawl rate from 1.9% to 1.3% for the second half of the year, huge amounts of private capital began to flow into the country.

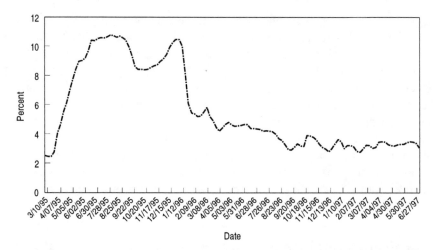

Figure 5.2. Premium on 3-month Hungarian treasury bills [based on comparison with 3-month LIBOR (London Inter-Bank Offered Rate), according to composition of Hungarian currency basket].

5.2.3   Reasons behind capital inflows

What were the factors behind the surge in private capital inflows? Part of the inflow was probably the return of the flight capital that had flowed away from the country in late 1994 and early 1995 because of devaluation expectations and fears of a BOP crisis. The stabilization package most likely contributed not only to the return of previous capital outflows but also to new inflows. Those international investors who considered Hungary an appropriate site for both direct and portfolio investments within the region may have postponed their decisions in view of the country's growing external imbalances. Since the messages of the stabilization package were that the government considered the correction of macroeconomic imbalances a major priority, and that it was capable of avoiding the disruptions associated with a BOP crisis, these investors' attitudes changed rather quickly. In addition, a substantial portion of the capital inflows is likely to have been related to the exceptionally high interest premium that emerged in Hungary. In the second half of 1995, the premium – that is, the difference between annualized domestic interest rates (e.g., on treasury bills) corrected for the pre-announced devaluation, on the one hand, and foreign interest rates, on the other – was in the range of 8–11% (see *Figure 5.2*).

Sterilizing the monetary impact of private capital inflows became a major goal of monetary (and overall economic) policy. The "crawling band" turned out to be more of a "crawling peg": the exchange rate on the interbank foreign exchange market remained more or less continuously on the lower side of the band, indicating pressure for nominal appreciation. This implied a constant obligation for the NBH to intervene on the foreign exchange market, that is, to buy foreign exchange and sell domestic currency, which most likely would have led to a marked increase in the domestic money supply. However, such an increase in the money supply would have jeopardized the attainment of the goals of the stabilization policy. The main dangers were considered to be the following: (i) a decrease in short-term domestic interest rates, involving the risk of a turnaround in capital inflows and a fall in domestic savings; (ii) a further acceleration in inflation; and (iii) a reversal of the improvement in the current account. For these reasons, the NBH pursued a policy of sterilized intervention, as discussed below.

5.3   Net Capital Inflows, Intervention, and Sterilization: A "Sources" and "Uses" Approach

In the following, we present the core of a conceptual framework for analyzing the aspects of capital inflows most relevant for understanding recent developments in Hungary. On occasion, we shall refer to specific developments in Hungary to indicate the empirical relevance of the framework. As the statistical analysis that follows relies on BOP statistics, the framework applies definitions that correspond to those of the BOP.

5.3.1   Net capital inflows and intervention by the central bank

Net Capital Inflows, Net Resource Transfers, and Financial Transfers

Our framework aims to capture some of the essential features and possible effects of capital inflows that are likely to be relevant for a country: (i) that runs current account deficits; (ii) that has large foreign debts; (iii) the bulk of whose external debt has been incurred by the public sector; (iv) a significant part of whose foreign capital inflows consist of privatization revenues accruing to the public sector; and (v) where the private sector also experiences large capital inflows.

Net capital inflows (*NCI*) are defined as the balance on the capital account (or, according to more recent BOP terminology, the "financial account"). *NCI* may involve either foreign equity (*FDI*) or loans (which include portfolio investment). The latter results in an increase in the country's external debt, whereas the former does not. *NCI* can be "used" either for financing the deficit on the current account (*CAD*) or for increasing the foreign exchange reserves of the CB (*dR*):

$$NCI = FDI + NFB + \ldots = CAD + dR + \ldots, \qquad (5.1a)$$

where, on the sources side, *FDI* and *NFB* indicate the net inflow of FDI and net foreign borrowing (inclusive of portfolio investment),[9] respectively. The identity never holds in practice (hence, the ellipses on both sides), partly due to incomplete recording and partly because agents may wish to conceal the existence, size, or nature of their transactions. The item that bridges the statistical gap between the sources and uses is "net errors and omissions" (NEO). For simplicity, we shall consider NEO as a capital inflow; we will have more to say on this in the context of Hungary below.

On the uses side, the current account deficit can be broken down into two components: the primary (or noninterest/noncapital income) deficit (*PD*), and net interest payments (inclusive of profit transfers). We refer to the latter as net factor payments abroad (*NFP*). Thus, the sources and uses of net capital inflows are:

$$FDI + NFB + NEO = PD + NFP + dR. \tag{5.1b}$$

The primary deficit of the current account may be interpreted as a deficit in visible and invisible trade and, therefore, as a net resource transfer (*NRT*) from abroad; we interpret a surplus as a resource transfer by the domestic economy.

Subtracting *NFP* from both sides of the equation offers a measure of net financial transfers (*NFT*) to or from the economy:

$$NCI - NFP = NFT = NRT + dR. \tag{5.2}$$

This identity states the simple fact that only net capital inflows less net interest payments made abroad constitute a net financial transfer to the country; a negative net financial transfer must be covered by a net resource transfer abroad and/or a drawing down of international reserves. These identities are helpful in analyzing capital inflows to countries with large external debt and debt service obligations.

Capital Inflows and Outflows of the Public and the Private Sectors

Statistics on total net capital inflows (total inflows into the economy), as well as figures on net financial transfers to and from the economy, are likely to be misleading if net inflows to certain sectors are accompanied by outflows or large variations in inflows to other sectors. In this respect, and as already emphasized, the most important distinction is that between the (capital and current account) transactions of the public (pu) and the private (pr) sectors. For the purposes of the present analysis, the public sector is defined to include the general government and the CB, but not state-owned companies.

We focus on how capital inflows to the private sector may be "used" by the two sectors and decompose (5.1b) into the following:

$$FDIpr + NFBpr + NEO - CADpr = CADpu - (FDIpu - dNFApu), \qquad (5.3)$$

where *FDIpu* indicates the foreign exchange (forex) privatization revenues of the government; *NFApu* is the net foreign asset position of the public sector (i.e., $dNFApu = dR - NFBpu$); and *CADpu* indicates net factor (interest) payments on foreign public debt. The left-hand side of the equation shows the size of net private capital inflows not "used" by the private sector (i.e., not going to finance its own current account deficit). The right-hand side indicates that the part of net capital inflows to the private sector not used by that sector may finance the public sector's current account deficit and/or an increase in the public sector's net foreign assets (debt repayment and/or reserve accumulation), corrected for forex privatization revenues.

Intervention by the Central Bank

As emphasized above, the distinction between the private and public sectors is important for clarifying the monetary implications of capital inflows to Hungary. To see why, we briefly describe two important developments.

First, since March 1995 Hungary has maintained a quasi-fixed (crawling) exchange rate mechanism with a relatively narrow band, which implies that the CB has been obliged to intervene (purchase foreign exchange) whenever the market rate reached the lower side of the band. As a practical matter, the market rate has almost always been at or near that side since mid-1995. Second, the foreign transactions of the government sector in 1995 and 1996 were characterized by large net interest payments (*CADpu*), very significant repayments – and prepayments – of foreign public debt (*–NFBpu*, involving the increase of *dNFApu*), and substantial privatization revenues (*FDIpu*). As neither the public sector's demand for, nor supply of, foreign exchange manifested itself on the domestic foreign exchange market, a significant portion of the sources and the uses of total net capital inflows bypassed this market.[10] Therefore, CB intervention due to capital inflows (and the increase in base money from this source) depended on the size of net capital inflows to the private sector on the one hand, and the private sector's uses of these inflows on the other.

This implies that equation (5.3), indicating the potential "uses" of net private capital inflows by the public sector, can also be considered a rough indicator of the scale of CB intervention[11] related to capital inflows [*INTnci(1)*], at least in the Hungarian context. Thus, $INTnci(1) = NCIpr - CADpr$, an equation which shows that we can approximate the scale of CB intervention as the difference between the net foreign capital inflow to the private sector and that sector's current account deficit.

For this formula to show exactly the amount of CB intervention due to capital inflows the following conditions must hold:

- Privatization revenues in forex are not converted to domestic currency, but are kept in a special account and used for repaying foreign public debt.[12]
- The private sector's current proceeds from abroad (e.g., from exports of goods and services) are converted into domestic currency and current foreign payments are made by purchasing foreign exchange.
- Capital inflows to the private sector (those involving an inflow of foreign exchange) are converted to domestic currency; if there are capital outflows from the private sector, they necessitate the conversion of domestic currency into foreign exchange.

The importance of the second and third conditions above derives from the fact that in Hungary (as in most transition countries), the household and business sectors hold considerable foreign exchange (forex) deposits with domestic commercial banks, which, in turn, hold forex deposits with the CB and banks abroad.[13]

While actual developments may diverge somewhat from the second condition, under normal circumstances the net effect of such divergence is not likely to be significant. The second part of the third condition, however, did not hold for Hungary in 1996. Some of the private banking sector's capital exports did not involve the purchase of foreign exchange, but rather the direct withdrawal of foreign exchange deposits from the CB. Thus, part of the private demand for foreign exchange also bypassed the forex market. In this case, the difference between net foreign capital inflows to the private sector and the private sector's current account deficit understates the size of CB intervention due to capital inflows. This is because the sale of foreign exchange from net capital inflows by the corporate sector was not matched by the purchase of foreign exchange by the banking sector for capital exports. As a result, the purchase of foreign exchange by the CB (i.e., its intervention) was larger than it would have been if commercial banks had purchased the foreign exchange for their capital exports on the market, rather than directly drawing on their forex deposits with the CB.

Under such conditions, these banking sector capital exports ($CXpb$) must be added to the first measure of CB intervention in order to better approximate the scale of intervention related to net capital inflows; that is, $INTnci(2) = INTnci(1) + CXpb$. Although we do not have direct information on the amount of foreign exchange that commercial banks shifted abroad (from forex deposits), we can use their net foreign lending (negative net foreign borrowing, $-NFB$) as a proxy for private capital exports without currency conversion. In this case, $INTnci(2) = NCIpr - CADpr - NFBpb$. The last term on the right-hand side (net foreign borrowing by the banking sector) is assumed to have a negative value, so its presence, other things being equal, increases CB intervention.

5.3.2   Intervention and sterilization

"Domestic" Intervention

In the previous section, we addressed only the foreign component of CB intervention, that is, that related to capital movements across national borders. However, in Hungary the conversion into domestic currency of commercial banks' foreign exchange deposits held with the CB has also contributed to the total amount of foreign exchange that the CB has purchased. Conversion of commercial banks' foreign exchange deposits at the CB reflected the earlier conversion of funds held by households and companies in commercial banks. The latter was motivated by the same circumstance as certain capital inflows, namely, the premium on assets denominated in domestic currency. In addition, part of the interest payments by the CB on those deposits may have been converted.[14] Taking domestic conversion into account, total CB intervention is:[15]

$$INTcb = INTnci + INTdom. \tag{5.4}$$

The first component of CB intervention – the purchase of the foreign exchange arising from capital inflows – involves an increase in the CB's net foreign assets (*NFAcb*), while the second component is associated with an increase in its domestic net foreign exchange assets (*DNFXAcb*).[16] Disregarding other factors, capital exports by commercial banks from their foreign exchange deposits involve a fall in *NFAcb*. However, they also entail an equal increase in *dNFXAcb* (because the net domestic forex liabilities of the CB decrease). Therefore, such capital exports do not affect the sum of *NFAcb* and *dNFXAcb*, which is the net foreign exchange asset position of the CB (*NFXAcb*).

Accordingly, total CB intervention is related (but not equal) to the increase in the net foreign exchange assets of the CB (*dNFXAcb*). The difference between the two is related, as discussed above, to the net effect of the asset transactions of the (non-CB) government sector. That effect includes privatization proceeds, the net repayment of the central government's foreign debts (*–NFBg*), and the public sector's current transactions. The last of these amounts to the net foreign interest payments made by the CB and the government. Accordingly, the relationship between total CB intervention and *dNFXAcb* is:

$$INTcb = dNFXAcb - (FDIpu - CADpu + NFBg).[17] \tag{5.5}$$

It is easy to see that in Hungary CB intervention (disregarding public sector transactions not involving purchases or sales on the forex market) is associated with an increase in *NFXAcb*, rather than in *NFAcb*. That leaves us with one additional important question to address, namely, whether the two components of intervention – the one related to net capital inflows (*INTnci*) and the other related to domestic conversion (*INTdom*) – have similar domestic monetary effects.

The answer depends on whether or not foreign exchange deposits with the CB constitute a component of the monetary base. If they do, we must make a fundamental distinction between *INTnci* and *INTdom*. Intervention resulting from capital inflows would increase base money, while "domestic intervention" would not do so, but result only in a change in the composition of base money. If, on the other hand, the monetary base does not contain commercial banks' forex deposits with the CB, the total amount of CB intervention is the appropriate indicator of the monetary impact of intervention.

In its regular publications, the NBH considers commercial banks' forex deposits as a component of the monetary base.[18] However, the real question is whether or not forex deposits with the CB have the fundamental attributes of base money: do they serve as a basis for "credit multiplication" and are they a source of seigniorage revenue? Within the Hungarian monetary framework the answer to both questions is clearly negative, as the forex deposits of commercial banks do not belong in base money.[19] As a result, "domestic intervention" has the same effect on money creation as intervention resulting from capital inflows. It appears that this has been the CB's view in practice: it does not seem to have cared whether foreign exchange was of domestic or foreign origin when pursuing sterilized intervention.

Sterilization

In this chapter, we interpret "sterilization" in the narrow sense of the term: it is understood as the net effect of CB (or non-CB) measures that result in a difference between CB intervention (involving a potential increase in the monetary base as a result of purchases of foreign exchange by the CB) and the actual increase in the monetary base (*MB*). Therefore, we define sterilization (*STER*) as:

$$STER = INTcb - dMB. \tag{5.6}$$

We are, of course, relying on *ex post* information, so we do not know how much of the sterilized amount would actually have contributed to the increase in *MB* and/or to the current account deficit.[20] Nor do we know how intervention would have evolved in the absence of sterilization; we shall return to these points.

All instruments of sterilization involve an increase in the net foreign exchange assets of the public sector and a corresponding increase in its net domestic currency liabilities. It is important to stress that currency denomination, rather than the residence status, is relevant from the point of view of sterilization. (Nonresidents may legally hold long-term government paper, but there is no information on the actual amount of public debt denominated in forints held by nonresidents.)

In Hungary both the CB and the government took part in sterilizing the monetary consequences of capital inflows (the latter by "overfunding" the public sector deficit), but the impacts of the two are not directly comparable. CB actions affect the monetary base, but this is not necessarily the case for sterilization by the government.[21]

The CB's sterilization instruments included sale of government paper in its portfolio and the reduction of the stock of refinancing credits. However, its most important tool was increasing the stock of passive repo (repurchase) arrangements, which actually means negative refinancing by the CB. Once again, we call attention to a difference between the NBH's actual practices and a written interpretation of what it does. NBH's regular publications include statistics on the stock of passive repo in the monetary base. This practice is misleading: the stock of passive repo was built up in order to prevent an increase in base money.

As we shall see in the following, in Hungary sterilization has had a considerable impact on the effect on the monetary base of net capital inflows and domestic conversion. The major part of CB intervention was sterilized in both 1995 and 1996.

5.4   Net Capital Flows in 1995 and 1996

Relying on official BOP statistics, we now attempt to identify the size, uses, and sectoral composition of net capital inflows to Hungary in the period 1995–1996.

5.4.1   Sources, uses, and sectoral composition of net capital inflows, 1995–1996

Overall Net Capital Inflows

We present statistics on the sources and uses of net capital inflows to Hungary in US dollars in *Table 5.3*. We show their sectoral composition in *Table 5.4*, and their size in Hungarian forints and percentage of GDP in *Table 5.5*.

While total net capital inflows to Hungary amounted to $7 billion (or 17% of GDP) in 1995, they were only $0.2 billion (or 0.6% of GDP) in 1996. Before we interpret this fall as a fundamental change in the situation, it is useful to take a closer look at the sources and uses of net capital inflows in 1995 and 1996.

As shown in *Table 5.3*, in 1995 net foreign direct investment (FDI) reached 11% of GDP, and net foreign borrowing 3.1% thereof. As for the uses of the inflow, the

Table 5.3. Sources and uses of net capital inflows to Hungary.

	Sources		Uses		
	Net capital inflows (FDI + NFB + NEO)	=	Current account deficit (primary deficit + net interest payment)	+	Change in international reserves
1995 US$ billion	7	=	2.5	+	4.5
US$ billion	(4.4 + 1.4 + 1.2)	=	(0.7 + 1.8)	+	
% of GDP	17.0	=	5.4	+	11.6
% of GDP	(11 + 3.1 + 2.9)	=	(1.3 + 4.1)	+	
1996 US$ billion	0.2	=	1.7	+	–1.5
US$ billion	(2.2 – 3.8 + 1.8)	=	(0.25 + 1.45)	+	
% of GDP	0.6	=	3.9	+	–3.3
% of GDP	(4.9 – 8.6 + 4.3)	=	(0.6 + 3.3)	+	
1995 + 1996 US$ billion	7.2	=	4.2	+	3
US$ billion	(6.6 – 2.4 + 3)	=	(0.95 + 3.25)	+	
	Net financial transfer (NCI – NFP)	=	Net resource transfer + change in international reserves (primary deficit)		
1995 % of GDP	17 – 4.1 = 12.9	=	1.3	+	11.6
1996 % of GDP	0.6 – 3.3 = –2.7	=	0.6	+	–3.3

Abbreviations: FDI, foreign direct investment (net); NFB, net foreign borrowing (including portfolio investment; NEO, net errors and omissions; NCI, net capital inflow; NFP, net factor payments.

Source: Author's calculations, based on NBH statistics.

current account deficit was 5.4% of GDP and the increase in forex reserves reached 11.6% thereof. In 1996, FDI was half of its 1995 level and net foreign borrowing was –8.6% of GDP. On the "uses" side, the current account deficit fell to 3.9% of GDP, but international reserves also declined, by 3.3% thereof. The item that bridges the difference between the sources and the uses of net capital inflows is net errors and omissions, which were 2.9% of GDP in 1995 and 4.3% thereof in 1996.

At this point, a note on the possible contents of NEO is in order. Nothing certain can be said about the unrecorded transactions that are lumped together in this item. However, there are indications that at least some (small) portion of NEO may cover unrecorded service exports.[22] The other part consists of net capital inflows, which consist not only of short-term (speculative) capital, but most likely portfolio investments as well.[23] In addition, the return of former flight capital may also have contributed to the increase in NEO. However, since we lack sufficient information to make any kind of revisions to the official BOP statistics, we note only that not all of NEO was capital inflow; some of it was portfolio investment.

We turn next to net financial transfers and net resource transfers. The respective figures are found toward the bottom of *Table 5.3*. In 1995, the net financial transfer (NFT) to the country was almost 13% of GDP, while in 1996 NFT became negative (–2.7% of GDP). As for net resource transfers (NRT), the primary deficit on the current account was surprisingly small in both years, especially when compared with net capital inflows (in the 2 years taken together). The discrepancy between net capital inflows and resource inflows may have been even more significant, as NEO is likely to have included items that constituted primary revenues.

In the following section, we shall try to explain both why 1996 was so different from 1995 with respect to net inflows and the discrepancy between net financial and resource inflows.

Sectoral Composition

In *Table 5.4* we distinguish between net capital inflows to the public and the private sectors; the definitions regarding sectors and other items correspond to those given in Section 5.3, the only difference being that the current account balance has the conventional sign.

The most important feature revealed by the table is that the difference between 1995 and 1996 with respect to the size of net inflows was due to developments in the public sector. In 1995, the government recorded privatization revenues (i.e., FDI to the public sector) of $3 billion (row I/2), and repaid a small amount of debt (row I/1), so the net capital inflow to the public sector (*NCIpu*) was $2.9 billion.[24] In 1996, privatization revenues were much smaller, while extremely large debt repayments ($3.5 billion) were made. As a result, the size of net capital outflows from the public sector ($2.9 billion) almost exactly corresponded to that of net inflows

Table 5.4. Sources, uses, and sectoral breakdown of capital inflows to Hungary, 1995–1996 (billion US$).

		1995			1996			1995 + 1996		
		Public	Private	Total	Public	Private	Total	Public	Private	Total
I	Sources									
I/1 (=1a + 1b)	Net borrowing	-0.13	1.50	1.37	-3.52	-0.27	-3.79	-3.65	1.23	-2.42
	of which									
I/1a	Banks	–	0.50	0.50	–	-0.75	-0.75	–	-0.25	-0.25
I/1b	Companies	–	1.00	1.00	–	0.49	0.49	–	1.49	1.49
I/2	FDI	3.02	1.39	4.41	0.58	1.41	1.99	3.60	2.80	6.40
I/3	Capital transfers	–	–	–	0.02	0.13	0.15	0.02	0.13	0.15
I/4	NEO	–	1.22	1.22	–	1.86	1.86	–	3.08	3.08
I/1 + 2 + 3 + 4	Net capital inflows	2.89	4.11	7.00	-2.92	3.13	0.21	-0.03	7.24	7.21
II	Uses									
II/1	Current account	-1.40	-1.08	-2.48	-0.97	-0.71	-1.68	-2.37	-1.79	-4.16
	of which									
II/1a	Net interest + profits	-1.39	-0.40	-1.79	-0.97	-0.46	-1.43	-2.36	-0.86	-3.22
II/1b	Primary balance	-0.01	-0.68	-0.69	0.00	-0.25	-0.25	-0.01	-0.93	-0.94
	Memo: net financial transfers	1.50	3.71	5.21	-3.89	2.67	-1.22	-2.39	6.38	3.99
II/2	Over/underfinancing (change in reserves)	1.49	3.03	4.52	-3.89	2.42	-1.47	-2.40	5.45	3.05
II/2 – II/1	Net capital inflows	2.89	4.11	7.00	-2.92	3.13	0.21	-0.03	7.24	7.21

Abbreviations: FDI, foreign direct investment (net); NEO, net errors and omissions.
Source: Author's calculations, based on NBH statistics.

in 1995. The cumulative net inflows to the public over the 2 years taken together were virtually zero, with all of the cumulative net inflow going to the private sector.

We can interpret these developments as follows. Over the 2 years, the public sector realized privatization revenues from abroad of $3.6 billion, which it used entirely to reduce the foreign public debt. At the same time, capital continued to flow to the private sector. *FDIpr* was $1.4 billion in both years; and although the figures show a decline in companies' net foreign borrowing (which is understood to include portfolio investments), much of the difference between the 2 years' figures is likely to be "embodied" in the increase in NEO.

With respect to the private sector, the only significant change between 1995 and 1996 was related to capital flows to and from the banking sector. Net foreign borrowing by banks was $0.5 billion in 1995; in the next year they were net lenders to foreigners of about $0.75 billion. As already mentioned, this change was mainly due to commercial banks shifting part of the forex deposits that they had held with the NBH to banks abroad.[25] Disregarding this factor, which had neither monetary nor real implications, both the size and composition of net capital inflows to the private sector factor were remarkably similar in the 2 years under review.

How were net capital inflows "used" by the two sectors? The answer depends on whether 1995 and 1996 are viewed separately or as a single period. Under the first interpretation, 1995 was characterized by substantial "overfinancing" of both sectors' current deficits, resulting in a massive increase in the forex reserves. In 1996, the public sector's current deficit (net interest payment abroad) was grossly "underfinanced" due to the accompanying debt reduction; the gap was covered by an "overfinancing" of the private sector and a fall in international reserves. If we focus on developments over the 2 years taken together, we can conclude that the public sector's capital account was balanced, and that net capital inflows to the private sector financed the current deficits of the private and public sectors and a $3 billion increase in international reserves. Most of the current account deficit in both years was due to large (although declining) foreign interest payments by the public sector. In 1995 and 1996, the private sector's primary deficit represented 16% and 8%, respectively, of the net foreign capital inflows to this sector. (Remembering the likely composition of NEO, the ratio may even be smaller.)

We can conclude that a very small portion of net private sector capital inflows could have contributed to investment and/or consumption, which is a clear indicator that capital inflows were extensively sterilized.

5.4.2   The domestic monetary impact of capital inflows

When discussing the domestic monetary impact of net capital inflows on the basis of balance of payments figures, we can only address their *ex post* "revealed" impact:

had the authorities pursued different policies, both the current account and capital flows would have behaved differently. In the discussion that follows, we rely on *Tables 5.4* and *5.5*; the latter presents the same items as the former, but expressed in domestic currency and in relation to GDP.

Although the public sector was a net recipient of foreign capital flows in 1995, and a source of net capital outflows in 1996, this difference is irrelevant as regards the monetary effects of capital inflows. Privatization proceeds from abroad did not increase the money supply, and repayments of foreign public debt also did not reduce this. However, the net foreign interest payments made by the NBH and the government did affect monetary aggregates: the domestic counterpart of this item was covered by domestic interest payments made to the NBH and foreigners by the government (financed by issuing government paper). As a result, the counterpart of public sector net foreign interest payments was more or less automatically sterilized.

This discussion seems to imply that the monetary impact of net foreign capital inflows depends entirely on the size of net inflows to the private sector minus the overall (public plus private) current account deficit. However, this is not necessarily the case, for two reasons. First, the timing of domestic government interest payments to the NBH may significantly differ from that of foreign interest payments by the NBH. Second, and more importantly, "sterilization" by the government may affect monetary aggregates differently from the more conventional sterilization of private capital inflows. (We shall return to this point below.)

Therefore, in the following discussion, we disregard the "automatic" sterilization of public sector interest payments and focus on the monetary impact of net private capital inflows. What is not "used" by the private sector for financing its current account deficit results in intervention by the CB: the corresponding amounts are shown in row II/2 (column "private") of *Tables 5.4* and *5.5*.

In 1995 the domestic monetary impact of capital inflows – the potential increase in base money due to actual capital inflows – largely corresponded to the figures in the tables ($3.03 billion or 401 billion forints). However, in 1996, when commercial banks shifted some of their domestic forex deposits abroad, the portion of the capital inflow that affected the domestic money supply must have been larger. We can estimate the monetary effect of capital inflows in that year by not subtracting the net capital outflows from the banking sector; thus, $2.42 billion + $0.75 billion = $3.17 billion (489 billion forints).

The domestic component of intervention is then the difference between total intervention (452 billion forints and 589 billion forints in 1995 and 1996, respectively) and intervention related to net capital inflows (51 billion forints in 1995 and about 100 billion forints in 1996).

Table 5.5. Sources, uses, and sectoral breakdown of capital inflows to Hungary, 1995–1996 (billion HUF and % of GDP).

		1995 (HUF)			1996 (HUF)			1995 (%)			1996 (%)		
		Public	Private	Total	Public	Private	Total	Public	Private	Total	Public	Private	Total
	Sources												
I/1(=1a + 1b)	Net borrowing	-17.8	186.3	168.5	-532.8	-37.8	-570.6	-0.3	3.4	3.1	-8.0	-0.6	-8.6
	of which												
I/1a	Banks	–	58.3	58.3	–	-113.7	-113.7	–	1.1	1.1	–	-1.7	-1.7
I/1b	Companies	–	128.0	128.0	–	75.9	75.9	–	2.3	2.3	–	1.1	1.1
I/2	FDI	418.8	180.0	598.8	89.2	216.1	305.3	7.6	3.3	10.9	1.3	3.3	4.6
I/3	Capital transfers				3.4	20.6	24.0	–	0.0	0.0	0.1	0.3	0.4
I/4	NEO		159.5	159.5	–	284.3	284.3	–	2.9	2.9	–	4.3	4.3
I/1 + 2 + 3 + 4	Net capital inflows	401.0	525.8	926.8	-440.2	483.2	43.0	7.3	9.6	16.9	-6.6	7.3	0.6
	Uses												
II/1	Current account	-171.6	-125.0	-296.6	-146.6	-109.0	-255.6	-3.1	-2.3	-5.4	-2.2	-1.6	-3.9
	of which												
II/1a	Net interest + profits	-170.1	-54.2	-224.3	-146.6	-70.9	-217.5	-3.1	-1.0	-4.1	-2.2	-1.1	-3.3
II/1b	Primary balance	-1.5	-70.8	-72.3	0.0	-38.1	-38.1	0.0	-1.3	-1.3	0.0	-0.6	-0.6
	Memo: net financial transfers	230.9	471.6	702.5	-586.8	412.3	-174.5	4.2	8.6	12.8	-8.9	6.2	-2.6
II/2	Over/underfinancing (change in reserves)	229.4	400.8	630.2	-586.8	374.2	-212.6	4.2	7.3	11.5	-8.9	5.6	-3.2
II/2 – II/1	Net capital inflows	401.0	525.8	926.8	-440.2	483.2	43.0	7.3	9.6	16.9	-6.6	7.3	0.6

Abbreviations: HUF, Hungarian forints; FDI, foreign direct investment; NEO, net errors and omissions.
Source: Author's calculations, based on NBH statistics.

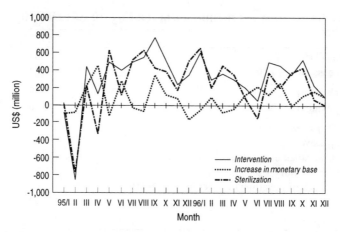

Figure 5.3. Intervention, sterilization, and increase in monetary base.

5.5 Size, Effectiveness, and Costs of Sterilization

5.5.1 Size, instruments, and agencies of sterilization

The potential increase in base money in 1995 as a result of CB intervention was 452 billion forints ($3.38 billion) and the actual increase was 113 billion, so 339 billion forints (75% of intervention) were sterilized. The corresponding figures for 1996 are as follows: intervention: 589 billion forints ($3.89 billion); increase in base money: 141 billion forints;[26] sterilization: 448 billion forints (76% of intervention). Sterilization represented 64% of net private capital inflows in 1995 and 75% thereof in 1996 (as corrected for net capital exports of the banking sector). *Figure 5.3* shows monthly developments in intervention, sterilization, and changes in the monetary base. In most of the period, intervention and sterilization moved parallel to each other.

Table 5.6 shows the instruments of sterilization and their magnitudes. While in 1995 the major instrument of sterilization was a decrease in the stock of refinancing credits to commercial banks, by 1996 this source was "depleted" and passive repo became the most important channel for withdrawing domestic liquidity. The government's role in sterilization is indicated by the increase in the balance of the Treasury's account at the NBH; such "overfunding" of the public deficit also increased in 1996. However, as pointed out above, the latter indicator understates the actual amount sterilized by the government, as the government additionally sterilized private capital inflows in an amount equal to the sum of its own and the NBH's net foreign interest payments (by collecting taxes and/or issuing government paper to finance the domestic currency counterpart of interest paid abroad). This is likely to be the main item behind the term "other" sterilization in *Table 5.6*.

Table 5.6. Intervention and sterilization in Hungary, 1995–1996 (billion HUF).

	1995	1996
Intervention (1)[a]	452	589
Change in base money (2)[b]	113	141
Sterilization (3 = 1 − 2)	339	448
Sterilization ratio (4 = 3/1)	0.75	0.76
Instruments of sterilization		
Change in passive repo	50	164
Decrease in the stock of NBH credits to commercial banks	105	24
Change in the Treasury's account held with NBH	26	71
Decrease in stock of government paper held by NBH	64	72
Other	94	117
Total sterilization	339	448

[a]Intervention is defined as the puchase of foreign exchange by NBH on the foreign exchange market.
[b]Currency plus commercial bank's domestic currency deposits with NBH.
Source: Author's calculations, based on Barabás and Hamecz (1997) and NBH (1996, 1997).

The sterilization of three-fourths of intervention appears to have been excessive and perhaps inefficient, in that it entailed fiscal costs. Determining whether this was the case would require further analysis. However, before discussing these issues, we must make two additional points. First, the NBH's sterilization objectives were not explicitly defined in quantitative terms. Its overt goals were to avoid an "excessive" or overly rapid fall in domestic nominal interest rates (arising from intervention) and to maintain an "adequate" differential between foreign and domestic interest rates. As the NBH formulated no explicit targets for monetary aggregates, the scale of its sterilization activities cannot be compared to its monetary policy intentions.

Second, Hungarian institutional arrangements – according to which most foreign public debt was held by the CB – raise a tricky question: can the observed activities of the CB be properly described as intervention and sterilization?[27] If we take a closer look at the size of the net financial transfer abroad by the public sector in 1996 (see *Table 5.5*), we observe a striking similarity with the magnitude of CB intervention that same year (587 billion forints vs. 589 billion forints). Recall that in Hungary the bulk of the public sector's net foreign financial transfer, that is, foreign debt service, is made by the CB. The latter makes foreign payments directly from its international reserves; the government in turn buys the foreign exchange necessary for its own foreign debt service from the CB.

Suppose, however, that the government had serviced all of the foreign public debt and purchased the necessary foreign exchange on the forex market. In that case, the amount of foreign exchange bought by the government for making net foreign payments (including debt repayments) would have corresponded to the level of intervention by the CB. This suggests that, had institutional arrangements been different, CB intervention would have been nil and there would have been no need for sterilization in 1996. Practically all "sterilization" would have been carried out by the government by issuing domestic bonds to cover its foreign debt service; however, we would not have considered such actions sterilization, but rather domestic financing of the public sector's foreign obligations. This implies that the widely held view that there was constant pressure for a nominal appreciation of the forint may require reappraisal.

A problem with this interpretation is that if one assumes that the government buys all of the foreign exchange on the market, one should also assume that all privatization revenues are sold on the market as well. Since the latter were used for debt repayment, the potential net impact of government sales and purchases of foreign exchange over the 2 years would have largely corresponded to the impact of net interest payments, rather than to the public sector's total debt service. Nonetheless, the proposition that part of the observed "market intervention" by the CB actually constitutes the purchasing of foreign exchange for servicing public debt is certainly valid.

Another problem with this interpretation is that, within the institutional framework that existed until the end of 1996,[28] the public sector's net financial transfers abroad – in particular, the decrease in gross foreign public debt – may have been a consequence of intervention. The mechanism could have been as follows: as a result of intervention, the international reserves increase, but the yield on international reserves is significantly lower than the interest paid on outstanding foreign public debt. This leads to a reduction in such debt. In such a case, we would expect a close correlation between intervention, the change in reserves, and the reduction of foreign public debt. Developments in these items are shown in *Figure 5.4*.

Clearly, debt repayment by the public sector was not independent of intervention, especially in 1996.[29] The public sector's decisions concerning debt repayments indeed appear to have been related to intervention. However, such decisions do not seem to have been related to changes in reserves, which are likely to be affected by other factors, of which the most obvious candidate is net capital exports by the commercial banking sector. This supposition is reinforced by *Figure 5.5*, which presents net capital exports by commercial banks and the change in reserves. These data lend some support to the notion that public sector debt repayments were related to intervention proper, and that the CB disregarded temporary changes in reserves due to movements of funds by commercial banks. This suggests that the market exchange rate would not have exhibited totally different behavior if the public sector had purchased the foreign exchange for financing the reduction of its foreign debt.

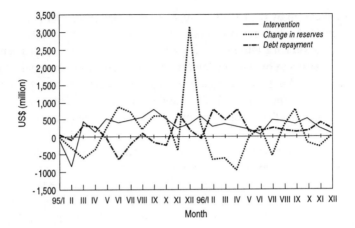

Figure 5.4. Intervention and public debt repayment.

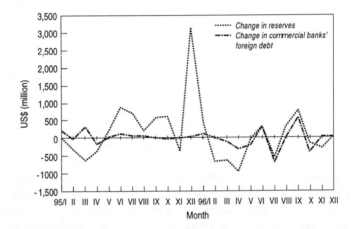

Figure 5.5. Change in reserves and commercial banks' net foreign debt.

5.5.2 "Effectiveness" of sterilization

The "effectiveness" of sterilization is an ambiguous concept. In what follows, we present three approaches. The first is based on a comparison of the actual objectives of sterilization with actual outcomes. The second addresses this question from a different angle: whether or not sterilization contributes to the continuation of the very inflows that have been sterilized. Finally, one can ask whether sterilization, which results in the maintenance of high interest rates at home, curbs or increases domestic demand.[30]

If the benchmark for effectiveness is a comparison of policy targets and out-comes, Hungarian sterilized intervention fares relatively well. As mentioned, the main objective of this policy was to keep the fall in interest rates within limits, and in that it succeeded. That is not to say that interest rates did not decline: between the end of 1995 and the end of 1996 they fell from 30–32% to 21–23%, while the inflation rate on a December-to-December basis decreased from 28.3% to 19.8%.

As for the question of whether sterilization causes a further inflow of capital, the tentative results, based on an econometric analysis by Árvai (1997), suggest what one would expect: the sterilization of FDI may be effective, but the mainte-nance – or more gradual decrease than in the absence of sterilization – of the dif-ferential between domestic and foreign interest rates contributes to a further inflow of capital.

The last approach (Simon, 1996) is unconventional. Suppose that sterilization results in higher domestic real interest rates, or in an interest premium related to the differential between domestic and foreign interest rates, on the one hand, and a pre-announced crawl on the other. Domestic demand and/or the net government interest expenditures paid to nonresidents may actually increase. In this case, at some point, sterilization could turn out to be not simply inefficient, but even counterproductive.

As a practical matter, however, the effects of sterilization in Hungary appear to have corresponded to the conventional notions. It was effective in restraining domestic demand, curbing the fall in interest rates, and decreasing the current ac-count deficit, but it is likely to have contributed to further inflows of short-term capital into the country.

5.5.3 Costs of sterilization

The costs of sterilization are not clear-cut. Such costs are divided below into three distinct categories: (i) nominal fiscal costs; (ii) real costs; and (iii) structural, indi-rect, and macroeconomic costs.

Nominal Fiscal Costs

When discussing the costs of sterilization, one usually focuses on the nominal fiscal costs.[31] These derive from the difference between two variables. The first is the domestic interest paid on the increment to net domestic public sector liabilities – including passive repo, but excluding the components of base money, as defined above – due to sterilization. The second is the foreign interest earned or forgone on the increment to the public sector's net foreign exchange assets resulting from intervention.

In 1995, sterilization, as measured by the difference between CB intervention and the increase in base money, was 339 billion forints; the corresponding figure in 1996 was 448 billion forints. Under certain assumptions, the associated direct nominal costs can be estimated by comparing the relevant foreign and domestic interest rates. In what follows, we focus on the costs in 1996.

Assuming that sterilization was spaced out more or less evenly over 1996, the average additional stock (on which interest was paid during the whole year) was 224 billion forints. Estimating the relevant average domestic interest rate at around 24–25%, and the foreign rate at 4–5%, the direct nominal fiscal cost of sterilization was about 44 billion forints ($224 \times 0.2 = 45$) or 0.7% of GDP. If we take into account the fact that the costs of sterilization carried out in 1995 (339 billion forints) had to be borne in 1996 as well, the cumulative nominal costs may have reached 113 billion forints or 1.6% of GDP. However, these figures most likely overstate the nominal costs of sterilization. The relevant foreign interest rate may have been higher than 4–5%, as the foreign exchange purchased through intervention was extensively designed for repaying or prepaying foreign public debt, which generally carries a much higher interest rate than foreign exchange reserves.

Sterilization implies an indirect fiscal cost as well; the maintenance of an interest rate on the total stock of government debt, which is higher than would be the case in the absence of sterilization (see Simon, 1996).

Real Costs

The large direct and indirect nominal fiscal costs of sterilization do not necessarily imply similar real costs. Sterilized intervention involves a change in the composition of net public liabilities. In Hungary, the share of net public debt in foreign currency decreased, while that of net debt denominated in domestic currency increased. Although nominal interest rates in Hungary are much higher than abroad, so is the rate of inflation. Therefore, the increase in nominal interest payments on public debt due to sterilization is almost fully compensated by inflationary erosion of the change in domestic debt. In what follows, we focus on the real costs in 1996.

We may interpret the real costs of sterilization in two ways. On the one hand, we may compare the relevant foreign and the domestic real interest rates; such a comparison indicates that sterilization on average did not result in real losses for the Hungarian government in 1996. Inflation in 1996 was 23.6%, the relevant domestic real interest rate was about 0.5–1.5%, which – especially in the case of foreign debt repayment – was lower than the relevant foreign rate in real terms.

On the other hand, we may interpret the real cost of sterilization as the premium paid by the public sector over the difference between domestic and foreign nominal interest rates, corrected for the expected or actual change in the exchange rate. As we can estimate the average premium in 1996 at 4–5%, the cost of sterilization on this interpretation was about 10 billion forints (224×0.045) or 0.15% of GDP for 1996, and 25 billion forints or 0.35% of GDP cumulatively over 1995–1996.

Structural, Indirect, and Macroeconomic Costs

While the real fiscal costs of sterilized intervention do not appear to have been significant in Hungary, sterilization may carry other types of costs that are difficult to quantify. Sterilization means, among other things, that rather than extending loans to the private sector, commercial banks buy government paper and/or keep money with the CB in the form of passive repurchase arrangements. This is not likely to affect those sectors or businesses that are in a position to draw on foreign capital, whether they are foreign-owned companies in the country or domestic firms engaging in foreign borrowing. This development mainly affects activities oriented toward the domestic market and/or where foreign capital is absent. Thus, one of the consequences of large-scale sterilized intervention may be a strong polarization within the business sector between those able and unable to raise foreign capital for investments. While overall investment activity stagnated in 1996, there was an investment boom in several sectors where foreign capital was dominant.

In a country such as Hungary, where inflation is significantly higher than abroad, large-scale sterilized intervention entails a significant increase in nominal interest payments by the public sector (inclusive of the CB). As a result, current nominal public expenditures increase, and the public sector's nominal deficit may also expand. However, as mentioned in point (ii), this is simply due to a swapping of foreign debt carrying a low nominal interest rate for domestic debt with a much higher one. As such, it does not necessarily affect the size of real expenditures or the public sector's real (operational) deficit.[32] Therefore, an increase in the nominal deficit arising from sterilization does not in itself warrant a fiscal correction. If, however, the economic nature of this component of the deficit is misunderstood, and it is offset by expenditure cuts and/or increases in taxation, the social and economic costs may be substantial. The relevance of this point for Hungary is indicated by the fact that the primary (noninterest) surplus of the general government reached 4.4% of GDP in 1996, exceeding the original target by 0.7 percentage points.[33]

A potential further macroeconomic cost of sterilized intervention may occur when there is "excessive" sterilization, which hinders investments and economic growth. Whether we consider sterilization to be excessive is, of course, a matter of judgment and interpretation; such a determination should be based on the country's overall macroeconomic performance. Hungary's poor results in 1996 with respect to economic growth (1.3% in real terms), combined with a smaller than targeted current account deficit, may be a sign of overly restrictive overall macroeconomic policies. However, it would not be reasonable to blame monetary policy solely for this.

5.6   Other Policy Responses to Capital Inflows and Concluding Remarks

The problems related to sterilized intervention were the focus of our discussion of the policy responses to capital flows to Hungary. This was because such intervention was the major policy response there. Although the authorities took some other steps, the importance of those moves in limiting the macroeconomic effects of capital inflows was minor.

As for exchange rate policy, the rate of crawl was decreased in 1996 to 1.2% per month (from 1.3% in the second half of 1995); that rate was maintained throughout the year. Although these steps (just as the further decrease of the crawl to 1% in 1997) were not in direct response to capital inflows, they were supported by the continuing inflow of foreign capital.

The same holds for the progress made on external financial and trade liberalization. The authorities took several important measures to liberalize financial outflows. In line with the declaration of the convertibility of the forint at the end of 1995, the ceiling on the conversion of domestic to foreign currency by households was abolished and the rules governing the making of several types of financial investments abroad by both households and businesses were liberalized.

With regard to trade policy, the authorities in 1996 began the gradual removal of the import surcharge (introduced in March 1995), abolishing it altogether in mid-1997. Meanwhile, in accordance with agreements with the EU, they began to make significant reductions in tariff rates. The short-term impact of trade liberalization on capital inflows is ambiguous. In any case, it is useful to note that any worrisome implications of such liberalization for the balance of payments were mitigated by the inflows of foreign capital.

These policy measures did not significantly affect the size or uses of net capital inflows in the period under review. However, the combined effect of the decrease in the rate of crawl of the exchange rate, the tariff reductions, and the total removal of the import surcharge most likely contributed to the increase in imports in 1997.

The authorities took no direct or indirect steps to discourage capital inflows. Policymakers were most probably influenced by memories of the time when it was necessary to raise foreign capital for financing current account deficits; they were reluctant to introduce measures that could have scared off foreign investors. Still, the fact that the premium component in Hungarian interest rates had become negligible by the end of 1996 indicates that policymakers did not wish to further stimulate inflows that they would have had to sterilize.

Capital inflows to Hungary during 1995–1996 did not seem to have direct macroeconomic effects. The reason for this was the extensive sterilization of these flows. Therefore, unlike in many other countries experiencing large net capital inflows, macroeconomic outcomes were largely influenced by such internal developments as the fall in real incomes and consumption. These outcomes were also affected by policy measures – especially fiscal policy – and by measures aimed at offsetting the effects of capital inflows.

In 1997, the Hungarian economy showed clear signs of recovery, with GDP growth at 4.4%. This is closely related to expansion of the output and exports of partly or fully foreign-owned companies. The volume of total exports increased by 25% and that of engineering exports by 50% in the first half of 1997; the latter was mainly due to foreign investors. The activities of these companies have clearly had a major impact on overall economic performance, suggesting that it is neither the amount of total inflows, nor the extent of their sterilization, that matters for the macroeconomy, but rather the quality and the composition of the inflows.

In Hungary, extensive sterilization of capital inflows does not seem to have hindered the increase in productive capital, in particular that of the exporting sectors. Whether or not the other sectors will be able to catch up depends on their ability to draw upon either domestic or foreign capital. The latter form of capital may be preferable, because it is more likely to involve new technology. In any case, this discussion clearly demonstrates the limitations of the forgoing analysis, which has focused on macroeconomic developments arising from capital inflows, to the neglect of the accompanying structural changes in the real economy.

Acknowledgments

I am grateful to János Gács and Michael Wyzan for their comments and suggestions, as well as to David Begg and Charles Wyplosz, the discussants of the first version of the chapter. Although I received significant assistance from several persons at the NBH, the views expressed and interpretations offered in this chapter are the author's alone and may diverge from official views and interpretations. The standard disclaimer is especially important in the present instance, because I received great help in my work from several persons at the NBH. I am obliged to Judit Neményi, István Székely, István Hamecz, and Gyula Barabás for useful discussions and the provision of important data; I also received some essential statistics from Mihály Durucskó and Erika Vörös. None of these persons is responsible for the content of this chapter.

Notes

[1] For a history of Hungarian debt accumulation see, e.g., Oblath (1993a).

[2] See, e.g., UN/ECE (1996), Table 5.2.1, which shows that in the first half of 1996 there was a net capital outflow from Hungary of \$0.7 billion or 3% of GDP. The table includes figures for other East European countries in the first half of 1996. Bulgaria

also experienced a net capital outflow of $0.7 billion. This seems to suggest that the experiences of Hungary and Bulgaria regarding net foreign capital flows were similar during that period. However, this interpretation would be misleading: while Bulgaria suffered major capital flight, Hungary experienced a large inflow of private capital, while the public sector repaid part of its foreign debt.

[3] Some further important issues of recent capital inflows to Hungary, in particular the distinction between short-term (potentially speculative or transitory) and longer-term inflows, are taken up by Barabás and Hamecz (1997).

[4] See, e.g., Schadler *et al.* (1993), Corbo and Hernández (1996), and Fernández-Arias and Montiel (1996), for reviews and analytical treatments of related experiences.

[5] In December 1996, cumulative nondebt-related foreign capital inflows through the banking system were $14.7 billion, including owners' credits ($1.4 billion) and the government's privatization revenues ($5.7 billion); however, even excluding these items, the cumulative inflow was $7.6 billion. Hungary's foreign direct investments abroad were close to $0.5 billion, so net versions of these items can be attained by subtracting that figure from each of them. In addition, there was an inflow of FDI in kind, the cumulative sum of which was about $1 billion. (This was recorded in the trade balance, based on customs statistics, but not in the balance of payments statistics, where actual payments related to exports and imports are reported. Thus, total gross cumulative FDI inflows exceed $15 billion.)

[6] Between 1990 and 1993 the real appreciation of the forint was 7% on the basis of industrial prices, but more than 30% according to unit labor costs, and 19% based on GDP deflators. It should be noted that the real exchange rate (RER) index based on industrial price indices is just as poor a guide for assessing price competitiveness as the one based on the consumer price index (CPI); the latter indicated a real appreciation of 23%. While the industrial price index is strongly influenced by the nominal exchange rate index, the RER based on the CPI is dominated by structural changes (restructuring of economic activity toward the previously underdeveloped service sector) and increases in indirect taxes. The relevant RER index under these circumstances is the one based on unit labor costs. See Oblath (1993b) for a detailed description of trade liberalization and exchange rate policy in the early years of the transition.

[7] The main theoretical justification for distinguishing between privatization revenues and other forms of FDI is that while the former involve only a change in the composition of net government assets (between real and liquid assets, and hence a decrease in the net foreign debt of the government sector), other forms of FDI increase the volume of capital investment.

[8] See OECD (1995) on this point.

[9] Net foreign borrowing is defined as conventional net borrowing (the difference between credits received and extended) minus net payments of principal (i.e., debt repayment).

[10] The public sector's demand for foreign exchange stemmed from net interest payments on foreign public debt (*CADpu*) plus the fall in net foreign public debt (*–dNFApu*). Neither the CB nor the government buys forex on the market for conducting these transactions. Therefore, these transactions simply decrease the level of foreign exchange reserves, without a corresponding increase in the supply of domestic currency on the forex market. As for the supply of foreign exchange offered by the public sector, privatization revenues (*FDIpu*) are not sold on the forex market, so they increase the CB's international reserves, without creating a corresponding market demand for domestic currency.

[11] In the discussion that follows, the term CB intervention is defined as the purchase of foreign exchange by the CB. During every month from March 1995 through December 1996, the NBH was a net purchaser of foreign exchange.

[12] This was more or less the case in Hungary, where an agreement was reached in 1996 on using privatization revenues mostly for repaying foreign debt, rather than for financing public expenditures.

[13] In Hungary, according to figures for December 1996, the share of forex deposits in the total deposits held with commercial banks was 36% for the household sector, and 27% for the business sector. As for commercial banks, 45% of the total deposits that they held with the CB were in foreign exchange. In December 1995, this ratio was much higher (74%); the reasons for this change are addressed further in the text.

[14] We have no information on the scale of the conversion of interest payments on forex deposits held with the CB, but it does not appear to have been significant.

[15] In the following equations we do not make an explicit distinction between *INTnci(1)* and *INTnci(2)*. *INTnci* is understood to be one or the other concept, depending on which of the two is empirically relevant.

[16] The domestic net foreign exchange assets of the CB are defined as the difference between domestic foreign exchange credits extended by, and domestic foreign exchange deposits held with, the CB. At the end of 1996, *dNFXAcb* was –677 billion forints, of which credits were 14 billion forints and debits 691 billion forints.

[17] The last term on the right-hand side had a negative sign in the period under review.

[18] "Beside the coins and bank notes in circulation, we include in the monetary base all claims of commercial banks vs. the CB: financial institutions' both forex and domestic currency deposits – inclusive of deposits placed in the framework of passive repurchase arrangements – bonds issued abroad, but in the portfolio of domestic (resident) banks, as well as consortial credits extended by resident banks to the CB". (NBH Monthly Report, 1997, No. 2, footnote on p. 33.)

[19] Barabás and Hamecz (1997) make this point very clearly.

[20] Here we are simply referring to an *ex post* relationship; that which would have contributed to the current account deficit simply could not have involved sterilization. This statement does not imply that the capital inflows directly affected the current account.

[21] The idea here is that while the CB can take steps that directly change base money, the issuing of government paper above its actual financing requirements may change broader monetary aggregates. We will return to this subject in the text.

[22] According to a recent (cautious) estimate by Klauber (1997), the surplus on "travel" is likely to have been above $2 billion in 1996. The official figure was $1.2 billion, while "(unrequited) current transfers", which are known to include service exports, were $0.9 billion. If part of "current transfers" did involve actual current transfers, some component of net service exports (i.e., the actual surplus on "travel") had to show up in NEO.

[23] The large amount of foreign capital that flowed into the Budapest Stock Exchange in 1996, and the comparatively small size of recorded portfolio investment, suggests that a significant part of NEO may be investment that is unrecorded.

[24] To simplify the presentation, we base our discussion on the figures expressed in dollars. We present the corresponding figures expressed in forints and in relation to GDP in *Table 5.5*.

[25] This shift was due to changes in reserve regulations, which significantly reduced the incentives for banks to hold forex deposits with the NBH. Banks took advantage of the opportunities offered by the liberalization of capital exports. However, at the end of each quarter, they temporarily increased their forex deposits with the CB.

[26] The change in base money is based on a correction by Barabás and Hamecz (1997), who subtract the increase by banks in their stocks of passive repo on the last day of the year.

[27] See Barabás and Hamecz (1997).

[28] In January 1997, the net foreign debt held by the NBH was transferred to the Hungarian government: part of the government's liabilities to the CB, in the amount of the CB's net foreign debt, was replaced by forex-denominated government liabilities.

[29] The figure depicts net repayments by the CB, but similar developments characterized the overall public sector.

[30] Árvai (1997) and Simon (1996) address the second and third questions.

[31] These costs are considered "fiscal" because, in line with arrangements in Hungary, the deficit on the CB's profit and loss account (e.g., due to sterilization) is covered by a transfer from the government. Accordingly, these costs show up either as a decrease in CB profits transferred to the government, or as a government expenditure corresponding to the current loss of the CB.

[32] See Tanzi *et al.* (1993) for a discussion of the operational deficit. In this case, while the nominal deficit (or its ratio to GDP) increases, the real deficit may even decrease. For the relevance of the operational deficit for Hungary, see Oblath (1996).

[33] The overall deficit of the general government (Government Financial Statistics definition, disregarding privatization revenues) was 3.3% of GDP, rather than the targeted 4%.

References

Árvai, Zs., 1997, The econometric analysis of capital inflows and sterilisation policy, *NBH Discussion Papers*, No. 1997/5 [in Hungarian].

Barabás, Gy., and Hamecz, I., 1997, Capital inflows, sterilization, and the money supply, *NBH Discussion Papers*, No. 1997/3 [in Hungarian].

Corbo, V., and Hernández, L., 1996, Macroeconomic adjustment to capital inflows: Lessons from recent Latin-American and East-Asian experience, *World Bank Research Observer*, **11**(1):61–85.

Fernández-Arias, E., and Montiel, P.J., 1996, The surge in capital inflows to developing countries: An analytical overview, *World Bank Economic Review*, **10**(1):51–77.

Klauber, M., 1997, The effect of household foreign-currency transactions on the balance on invisible trade, unpublished manuscript, KOPINT-DATORG, Budapest, Hungary [in Hungarian].

National Bank of Hungary (NBH), 1996, *Annual Report 1995*, NBH, Budapest, Hungary.

National Bank of Hungary (NBH), 1997, *Annual Report 1996*, NBH, Budapest, Hungary.

Oblath, G., 1993a, Hungary's foreign debt: Controversies and problems, in D.M.G. Newbery and I.P. Székely, eds., *Hungary: An Economy in Transition*, Cambridge University Press, Cambridge, UK.

Oblath, G., 1993b, Real exchange rate changes and exchange rate policy under economic transition in Hungary and Central Eastern Europe, in J. Gács and G. Winckler, eds., *International Trade and Restructuring in Eastern Europe*, International Institute for Applied Systems Analysis, Laxenburg, Austria.

Oblath, G., 1996, Macroeconomic effects of fiscal deficits in Hungary, *Russian and East European Finance and Trade*, May–June.

Organisation for Economic Co-operation and Development (OECD), 1995, *Economic Surveys: Hungary 1995*, OECD, Paris, France.

Schadler, S., Carkovic, M., Bennett, A., and Khan, R., 1993, Recent experiences with surges in capital inflows, *IMF Occasional Paper No. 108*, International Monetary Fund, Washington, DC, USA.

Simon, A., 1996, Sterilization, interest-rate policy, the budget deficit, and the balance of payments, *NBH Discussion Papers*, No. 1996/3 [in Hungarian].

Tanzi, V., Blejer, M.I., and Tejeiro, M.O., 1993, Effects of inflation on measurement of fiscal deficits: Conventional versus operational measures, in M.I. Blejer and A. Cheasty, eds., *How to Measure the Fiscal Deficit*, International Monetary Fund, Washington, DC, USA.

United Nations Economic Commission for Europe (UN/ECE), 1996, *Economic Bulletin for Europe*, **48**, UN/ECE, New York, NY, USA.

Appendix: Variable names and abbreviations

CAD	Current account deficit
CADpr	Current account deficit of private sector
CADpu	Net factor (interest) payments on foreign public debt
CB	Central bank
CX	Capital exports
CXpb	Capital exports of banking sector
FDI	Foreign direct investment
FDIpr	Conventional foreign direct investment
FDIpu	Forex privatization revenues of government
INT	Central bank intervention
INTcb	Total (foreign and domestic) central bank intervention
INTdom	Domestic central bank intervention
INTnci(1)	Central bank intervention related to capital inflows
INTnci(2)	Central bank intervention related to capital inflows plus capital exports of the banking sector
MB	Monetary base
NCI	Net capital inflows
NCIpr	Net private capital inflows
NEO	Net errors and omissions
NFA	Net foreign assets
NFAcb	Net foreign assets of central bank
NFApu	Net foreign assets of public sector
NFB	Net foreign borrowing
NFBg	Net foreign borrowing by government
NFBpu	Net foreign borrowing by public sector
NFBpb	Net foreign borrowing by banking sector
NFP	Net factor payments abroad
NFT	Net financial transfers from abroad
NFXAcb	Net foreign exchange assets of central bank
NRT	Net resource transfers from abroad
PD	Primary deficit
R	Central bank's foreign exchange reserves
STER	Magnitude of sterilization

Note: A *d* before a variable name in the text and formulae indicates an absolute change in the relevant variable.

Chapter 6

Financial Inflows to Poland, 1990–1996

Paweł Durjasz and Ryszard Kokoszczyński

6.1 Introduction

The problem of large foreign exchange inflows to Poland has been evident since 1994, although only in 1995 did the magnitude of those inflows become a major issue for financial policy. Such inflows were mainly caused by a large, unsustainable current account surplus, resulting primarily from net inflows from unclassified transactions. Capital inflows have been significant only since the second quarter of 1995, after the conclusion of the agreement with the London Club in October 1994 and the resulting improvement in Poland's credit standing. Thus, the period from 1995 onward is the major subject of our study. We present this episode within the broader context of the entire decade of the 1990s; without such background, it would be difficult to analyze the relevant causal relations and policy reactions.

This chapter is organized as follows. Section 6.2 presents an overview of the financial inflows from 1990 through 1996, including a detailed presentation of the period 1994–1996, when inflows were most intensive. Section 6.3 lays out the major causes of these inflows. In Section 6.4, we describe the challenges posed by these inflows and the measures that the Polish authorities have used to address them. In Section 6.5, we evaluate the effects of the capital inflows and the policy responses to them. Section 6.6 provides a conclusion.

An earlier version of this chapter was published in *Empirica*, Volume 25, Number 1, 1998, Kluwer Academic Publishers.

Table 6.1. Selected balance of payments components in Poland (in million US$).

	1990	1991	1992	1993	1994	1995	1996
Current account[a]	597	–1,979	913	–579	2,267	5,455	–1,352
Percent of GDP	1.0	–2.6	1.1	–0.7	2.4	4.6	–1.0
Trade balance	2,214	51	512	–2,293	–836	–1,827	–8,154
Percent of GDP	3.8	0.1	0.6	–2.7	–0.9	–1.5	–6.1
Net unclassified current account							
transactions	–119	– 620	1,182	1,750	3,211	7,754	7,153
Capital account[a,b]	1,580	1,113	–440	573	–519	3,480	4,422
Percent of GDP	2.7	1.5	–0.5	0.7	–0.6	2.9	3.3
IMF credits	479	322	0	–138	610	–1,400	0
Increase in gross official reserves	2,177	–866	473	–6	1,748	8,935	3,070
Increase in net international reserves		–1,317	1,615	635	2,535	9,146	1,231
Gross official reserves	4,680	3,814	4,287	4,281	6,029	14,963	18,033
Net international reserves	7,822	6,505	8,120	8,755	11,290	20,436	21,667
Gross official reserves							
(in months of imports)	6.5	3.6	3.8	3.2	4.1	7.3	6.6

[a] In January 1996, a new item, "Unclassified transactions on current account: net" was introduced in the current account. It is the equivalent of the previous "Purchase/sale of foreign currencies", included in "Other short-term capital". Previous figures have been adjusted for purposes of comparison.
[b] Defined as "Increase in gross official reserves" minus "Current account".
Source: NBP data, based on banking statistics.

6.2   Size, Timing, and Structure of Financial Inflows

Table 6.1 contains basic information on Poland's balance of payments (on a cash basis) for 1990–1996. The surplus on the capital account – measured as the difference between the increases in gross official reserves (GOR) and the current account balance – was markedly higher during 1990–1991 and 1995–1996 than in the rest of the period. In the first of these periods, capital inflows occurred mostly due to large exceptional financing: Poland had not been servicing its debt to official creditors since 1981, and had partially suspended servicing of its debt to private creditors in 1990, when the stabilization package was introduced.[1] A resumption of large-scale net capital inflows began only in 1995 and these inflows have gained momentum since then.

A significant accumulation of gross official reserves occurred in 1990 and during 1994–1996. The stabilization package introduced at the beginning of January 1990 included *inter alia* a sizable devaluation of the zloty, liberalization of foreign trade, the introduction of so-called internal current account convertibility, and the implementation of measures designed to reduce internal demand. All of these resulted in an unexpected trade surplus equal to 3.8% of gross domestic product (GDP), leading to a current account surplus (which was complemented by a positive capital account).

During the second period, which was characterized by reserve accumulation, the relative contributions of the current account and capital flows evolved over time. In 1994 and 1995, a rapidly expanding current account surplus was the main factor behind an increase in official reserves. There was a net capital outflow equal to 0.6% of GDP in 1994, although by 1995 the capital account deficit had turned into a sizable surplus, which contributed – along with current account inflows – to an unprecedented rise in the foreign exchange reserves. In 1996 and 1997 capital inflows were able to finance both a current account deficit and a more moderate increase in the official reserves.

The difference between the changes in GOR and the net international reserves (NIR)[2] of the banking system reflects, to a certain extent, domestic banks' perceptions of exchange rate risk. Until 1994 (with the exception of 1991), NIR grew faster than GOR, as banks preferred to keep long open foreign exchange positions, in order to exploit the eventual gains from step devaluation. In 1995 and 1996, the opposite pattern can be observed. If Poland had not repaid a loan from the International Monetary Fund (IMF) earlier than scheduled, GOR would have risen by an additional $1 billion in 1995, so the increase in GOR would have exceeded the rise in NIR. Expectations that the zloty would appreciate became widespread, causing banks to reduce their foreign exchange positions in anticipation of higher yields on their zloty holdings; this process continued until at least the second quarter of 1996.

The spectacular rise in the current account surplus in 1994 and 1995 was associated with a surge in net cash inflows in convertible currencies. Until 1996, this buildup of cash purchased by the banking system from foreign exchange bureaus and individuals was recorded as a short-term capital item. However, the Polish authorities, foreign investors, and international financial institutions were all aware that these inflows were in large part the net result of unclassified current transactions. Such transactions consist mainly of cross-border trade with Germany and the purchase of goods in Poland by residents of Russia, Ukraine, and Belarus. Faced with this classification problem, the National Bank of Poland (NBP) decided at the beginning of 1996 to record data on the purchase and sale of foreign currencies by the banking system as "unclassified transactions on the current account". In this chapter, we have adjusted the data for earlier years in the same manner.

It is extremely difficult, if not impossible, to gather precise statistical evidence on the sources of these cash inflows. It seems that even the most comprehensive survey, made semi-annually by the Główny Urząd Statystyczny (GUS or Central Office of Statistics), which relies on voluntary replies from people crossing the borders, is bound to underestimate the purchases made by visitors from the East.[3] Because their activities are often semilegal, they have an incentive to underreport their expenditures in Poland. Some evidence of this underreporting can be found when results of the GUS survey are compared with the NBP's data on the regional

Table 6.2. Composition of capital flows to and from Poland (in million US$).

	1990	1991	1992	1993	1994	1995	1996
Capital account[a,b]	1,580	1,113	–440	573	–519	3,480	4,422
Net long-term credits[c]	160	482	140	10	–814	228	–177
Drawings of received long-term credits	428	786	562	922	894	702	819
Net short-term credits	–332	–38	–136	–53	–53	66	80
Net foreign direct investment	10	117	284	580	542	1,134	2,741
Net portfolio investment					–624	1,171	241
Net inflow into T-bills[d]						915	–178
Net equity						234	689
Errors and omissions	360	–713	50	589	–228	–27	480
Exceptional financing	7,755	6,569	2,500	1,376	690	17	5
Other capital inflows[e]	–6,373	–5,744	–3,278	–1,929	–32	891	966

[a] In January 1996 a new item, "Unclassified transactions on current account: net" was introduced in the current account. It is the equivalent of the previous, "Purchase/sale of foreign currencies", included in "Other short-term capital". Previous figures have been adjusted for purposes of comparison.
[b] Defined as "Increase in gross official reserves" minus "Current account".
[c] Includes credits due and paid only.
[d] As estimated by NBP's Monetary Policy Department.
[e] Includes valuation changes and IMF credits.
Source: NBP data based on banking statistics.

distribution of cash inflows. According to these data, the share of the eastern and central provinces in generating these inflows is significant, whereas according to the results obtained by the GUS, the western border is the main source of revenues from unregistered exports.

We present the composition of the capital account in *Table 6.2*. Detailed data on portfolio investment are available only since 1995. However, before 1995, portfolio inflows, with the exception of investments in equity, were negligible. The net portfolio outflow recorded in 1994 reflects the purchase of the collateral necessary to effect the agreement with the London Club.

Foreign direct investment (FDI) was the most important type of net capital inflow in the period described here, followed by net portfolio investment, which was concentrated mainly in 1995. It is also evident that surges in these two kinds of foreign inflows were mainly responsible for the significant increase in the capital account surplus in 1995 and 1996. Net FDI inflows have more than doubled every year since 1994. Thus, the composition of the capital account has so far been favorable from the standpoint of the probability of a sudden reversal of capital flows. Net FDI inflows more than covered the current account deficit in 1996, while the net portfolio inflow that year was significantly lower than in 1995. This was partly the result of a net outflow of $178 million from the treasury bills market, compared to a $915 million net inflow in 1995. Foreign exchange proceeds from privatization (excluding banks) are estimated to account for nearly 20% of net FDI in the period in question. Taking into account that the most valuable companies (in telecommunications, copper processing, energy, insurance, and a number of banks) have yet to be privatized, one can expect a further intensification of FDI inflows in the coming years.

Although cumulative drawings of long-term credits during 1990–1996 were only slightly lower than FDI inflows, net inflows of long-term credits were close to zero, as Poland repaid approximately the same amount of funds to her creditors. During the first years of the transformation, the government was the main borrower. According to balance of payments statistics on a cash basis, over 1995–1996 slightly more than one-half of the total volume of long-term credit was drawn either by the banking sector or directly by companies. The share of enterprises in long-term foreign borrowing rose rapidly from only 0.9% in 1994 and 6.7% in 1995 to 33.1% in 1996, although the volume of this inflow was still relatively limited. The majority of these long-term credits were granted by such international financial institutions as the World Bank (the largest creditor), the European Bank for Reconstruction and Development, and the European Investment Bank. However, there has been a change in the composition of creditors since 1995, with the share of the international financial institutions in credits drawn recently falling below 50%.

Unexplained net inflows – leaving aside the problems associated with unclassified transactions on the current account – over 1990–1996 were relatively small, as evidenced by a cumulative balance of $511 million on errors and omissions. They seem to be rooted in methodological imperfections in the compilation of the balance of payments, rather than reflecting a failure to detect all inflows. Data obtained outside the banking system suggest, however, that companies may have obtained more foreign credits than banks have reported.

An intensification in capital inflows occurred during 1995–1996. However, by 1994, an increase in the foreign exchange reserves, and the resulting problems for monetary policy, were already in evidence. *Table 6.3* presents quarterly data on the composition of foreign exchange inflows from the beginning of 1994 until mid-1997. A rapid increase in the net international reserves occurred from the beginning of 1995 until the end of the first quarter of 1996. Capital inflows were especially strong in the second quarter of 1995. The first and most important component of these financial inflows was net unclassified transactions on the current account, which between the beginning of 1995 and the end of the first quarter of 1996 reached $9.6 billion, amounting to 83% of the increase in GOR.[4]

The second most important source of net inflows during this period was FDI, which amounted to $1.9 billion, or 16.5% of the rise in GOR. Portfolio inflows were only slightly behind, at $1.8 billion, or 16% of the increase in GOR. Net inflows into the treasury bills market were the most important component of portfolio

Table 6.3. Types of foreign exchange inflows to Poland (quarterly, in million US$).

Inflow	1994 I	1994 II	1994 III	1994 IV	1995 I	1995 II	1995 III	1995 IV	1996 I	1996 II	1996 III	1996 IV	1997 I	1997 II
Increase in net international reserves	843	469	1,286	-63	1,790	2,833	2,639	1,885	1,599	-494	-109	234	-594	1,512
Increase in gross official reserves	803	113	847	-15	1,545	3,154	2,260	1,976	2,589	88	-86	479	-36	1,691
Net unclassified current account transactions[a]	758	824	1,035	594	1,502	1,868	2,179	2,205	1,820	1,677	2,020	1,636	1,216	1,562
Capital account[b]	483	-800	-151	-229	648	1,476	668	688	2,438	511	-47	1,520	1,477	2,875
Net foreign direct investment	113	178	99	152	200	136	241	557	763	424	544	1,010	456	779
Net portfolio investment				-624	-112	352	732	199	631	-184	-320	114	408	1,071
Net equity					39	16	96	83	167	287	68	167	233	288
Net T-bills[c]					28	461	312	114	599	-27	-592	-158	50	379
Net long-term credits[d]	36	-151	-86	-831	89	185	40	-153	-141	38	-200	64	70	270
Other capital account items[e]	334	-827	-164	450	471	803	-345	85	1,185	233	-71	382	579	1,025

[a] In January 1996 a new item, "Unclassified transactions on current account: net" was introduced in the current account. It is the equivalent of the previous "Purchase/sale of foreign currencies", included in "Other short-term capital". Previous figures have been adjusted for purposes of comparison.
[b] Defined as "Increase in gross official reserves" minus "Current account".
[c] As estimated by NBP's Monetary Policy Department.
[d] Includes only repayments due and paid.
[e] Includes valuation changes and portfolio investment (the latter only until 1995).
Source: NBP data, based on banking statistics.

inflows. During this period of capital surge, there was only a $20 million net inflow of long-term credits (due and paid).

The most significant changes in the structure of capital inflows in 1996 were the growing importance of FDI and the sharp slowdown in net portfolio inflows. Inflows from unclassified transactions on the current account, despite some easing, remained the most important source of increases in the net international reserves. Since late 1996, net capital inflows have been increasing rapidly. Although in 1997 net FDI remained the most important contributor to inflows ($3.0 billion), net portfolio investment increased considerably (to $2.1 billion).

6.3   Major Causes of Inflows

The overview presented in the previous section illustrates clearly that 1995 was in many respects the turning point with respect to the Polish capital account. Until 1995, Poland – as a country that had reneged on servicing its foreign debt – did not have access to international private capital markets. Only after Poland concluded an agreement with private creditors comprising the London Club in October 1994, and received an investment grade rating from Moody's (announced by the Polish authorities in June 1995), did financial markets' perception of Poland as a high-risk country begin to change, leading to accelerated private capital inflows. These inflows were increasingly channeled outside the public sector. Poland has turned into a moderately indebted country, with total debt service due representing around 8–9% of exports of goods and services and net transfers (excluding unrecorded trade) in 1995–1996.[5]

Structural reforms improving Poland's attractiveness to foreign capital were carried out gradually, before the surge in capital inflows began. *De facto* current account convertibility for residents was introduced at the very beginning of the reforms. Capital inflows – with the guaranteed transfer of profits and repatriation of invested capital – were liberalized at a relatively early stage of the transformation; FDI and portfolio investment in equity were liberalized in 1991, as were inflows into the treasury securities market, without discrimination as far as maturity was concerned (in 1993).

Restrictions on contracting financial credits abroad by companies were liberalized in 1996, although even before that date the NBP had conducted a liberal policy on granting individual authorizations. Furthermore, the domestic financial market was substantially liberalized before capital inflows became significant. Since the beginning of 1993, the NBP has based its monetary policy on indirect market instruments, although changes in reserve requirements continue to play a role. However, these liberalization measures did not directly attract a significant amount of foreign capital until early 1995, despite other favorable conditions, such as visibly

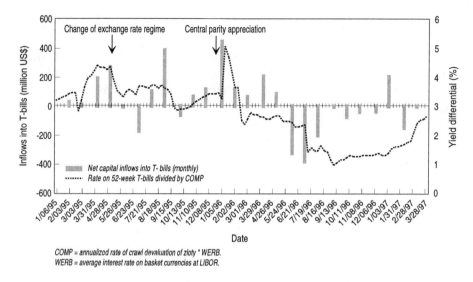

Figure 6.1. Yield differential and inflows into T-bills in Poland.

improving macroeconomic fundamentals (see *Table 6.4*) and relatively large interest rate differentials, reaching 9 percentage points at the beginning of 1994 (see
Figure 6.1 for the method of calculation).

The conclusion of the agreement with private creditors apparently was an important catalyst for FDI inflows. After the solution of the debt problem, and with
reassuring growth in the foreign exchange reserves, foreign investors could focus
more on the other positive developments in the Polish economy – mainly a market
with rapidly growing GDP per capita, with promising examples of pioneering investors. The big manufacturers who took the risk of investing in Poland in the early
years of reform have recently been followed by their competitors and subcontrac-
tors, as the case of the automotive industry illustrates. The agreement with private
creditors was also crucial to unleashing financing from Germany (Poland's most
important trade partner), as German companies had previously been constrained by
their banks' reluctance to finance projects in Poland.

Figure 6.1 illustrates the role played by the yield differential in attracting foreign investment into Polish treasury bills since the beginning of 1995. Although
there have been no restrictions on nonresidents' investments in commercial paper
and treasury securities of any maturity, investment in zloty-denominated treasury
bills has been the main channel used by foreigners for interest rate arbitrage. As
of December 1996, the value of outstanding treasury bills was not significantly
higher than the value of treasury bonds ($10.3 billion, compared to $8.0 billion), although the liquidity of the T-bill market was considerably larger. The average daily

Table 6.4. Basic economic indicators in Poland (real growth, previous year = 100 unless otherwise stated).

	1991	1992	1993	1994	1995	1996	Preliminary 1997
GDP	93.0	102.6	103.8	105.2	107.0	106.1	106.9
Industrial output	92.0	102.8	106.4	112.1	109.7	108.3	110.8
Agricultural output	98.4	87.3	106.8	90.7	110.7	100.7	99.9
Investments	95.9	100.4	102.3	108.1	117.1	119.2	120.0
Consumer price index (December–December)	160.4	144.3	137.6	129.5	121.6	118.5	113.2
Employment	95.6	97.2	98.3	101.1	100.3	103.5	100.6
Unemployment rate (%)	12.2	14.3	16.4	16.0	14.9	13.2	10.5
Exports (index calculated from US$ values)[a]	104.6	88.5	107.3	121.9	132.8	106.7	105.4
Imports (index calculated from US$ values)[a]	161.1	101.0	118.4	114.5	134.7	127.8	113.9
Trade balance (% of GDP)	0.07	0.61	–2.67	–0.90	–1.55	–6.10	–8.29
Current account balance (% of GDP)	–2.62	1.08	–0.67	2.45	4.62	–1.01	–3.16
Budget deficit (% of GDP)	3.8	6.0	2.8	2.7	2.6	2.5	1.3
Public debt (% of GDP)	81.4	85.2	88.7	72.3	57.9	51.1	49.2

[a] Customs data.

Sources: GUS, 1996; GCSS, 1997; NBP, various years.

turnover on the secondary market for T-bills reached the equivalent of $750 million in April 1997, compared with only $18 million for T-bonds. Thus, foreign investment in Polish T-bonds, which started to intensify in early 1997 from previously low levels, seems to have been motivated by longer-term considerations. The market for commercial paper, although developing relatively quickly, has been too small to attract significant inflows.

Portfolio capital – especially that flowing into the treasury bills market – has since the beginning of the second quarter of 1995 been attracted by expectations of a zloty appreciation and by higher yields on zloty investments. The expected interest rate differential in some subperiods of 1995–1996 was in fact much higher than presented in *Figure 6.1*, where the actual annualized rate of crawling devaluation of zloty was used as a proxy for the expected devaluation. But the virtual absence of exchange rate risk, accompanied by the high probability of appreciation of the zloty, was a strong incentive for foreign purchases of zloty-denominated treasury securities. Expectations that the zloty would appreciate in real terms arose when it became clear that the strong growth of the foreign exchange reserves, which fueled monetary growth – and possibly inflation – was the result of a significant current account surplus.[6] This surplus built up mainly due to a surge in net receipts from unclassified cash inflows, largely from unrecorded cross-border trade.

Inflows were heavily concentrated in the periods of strong expectations of zloty appreciation. Examples of such periods include the 6 weeks prior to the introduction of new, more flexible, and market-determined exchange rate arrangements in May 1995 (after which they partially reversed themselves)[7] and immediately after public statements on the strength of the zloty in September 1995. The authorities accepted the possibility of adverse effects from an inflow of portfolio capital before the introduction of the new exchange rate regime. This was the price that they consciously paid for the efficient and smooth (although time-consuming) introduction of the new exchange rate regime and subsequent zloty appreciation.

Gomulka (1997) has estimated the relationship between cumulative portfolio investment through period t, the level of NIR at the end of period $t - 1$, and the current expected rate of return using monthly data over 1995–1996. His work suggests that portfolio investment was not yet very sensitive to increases in yield differentials, so that the central bank had ample room for controlling domestic credit using interest rate policy.[8] Although net portfolio inflows were relatively small as a proportion of NIR accumulation (12% in 1995 and 16% in 1996), the NBP viewed foreign inflows into the treasury bill market in 1995 and early 1996 as seriously constraining the efficacy of interest rate policy.

A role in the intensification of capital inflows into Poland was also played by external factors such as low interest rates in the world's main financial centers. Another external factor was the "Tequila effect", which increased investors' interest in Central and Eastern Europe after the financial crisis in Mexico and the resulting disillusionment with Latin America. However, the timing and composition of capital inflows – namely, the dominant role played by FDI and the relatively modest inflows of portfolio investment – suggest that domestic factors were crucial here.

Interest-rate-sensitive inflows will most likely increase in the future. International borrowing by Polish residents (including companies, municipalities, and banks) has been relatively small until now, but by 1997, this channel of capital inflows had risen in importance, as the domestic cost of borrowing is rising. Poland is currently rated just above the investment grade threshold by major rating agencies. With country risk falling further, there is potential for increased capital mobility. Interest-rate-sensitive portfolio inflows into Poland will be additionally boosted in 1998 by the (planned) removal of restrictions limiting the external convertibility of the zloty. We also expect that the prospects of accession to the European Union (EU) and the further development of the capital market will be additional factors attracting both FDI and foreign investment in equity.

Large price differentials between Poland's and Germany's (and the EU's) home markets, originating from price differentials for nontradables, different taxation systems, and other policy-related distortions, provide an incentive for large numbers of Germans to engage in retail shopping in Poland. Although on average prices in Poland and Germany are gradually converging, there is still a relatively long list of goods whose prices differ significantly between the two countries (see Appendix). Trade-related tourism has also developed on Poland's southern border with the Czech and Slovak Republics. Tourists crossing Poland's eastern border (from Ukraine, Belarus, Lithuania, and Russia) frequently conduct purchases on a wholesale scale, fueled by the real appreciations of the local currencies, relative shortages of domestically produced consumer goods, and the emergence of a class of relatively wealthy citizens.

Taking into account our inability to precisely identify the origins of net cash inflows, we suspect that some of these inflows are in fact short-term capital movements attracted by the relative yields on zloty-denominated instruments or expectations that the zloty would appreciate. In that case, the relevant component of cash inflows should respond to yield fluctuations and show movements similar to those of net inflows into short-term debt instruments. However, monthly data show that net unclassified transactions on the current account are one of the least volatile components of the balance of payments, correlated neither with net inflows into treasury bills nor changes in the yield differential.

The NBP, on the basis of the existing evidence and research, attempted recently to identify the sources of net cash inflows (unclassified current account transactions). The analysis confirmed that most of the net cash inflows are the result of current transactions. According to these estimates, net cash inflows originating from net exports of goods and services (mostly tourism) amounted to $3.7 billion in 1995 (out of $7.75 million) and $5.6 billion in 1996 (out of $7.15 million). Part of the cash inflows is related to the repatriation of money earned abroad by Polish residents. An important share of net cash inflows ($2.6 billion) in 1995 most likely originated from the conversion of foreign currency into zlotys by the Polish non-bank and nongovernment sector. Such activities could be detected early in 1995, when residents sold foreign currency that they had accumulated earlier in anticipation of the denomination of the zloty (i.e., the introduction of the new zloty, which started at the beginning of 1995).[9] Polish residents also reduced their foreign currency deposits in favor of zlotys, as expectations of a nominal appreciation became widespread in 1995. Foreign portfolio investment, according to recent NBP estimates, was responsible for only $6 million in net cash inflows in 1995 and $60 million in 1996.

To summarize, each of the three major components of financial inflows has had rather distinct causes. First, net unclassified current account transactions have been stimulated primarily by price differentials. Second, FDI, which was responsible for the bulk of inflows, was induced by perceived country risk and market potential, signaled by the growth of the GDP. Finally, for net portfolio flows, the growth of, and price developments on, the Polish capital market were the prime determinants of flows into equity; for inflows to the Polish debt market, the interest rate differential was the most important factor. Net inflows into equity have been stable and expanding gradually.

6.4   Policy: Challenges and Responses

The government began to respond to the growth in the foreign exchange reserves in the second half of 1994, with a modest reduction in the rate of monthly devaluation of the zloty (from 1.6% to 1.5% in September, and to 1.4% in December). This cautious reaction was heavily influenced by the novelty of the phenomenon. The government's reluctance to make a larger adjustment in policy targets can be explained also by uncertainty concerning the London Club agreement, which it expected would be finalized in the second half of the year. Another factor explaining this somewhat passive approach was the fact that the authorities considered the main sources of the foreign exchange inflows – registered exports and the net outcome of cross-border trade – to be transitory. To summarize, the Polish authorities, influenced heavily by many years' experience with foreign exchange scarcity, were reluctant to interpret any new source of its inflow as permanent. Facing a still relatively large foreign debt and, after restructuring, a long, fixed timetable of debt service, the authorities reacted to the unexpected growth in the foreign exchange reserves by trying to minimize its negative impact rather than by attempting to control its causes.

When Poland finally reached an agreement with the London Club in October 1994, and the nature and magnitude of foreign exchange inflows made it clear that they were a long-term issue, the thrust of policy began to change. A new exchange rate regime was implemented and there were larger adjustments to the exchange rate that attempted to address the major sources of the inflows. To avoid the well-known Dutch disease – where a favorable development (e.g., an increase in foreign exchange receipts) leads to a large real appreciation of the currency – the authorities controlled the speed of the market-based adjustment of the exchange rate. In the meantime, to minimize the possible inflationary influence of this slow adjustment of the nominal exchange rate, the NBP expanded its sterilization operations.

6.4.1   Sterilization and its costs

The foreign exchange inflows, via an increase in commercial bank liquidity, put strong downward pressure on nominal interest rates on the money market. The NBP was concerned that this process, unless controlled, might depress the deposit rates banks offered their customers, leading to a fall in the savings ratio. Therefore, the NBP resisted the Ministry of Finance's arguments that it should lower interest

Table 6.5. Sources of money creation in Poland (%).

	1995	1996
Net international reserves	58.7	29.9
Net credit to the government	3.4	12.8
Credit to the nonfinancial sector	37.9	57.3
Companies	32.0	42.8
Households	5.9	14.6
Total	100.0	100.0

Note: "Other items net" excluded.
Source: NBP.

rates so as to limit the growth of NIR through increased domestic absorption and discourage portfolio inflows. The NBP's open market operations attempted to target a level of nominal interest rates high enough to maintain real positive rates on households' term deposits in commercial banks.

However, monetary policy in Poland in the 1990s is based on monetary targeting. Reserve accumulation is thus not only an obstacle to maintaining interest rates at a level high enough to stimulate savings, but also, other things being equal, a major factor driving up the growth of the money supply (see *Table 6.5*).

The NBP's obvious reaction was sterilized intervention. In the first half of 1994, when it still believed that capital inflows were temporary, open-market operations were mostly of a reverse-repo type. However, in the second half of the year, the NBP introduced the outright sale of T-bills from its portfolio. This being not enough to control liquidity (or the level of interest rates), the NBP reintroduced the outright sale of its own bills.[10] The volume of each type of operation is shown in *Figure 6.2*. We observe a similar response, i.e., outright sale of T-bills, in 1995, although the role of outright operations increased. The volume of sterilizing operations peaked in April 1996. With the stabilization of the foreign exchange reserves (beginning in the second quarter), the NBP was able to reduce the extent of sterilization in 1996.

We attempt here to estimate the costs of these sterilization efforts in a simple, even crude manner. The authorities' usual approach was not directed toward formal changes in official targets. To define the scope of sterilization, we compare the targeted and actual values of the money supply and NIR. The difference for the money supply in 1994 was 5.9 billion (new) zlotys, and 9.9 billion zlotys in 1995; the figures for NIR were 6.7 billion and 19.3 billion zlotys, respectively. If we assume that the sole reason for the fact that the growth of the money supply was higher than envisaged was unexpected growth in NIR, we can interpret the difference between these deviations from their respective targets as the amount successfully sterilized. Simple comparisons of these two sets of figures suggest that the sterilization efforts in 1995 were much more effective than in 1994.

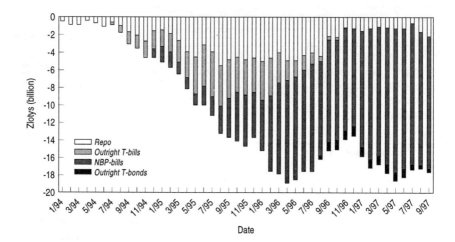

Figure 6.2. Open-market operations in Poland (monthly average of daily balances kept by banks with the NBP).

We obtained the costs of sterilization (defined in the above manner) by applying the interest rates used by the NBP in its open market operations; the weighted average interest rate was 26.9% in 1994 and 26.4% in 1995. If we also take into account the windfall gains on the larger stock of international reserves, we come up with the following crude estimates of the costs of sterilization: approximately 0.18 billion (new) zlotys in 1994 and 2.4 billion zlotys in 1995 (i.e., 0.08% and 0.84% of GDP, respectively). Of course, these are only estimates of the first-round effects. The increase in NIR in 1996 was smaller than targeted, so we do not carry out this exercise for that year.

The IMF adopted another approach for evaluating the effectiveness of sterilization in 1994–1996 in Poland and the Czech Republic (Rodlauer, 1996). The fund estimated a simple regression model, with the change in the central bank's net foreign assets (NFA) explained by the change in its net domestic assets (NDA), nominal income, and the foreign interest rate. With mobile capital, a decrease in NDA arising from open-market operations will lead to an increase in NFA; the regressor on NDA is the offset coefficient, a measure of the effectiveness of sterilization. The fund's preliminary (and not yet published) estimates show this coefficient to be in the range of –0.57 to –0.62 for Poland and approximately equal to –0.65 in the Czech Republic, where a coefficient equal to –1 means that sterilization is totally ineffective.

In 1995, the authorities, understanding the implications of sterilized intervention, and finally seeing financial inflows as not just a transitory phenomenon, reacted in a more comprehensive manner. In that year, policy concentrated on exchange rate changes, while in 1996 exchange rate policy was dominated by interest rate policy, and in 1997 both played a substantial role in controlling capital inflows.

6.4.2 Exchange rate policy and interest rate policy

In the face of the intensified accumulation of foreign exchange reserves at the beginning of 1995, which originated first of all in the current account surplus (suggesting that the zloty was undervaluated), the authorities could not avoid choosing between a nominal appreciation and higher inflation. However, an excessive real appreciation, pursued so as to maintain macroeconomic stability, could adversely affect the tradable-goods sector.

There was also a trade-off concerning the way to accomplish the appreciation of the zloty. Until 1995, the NBP had conducted its exchange rate policy within the framework of a preannounced crawling peg regime. The exchange rate mechanism was relatively inflexible: the exchange rate on the interbank foreign exchange market could fluctuate within ±2% around the rate announced daily by the NBP, reflecting daily movements in the cross rates among various foreign currencies. However, the extent of domestic market influence on the exchange rate was limited *de facto* to the 1% spread between the NBP's buy and sell rates. The NBP was constantly ready to effect transactions with foreign exchange banks.

A fast step appreciation within this framework would have quickly defused the expectations of appreciation, thus limiting possible short-term capital inflows. But such an exchange rate adjustment would have had negative implications, as previously the authorities had only devalued the zloty. A market-based appreciation also seemed attractive, because it provided an opportunity to flexibly manage exchange rate adjustment in an environment of rapid changes in productivity and in the structure of the economy. However, the size of the step appreciation would have had to be arbitrary. Moreover, in the face of important changes in the equilibrium real exchange rate, it was difficult to determine the desired real exchange rate and the rate of preannounced devaluation.

Appreciation in a "market way", through the implementation of a more market-determined, flexible exchange rate mechanism, would have been more time-consuming. However, it seemed desirable mostly because of the considerable scope of *de facto* capital account convertibility. In the first months of 1995, when the risk premium on investment in treasury securities began to shrink, the room for autonomy in interest rate policy was reduced. The effectiveness of monetary policy could be restored primarily by allowing the zloty to float, at least to a certain extent, within a wider band.

Letting the zloty appreciate in a market way, coupled with the creation of a more flexible exchange rate system, would have consequences beyond the problem of regaining control over the foreign exchange reserves. This systemic adjustment could at least, to some extent, shield monetary policy from the effects of interest rate arbitrage, improve the cross-border transmission of price signals, and contribute to the further development of the foreign exchange market.

The rate of crawl was reduced from 1.4% to 1.2% on 16 February 1995. Already on 6 March 1995, the NBP extended the spread between its continuously quoted buy and sell rates from 1% to 4%, covering the fully allowable margin of exchange rate fluctuations. This measure represented the most that the NBP could do independently in the area of exchange rate policy within the legal framework of the time. The exchange rate on the interbank market responded relatively quickly by appreciating to the fullest extent allowed relative to the NBP's new buy rate.

On 16 May 1995, the NBP abolished the limits on the fluctuation of exchange rates quoted by banks. The NBP has publicly committed itself to keeping exchange rate fluctuations on the foreign exchange interbank market within a band of $\pm 7\%$ around the central rate; since then the central rate has played only the role of a reference rate for establishing the band. Simultaneously, the NBP has limited its former direct, dominant role on the interbank market by withdrawing from the quotation of its rates. It retains, however, the ability to intervene on this market. Transactions between banks and the NBP – other than those resulting from interventions – are currently effected by means of a fixing held around 3 p.m. each business day, during which it balances the market. The central rate around which the band is determined continues to be devalued according to the former rules governing the crawling devaluation. The rate of crawl plays an active, forward-looking role, since the NBP sets it with respect to inflation targets and projected inflation abroad.

As a result of these changes, the zloty appreciated relatively quickly within the band, reaching the limit of 5% above the central rate, where the NBP's interventions kept it (see *Figure 6.3*). The implementation of the new system has been smooth and the commercial banks have welcomed it. The market-based real appreciation of the zloty has also been more difficult for exporters to contest than arbitrary exchange rate adjustments would have been. The exporters' lobby has voiced objections, but its supporters in the government have had little influence on exchange rate policy.

As was expected – given the size of the foreign exchange inflows – the measures undertaken between February and May could not restore equilibrium on the foreign exchange market immediately. Here it should be recalled that a net inflow of cash mostly from net unregistered exports and other current transactions was the most important factor behind the increase in the foreign exchange reserves. Therefore, the appreciation pressure continued until the second quarter of 1996. The

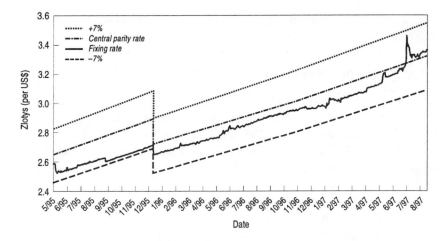

Figure 6.3. Zloty exchange rates since introduction of band.

NBP, in consultation with the government, intervened on the market to limit the size of the zloty's appreciation. This policy, aimed at enhancing the ability of the tradable goods sector to adjust to exchange rate changes, constrained exchange rate flexibility and reduced the effectiveness of monetary policy.

Confronted with a constant oversupply on the foreign exchange market in September 1995, the NBP allowed the zloty to appreciate by shifting its internal intervention limit to –6% from the central rate. In the face of the constant proximity of the market rate to the lower intervention band and the exchange rate mechanism's lack of flexibility, on 22 December 1995, the NBP revalued its central rate by 6%. The next day, the authorities allowed the market rate to appreciate, and it gained 2.5% against the new parity rate. Additionally, the NBP reduced the rate of crawl from 1.2% to 1% on 8 January 1996. The NBP's interventions kept the exchange rate within a margin of 2.5–3% of the central parity during the first quarter of 1996, but in the next quarter, the foreign exchange market began to stabilize and the exchange rate became more volatile and unpredictable. The NBP did not intervene on the market during the business day from 22 May 1996, until the end of that year.

The absence of such intervention was not the result of exchange rate policy alone. Favorable developments with respect to inflation made it possible to slowly reduce interest rates in the first half of 1996. In that way, the two major factors shaping capital inflows weakened. First, other things equal, lower interest rates reduced the yield in foreign currency on investments in fixed-income securities denominated in zloty. Second, lower interest rates stimulated the growth of domestic demand, which resulted in a larger deficit on the current account. As a result, since the second quarter of 1996, the growth of NIR has stabilized.

6.4.3   Other policy responses

In 1994 and 1995 commercial banks had been pressing the NBP for a decrease in the reserve ratio, which they considered too high: at the beginning of 1994, it was 23% for zloty demand deposits, 10% for zloty term deposits, and zero for foreign currency deposits. February 1994 saw the introduction of nonremunerated reserve requirements for foreign currency deposits, initially 0.5% for term deposits and 0.75% for demand deposits.[11]

However, in the autumn of 1994, the NBP cut the reserve requirements on zloty demand deposits from 23% to 20%, increasing at the same time the reserve ratio to 1% for both demand and term forex deposits. Another change in reserve requirements took place in February 1995, when the ratio for term deposits was cut from 10% to 9%. The main reason for this was the establishment of a new deposit insurance system financed by mandatory bank contributions; the cut in reserve requirements was to compensate for the increase in banks' costs arising from those new contributions.

It is clear that during 1994 and 1995 the NBP did not use reserve requirements to an appreciable extent to control the liquidity of the banking system. The major reason for this approach was the situation of the banking system. The NBP was in the process of restructuring banks' portfolios of bad loans, and it saw any measure increasing banks' costs as endangering that process.

It can be argued that monetary policy was not supported by other policies in dealing with increased foreign financial inflows. New foreign exchange regulations were issued at the beginning of 1995 in order to meet the *de jure* requirements of Article VIII on currency convertibility of the IMF's Articles of Agreement. However, the first adjustment of the foreign exchange system in response to the foreign exchange inflows came relatively late, on 10 December 1995, with the abolition of the requirement that exporters must sell foreign currency. The move was aimed at slowing the growth of official reserves and reserve money.

Further adjustments came in February, April, and May 1996, with the liberalization of some capital outflows. However, the authorities took these steps in order to achieve a level of capital account openness sufficient to gain membership to the Organisation for Economic Co-operation and Development (OECD), rather than to ease net capital inflows.[12] The government has introduced no direct or indirect controls on capital inflows, despite arguments from the NBP in favor of doing so.

During 1995–1997, the authorities introduced a number of trade policy measures aimed at stimulating imports and limiting the accumulation of international reserves. The import surcharge was gradually decreased from 6% to 5% at the beginning of 1995, to 3% at the beginning of 1996, and eliminated at the beginning of 1997. There was also a reduction in tariffs within the framework of the World Trade Organization and the association agreement with the EU. The weighted average tariff (including suspended tariffs), which was 11.6% at the beginning of 1994, was reduced at the beginning of 1995 to 9.4%, and to 8.2% at the beginning of 1996. However, these measures were introduced in order to honor the government's international obligations, rather than in response to the capital inflows problem.

There was also no significant fiscal adjustment during the period of intensive foreign exchange inflows. The treasury allowed the inflow of foreign investment into the T-bills market to depress interest rates on the primary market. That enabled it to obtain some savings on debt service costs, which reduced the budget deficit only to a limited extent relative to its planned level (see *Table 6.3*). The unexpected appreciation of the zloty, which reduced the zloty cost of foreign debt service, had a similar effect on the budget. A fair account must acknowledge that a large part of budgetary expenditures is determined by the government's long-term legal obligations, so there is relatively little freedom to adjust that side of the ledger. Exceptionally large foreign exchange inflows in 1995 required an immediate policy response, but fiscal policy has been difficult to adjust quickly due to both legal and political constraints.

6.5   Effects of Inflows and Policy Actions

The growth in the foreign exchange flows originated mostly in the real sector, and its influence on that sector's indicators has been positive (in quantitative terms) and beneficial (in qualitative ones). Capital inflows have contributed to increases in the demand for both domestically produced goods and imports.

In contrast to 1990–1993, when gross fixed investment declined as a percentage of GDP from 21% to 15.9%, during 1994–1996 this ratio started to rise, reaching 16.9% in 1995 and 19% in 1996. The share of personal consumption in GDP grew significantly over 1990–1992 and more moderately from then until 1994. In 1995, this share dropped from 64.3% to 62.1%, only to increase again to 64.2% in 1996, when real personal consumption increased faster (8.7%) than GDP (6.1%). Therefore, the period of increased net capital inflows (notably FDI) coincided with a rapid increase in investment activity, concentrated mainly in purchases of machinery and equipment. The share of these purchases in gross fixed investment increased from 36% in 1992 to around 60% in 1996. According to the Government Centre for Strategic Studies (GCSS, 1997), the share of foreign capital in the financing of investment in 1996 reached around 20%, against 13% in 1995 and 9.4% in 1994.

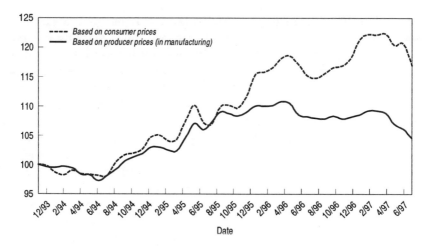

Figure 6.4. Real effective exchange rate of the zloty (December 1993 = 100).

However, the current account deficit that developed in 1996 was also associated with an increase in personal consumption.

In 1995 and the first quarter of 1996, large foreign exchange inflows – including net unclassified transactions on the current account – exerted significant appreciation pressure on the currency. As the profit margin on unrecorded exports is much higher than in official foreign trade, the dilemma facing exchange rate policy at the time resembled to some extent the Dutch disease. The authorities tried to prevent appreciation overshooting, but the stronger zloty (a 7% appreciation in real effective terms in relation to producer prices in 1995; see *Figure 6.4*) affected trade flows in the second half of 1995 and the first half of 1996. However, the deterioration in the recorded trade balance, especially in 1996, must also be seen as an adjustment necessary to stabilize the foreign exchange reserves and limit monetary expansion.

In 1995, exports (as recorded in the balance of payments statistics) increased by 35% in US dollar terms and imports (so recorded) rose by 39%. As a result, the trade deficit (excluding unrecorded trade) widened from 0.9% of GDP in 1994 to 1.5% of GDP in 1995. In 1996, the trade deficit grew rapidly to 6.1% of GDP. In 1996, with sluggish growth in the EU and especially Germany, and buoyant domestic demand (fed by markedly higher real wage growth), the growth of the volume of exports slowed to 9.7%, from 16.7% in 1995. Imports, also boosted by strong domestic demand, increased in dollar terms by 31.3%. Investment–goods imports were the most dynamic component in 1996, rising to 14% of total imports from 13% in the previous year. However, the share of consumer goods in imports also rose in 1996 to 18.5% from 17.8% the year before. An intensification of FDI added to this surge in investment–goods imports, while inflows on the treasury bills market probably mostly financed imports of consumer goods and related items.

As suggested earlier, the authorities did not intentionally adjust their targets in response to the surge in foreign exchange inflows. They perceived the deviations of the actual values of variables from their target values either as windfall gains, as in the case of increases in the foreign exchange reserves, or as the price to be paid for these inflows, as in the case of monetary growth. Faster growth of the money supply was definitely an important inflationary factor. However, the behavior of the exchange rate strengthened significantly the public's trust in the domestic currency. The year 1995 saw the denomination of the zloty, which was another important factor explaining this increase, so any precise delineation of the influences of individual factors is impossible. However, money demand studies conducted by the NBP (December 1996) showed that, for most of 1995, estimated money demand grew faster than the money supply. One possible interpretation of this result is that the deflationary impact of the zloty's appreciation more than offset the potential inflationary impact of the growth in the forex reserves.

The fiscal balances improved only slightly. Much of what the budget saved on public debt service costs (arising from lower interest rates on the T-bill market and slower devaluation as it affected foreign debt service costs) was spent on social programs such as education, health, and unemployment benefits.

The measures applied in response to the monetary shock originating from the growth of foreign exchange reserves seem to have been successful. The period 1995–1996 was the best that the Polish economy has experienced since the beginning of the reforms. In the year of the most difficult challenge, 1995, it was possible to achieve 7% GDP growth and simultaneously to reduce inflation from almost 30% at the end of 1994 to 21.6% at the end of 1995. This reduction in inflation was achieved despite rapid (38%, if adjusted for bank float in December 1994)[13] nominal growth of broad money during this period. This large increase in money supply has not been transformed into a money overhang due to the significant rise in the demand for real money balances.

Taking all of this into account, Poland managed not only to exceed its projected GDP growth rates in 1995 and 1996, but also to achieve a strong, long-term improvement in its external position, coupled with a significant increase in households' confidence in the zloty. A price was paid in the form of slower disinflation. The policies adopted have so far been successful in limiting the inflow of short-term portfolio capital without resorting to capital controls. Moreover, the central bank has managed to regain control over NIR and the money supply. Since the second quarter of 1996, NIR growth has stabilized, and nominal broad money growth in 1996 was lower by 9 percentage points than in 1995 (adjusted for bank float in December 1994).

However, a price (other than sterilization costs) was paid for this success. Lower nominal interest rates helped to limit the growth of international reserves but contributed to the growth of credit, which was 43% in 1996, compared with 18.5% consumer price inflation (on a December-to-December basis). The growth of real credit was so strong that, in the absence of fiscal consolidation, rising domestic demand became a new source of inflationary pressure and the major reason for the rapid swing in the current account.[14] The deterioration in the current account, from a surplus of 4.6% of GDP in 1995 to a deficit of 1% of GDP 1 year later, was spectacular. Although the level of current account deficit in 1997 (3.2% of GDP) is sustainable, the speed of its deterioration poses a challenge for policymakers.

In response to these developments, the NBP tightened monetary policy in December 1996. Money market interest rates have increased since then by more than 300 basis points. After some resistance, the treasury has also had to accept a fall in the prices of its bills. Higher yields on treasury securities again increase the risk of short-term capital inflows and require a more flexible exchange rate policy, that is, more volatility within the band. In order to increase the cost of credit, the NBP has increased its obligatory reserve requirements twice.[15] Further tightening came in August 1997, when the NBP hiked its headline rates by 2–2.5 points.

In September, the NBP made the unorthodox decision of collecting between 6 and 9 months' deposits from households. The move was aimed at sterilizing the impact of credits that the government had taken from the central bank, in order to provide liquidity for financing expenditures related to reconstruction and relief efforts after the disastrous flooding in the summer of 1997. The NBP also saw the collection of deposits with higher interest rates than those offered by commercial banks as a way to increase the pressure on banks to raise their interest rates on credits and deposits. The recent tightening of monetary policy has not provoked foreign capital inflows, thanks to the increased risk after currency crises in a number of emerging market economies and uncertainty over the results of the Polish general elections, which were held on 21 September 1997.

6.6   Conclusion

Foreign exchange inflows to Poland in the 1990s, and especially in 1994–1996, were not an orthodox problem of financial inflows resulting from interest rate differentials. They were the result of two separate but strongly interrelated developments. First, there was a current account surplus, which arose from a revival of economic growth spurred by increases in efficiency, while macroeconomic policy simultaneously controlled the growth of domestic demand. Second, Poland rejoined international private capital markets and regained a positive credit standing, which triggered substantial investment inflows.

There was also an important external dimension to this issue: low interest rates in the developed countries probably played a significant role in increasing the attractiveness of emerging markets to major institutional investors. However, since such factors are exogenously determined, an investigation of them would be beyond the scope of this chapter.

We can classify the major effects of these inflows into three broad groups: changes in the institutional framework brought about, to a large extent, by policy responses to the problem; changes in the stabilization path; and changes in the real economy. Among the major permanent changes brought about by capital inflows in the first of these groups are the exchange rate regime (i.e., the crawling band) introduced in May 1995 and rapid changes on both the money market and in the NBP's capacity to intervene there. However, although similar liquidity inflows are known to have been a cause of major problems for the financial sectors of other countries, the Polish case is different. A few years earlier, the country's banking system had gone through a period of considerable distress (see Wyczański and Gołajewska, 1996). A special restructuring program, combined with bank recapitalization, strengthened bank supervision, and a new regulatory framework, transformed Polish banking from its weak position in 1992–1993 into a strong and healthy sector by 1996.

Disinflation policy, formally a major part of any economic policy in transition countries in the 1990s, seemed to run into difficulty around 1993, as indicated especially by monthly data on the consumer price index. The disinflationary impact of real currency appreciation and import competition as a constraint on the price-setting behavior of Polish producers were important outgrowths of the strong disinflationary push in 1995 and 1996.

FDI and portfolio inflows played an important part in easing the financing constraints on investment in the industrial and service sectors. Banking sector restructuring, as mentioned earlier, made banks more risk-averse. Rapid economic growth, however, required a major increase in external financing. Budget spending is mostly for consumption purposes, therefore foreign investment was crucial to maintaining high growth rates for total investment and output.

Thus, we are able to say that most of the effects of financial inflows during the period analyzed in this chapter were beneficial to Poland. Developments in 1997 could, however, cast a shadow over the beneficial effects of the inflows. Domestic demand, financed in growing part by foreign investment, has caused a growing deficit on the current account, which if not contained might be a dangerous development. The NBP has tightened monetary policy and a fiscal adjustment is on the way.

Even so, it seems that capital inflows, after reaching 3.3% of GDP in 1996 and 5.1% in 1997, may reach 9% in 1998. Owing to the many uncertainties involved in making predictions about the more distant future, we can do little more than make informed guesses at present.

Let us start with external problems. The turmoil in various emerging markets in the fall of 1997 made investors initially reluctant to make investments in any emerging markets. We believe, however, that after an initial period of great caution, investors will observe emerging markets with greater care and in more detail, and better understand the differences among them. That raises the possibility that large-scale inflows will resume into countries perceived as being in better shape than others. Several internal factors in Poland make it highly likely that it will fall into this category.

First, the new cabinet formed at the end of October 1997 announced macro-economic policies that tackle the daunting current account deficit and show an awareness of the need for structural changes. These moves should further strengthen the Polish economy's already good prospects, particularly with respect to its ability to generate sustainable economic growth. Second, based on the ex-periences of other countries on the eve of accession to the EU, such as Spain, we anticipate that investors will have favorable expectations concerning business op-portunities in Poland. Both of these factors support our expectation of a stable or increased inflow of foreign investment. In addition, we anticipate that several large privatization deals will occur over the next 2 to 3 years in such sectors as telecommunications, oil refining, and banking.

Another important source of capital inflows may be debt creation by both com-panies and the government. The latter is definitely less important, because of the public foreign debt inherited from the past: capital inflows stimulated by the Polish government have had, on average, a negative net effect on the foreign financing of the government sector. We observe, however, a growing interest in foreign debt financing among Polish companies. Currently, most of this interest is concentrated on the financial sector, although we expect nonfinancial companies to become more active in the near future. Nevertheless, if the current restrictive policies keep disin-flation on track and allow a current account adjustment in the near future, we expect declining interest rate differentials, which should substantially diminish Poland's attractiveness to foreign creditors.

Acknowledgments

The views in this chapter do not necessarily reflect those of the National Bank of Poland. We would like to acknowledge the assistance of Rafal Drosik, Dorota Wyżnikiewicz, Paulina Sotomska, Monika Kubasik, Paweł Michalik, and Bartek Rutkowski. We received helpful comments from Jacek Osiński, Anna Włostowska, and Barbara Kosek. The usual disclaimer applies.

Notes

[1] In this period, the item "exceptional financing" in the Polish balance of payments mostly reflected due and unpaid principal and interest on foreign credits.

[2] The net international reserves of the banking system, according to the IMF definition, are equal to the difference between reserve assets (monetary gold, holdings of special drawing rights, the reserve position in the IMF, holdings of foreign exchange in convertible currencies, and claims on nonresident financial institutions denominated in convertible currencies) and reserve liabilities (liabilities in convertible currencies to nonresidents with original maturities of up to and including 1 year, and liabilities arising from borrowing from foreign banks, institutions, and governments for balance of payments support).

[3] The GUS estimates gross unrecorded exports at $3.7 billion in 1995, while net cash inflows in convertible currencies amounted to $7.7 billion that year.

[4] The shares of these inflows in the increase in GOR amount to more than 100% because we do not present the factors reducing GOR here.

[5] In 1990 and 1991 total debt service due was 60% of exports of goods and services and net transfers, and in 1993 – before the agreement with the London Club – 32.5%. Gross external debt fell from a peak of 78% of GDP in 1990 to 30% in 1996.

[6] There was widespread belief that the current account surplus was temporary: comparable experiences of other countries suggested that the price differentials between Poland and its more advanced neighbors would have to decline in line with Poland's economic growth, cutting the distance between Poland and its neighbors. Moreover, in a small open economy – as Poland was and is – rapid growth is usually import-intensive.

[7] We describe this modification of the exchange rate regime in more detail in the next section.

[8] However, it can be argued that this kind of equation should instead have the net monthly inflow as an endogenous variable.

[9] Denomination was widely perceived as a signal that the zloty had become a strong currency and domestic inflation had largely been contained.

[10] These bills were introduced in 1990 to control the liquidity of the banking system in a situation where no treasury securities had been issued.

[11] Reserves were to be calculated and paid to the NBP in zloty, so their burden under a system of constant devaluation was higher than implied by these figures.

[12] Residents are allowed to purchase real estate abroad, to make direct investments abroad (in OECD member states without limit and up to ECU 1 million in countries with which Poland has signed mutual agreements on supporting and safeguarding investment), and to make some categories of portfolio investments. Economic entities are permitted to purchase treasury securities or bonds (but only those in which public trading is allowed) issued by companies or institutions based in OECD member

states. The maturity of such instruments may not be less than 1 year and the value of investments on the purchasing day may not exceed ECU 1 million. Furthermore, nonresidents may issue participation units in investment and mutual funds in Poland, as well as shares in companies based in OECD member states and in such countries with which Poland has signed mutual agreements on supporting and safeguarding investment. Securities in which the Securities Commission allows public trading may be issued up to a limit of ECU 200 million. Additionally, resident economic entities are permitted to contract or grant credits for the fulfillment of financial obligations under contracts for goods, services, and incorporeal chattels. They are also permitted to contract or grant financial loans with maturity dates of over 1 year.

[13] The denomination of the zloty, introduced on 1 January 1995, required some changes in banks' accounting and reporting systems, which decreased the banks' float, as shown in balance sheet data for the end of 1994. This was a once-for-all effect and time series are usually adjusted for this to make data comparable.

[14] The growing demand for credit has other, deeper rooted causes. On the one hand, households have experienced income growth and recently are more inclined to positively assess their future financial situations. There remains a significant pent-up demand for consumer durables. Enterprise profits are growing and these enterprises are interested in expanding their production capacities. On the other hand, the supply of credit may also be increasing, as banks have cleaned up their balance sheets and gained experience in assessing credit risk. With the falling yields on treasury securities over 1995–1996, banks found it more profitable to extend loans and are competing strongly in that market.

[15] In January 1997, the NBP raised the reserve requirement on zloty demand deposits by 3 points (to 20%), and that on foreign currency deposits by 2 points (to 4%). In April, it raised that requirement on zloty term deposits by 2 points (to 11%), and on foreign currency deposits by 1 point (to 5%).

References

GCSS (Government Centre for Strategic Studies), 1997, *The Assessment of the Social–Economic Situation in 1996 and Preliminary Forecasts for 1997*, March, Warsaw, Poland [in Polish].

Gomulka, S., 1997, *Managing Capital Flows in Poland*, London School of Economics, London, UK (mimeo).

GUS (Główny Urząd Statystyczny), 1996, *Cross-border Traffic and Spending by Foreigners in Poland in 1995*, Warsaw, Poland [in Polish].

NBP (National Bank of Poland), various years, *Annual Report*, Warsaw, Poland.

NBP (National Bank of Poland), 1996, *Inflation Report*, December, Warsaw, Poland.

Rodlauer, M., 1996, *Monetary Policy in Poland: Challenges and Options*, IMF Warsaw Office, Warsaw, Poland (mimeo).

Wyczański, P., and Gołajewska, M., 1996, *The Polish Banking System*, Friedrich Eber Foundation, Warsaw, Poland [in Polish].

Paweł Durjasz and Ryszard Kokoszczyński

Appendix

Ratio between selected retail prices of consumer goods and services in Germany and Poland, 1991–1996.

	Specification	Unit of measure	Average 1991	1992	1993	1994	1995	1996
1	Beef, bone-in	1 kg	3.60	3.42	3.09	2.90	2.91	2.79
2	Beef, boneless	1 kg	3.99	3.88	3.62	3.43	3.40	3.40
3	Pork, boneless	1 kg	3.71	4.21	4.08	3.59	3.60	3.15
4	Baked ham	1 kg	2.65	2.95	3.06	2.98	2.93	2.92
5	Chicken, dressed	1 kg	1.81	1.83	1.73	1.55	1.60	1.51
6	Delicatessen butter	1 kg	2.48	2.39	2.58	2.40	1.92	1.74
7	Vegetable butter	1 kg	1.50	1.50	1.37	1.33	1.30	1.11
8	Hard cheese	1 kg	3.44	2.88	2.79	2.78	2.46	2.20
9	Hen's eggs	10 eggs	1.96	2.38	1.65	1.61	1.90	1.81
10	White granulated sugar	1 kg	2.36	2.25	2.14	2.29	1.92	1.80
11	Pure table vodka	0.5 l	2.28	2.20	3.27	1.57	1.45	1.35
12	Light beer, 10–12%	0.5 l	1.17	1.14	1.19	1.34	1.30	1.15
13	Potatoes	1 kg	7.50	3.77	5.62	4.71	4.34	3.90
14	Carrots	1 kg	6.30	4.73	3.08	4.16	3.80	3.60
15	White cabbage	1 kg	7.27	4.50	4.25	4.12	4.10	4.00
16	Apples	1 kg	4.26	4.47	4.20	4.25	3.90	3.50
17	Assorted breads	1 kg	6.84	6.45	5.76	6.48	6.00	6.00
18	Wheat flour	1 kg	2.26	2.09	1.88	2.16	2.05	1.81
19	Women's sheer tights	1 pair	4.26	5.33	6.20	6.70	6.80	5.00
20	Men's suits	1 set	3.87	3.93	3.20	2.73	2.60	2.20
21	Men's underwear, cotton	1 pc	3.08	3.84	4.22	4.19	3.95	3.37
22	Bed lines	1 set	3.07	3.43	3.48	3.49	3.16	3.08
23	Women's scarves	1 pair	5.40	5.26	5.24	4.96	4.40	4.35
24	Men's shoes	1 pair	2.60	2.75	2.77	2.71	2.75	2.78
25	Children's shoes	1 pair	3.44	3.38	3.23	3.00	2.90	2.90
26	Sofa, two seater	1 pc	3.77	4.90	5.06	5.48	5.15	5.00
27	Table linen	1 set	5.82	6.74	5.81	5.49	4.90	4.45
28	Men's haircut	1 cut	7.23	9.30	9.18	9.00	7.00	6.30
29	Women's hair styling	1 styling	1.92	1.76	1.73	1.88	1.89	1.89
30	Gasoline	1 l	1.81	1.76	1.63	1.95	1.98	1.75

Sources: NBP staff calculations, on the basis of data from GUS; Statistisches Bundesamt in Wiesbaden, Germany; and *OECD Economic Outlook*, No. 59, June 1996 .

Chapter 7

Capital Inflows to the Baltic States, 1992–1996

Marta de Castello Branco

7.1   Introduction

This chapter explores the nature and effects of capital flows to the Baltic states during the period 1992–1996, as well as the policy responses that they elicited. The rest of this section provides some background information, while Section 7.2 studies the size and composition of capital flows during the period under analysis, within the limitations of the data.[1]   Section 7.3 evaluates the macroeconomic effects of the inflows, and Section 7.4 contrasts the policy responses in the three Baltic states. Section 7.5 offers concluding remarks.

After regaining independence in the fall of 1991, Estonia, Latvia, and Lithuania moved quickly to implement stabilization and reform programs to facilitate the transition to a market system. The adjustment programs were centered on price and trade liberalization, elimination of subsidies and subsidized loans, and tight fiscal and credit policies. The three countries also established current account convertibility and liberalized capital transactions.[2] Furthermore, in order to be able to run an independent monetary policy, they left the ruble zone and introduced their own currencies at an early stage of the reform process.[3] Although the common objective of monetary policy was price stability, different monetary and exchange regimes were chosen: currency board arrangements in Estonia and Lithuania (the latter effective from April 1994), and a managed float in Latvia until February 1994, when

169

Table 7.1. Selected economic indicators in the Baltic states, 1992–1996.

	1992	1993	1994	1995	1996
Real GDP growth (in %)					
Estonia	−21.6	−8.4	−1.8	4.3	3.9
Latvia	−35.2	−16.1	2.1	0.3	3.3
Lithuania	−21.3	−16.2	−9.8	3.3	4.7
Inflation (period average; in %)					
Estonia	1,069.0	89.0	47.7	28.9	23.1
Latvia	951.3	109.1	35.9	25.1	17.6
Lithuania	1,020.5	410.4	72.1	39.5	24.7
Inflation (end of period; in %)					
Estonia	942.2	35.7	41.6	28.8	15.0
Latvia	958.7	34.9	26.3	23.1	13.2
Lithuania	1,161.1	188.8	45.0	35.5	13.1
Fiscal balance *(cash basis; in % of GDP)*					
Estonia	−0.3	−0.6	1.3	−1.2	−1.5
Latvia	−0.8	0.6	−4.1	−3.3	−1.4
Lithuania	0.5	−5.3	−4.8	−4.5	−4.5
Current account balance *(in % of GDP)*					
Estonia	3.4	1.4	−7.4	−5.1	−9.7
Latvia	1.8	7.0	−0.2	−3.4	−4.1
Lithuania	n.a.	−3.0	−2.2	−10.2	−9.1
Gross international reserves *(in million US$)*					
Estonia	195.6	391.3	447.0	582.8	639.7
Latvia	153.6	509.6	626.0	583.2	772.5
Lithuania	105.7	412.3	654.4	821.2	836.3
Gross international reserves *(in months of imports of G&NFS)*					
Estonia	3.3	3.8	3.2	2.7	2.5
Latvia	1.5	4.8	4.7	3.0	3.1
Lithuania	1.1	2.0	3.0	2.5	2.0

Abbreviations: G&NFS, goods and nonfactor services; n.a., not available.
Sources: IMF (EU2 centralized database); and IMF staff estimates.

the lats was pegged to the IMF's Special Drawing Right (SDR). The operation of the currency boards in Estonia and Lithuania is described in the Appendix.

These stabilization efforts have paid off. Substantial gains have been made on the inflation front and output growth has resumed in all three countries (see *Table 7.1*). They have also made significant headway on structural reform, but much remains to be done to develop the appropriate environment for private sector growth, especially in Lithuania and Latvia.

Table 7.2. Balance of payments in the Baltic states, 1992–1996.

	Balance of payments (in million US$)					Balance of payments (in % of GDP)					
	1992	1993	1994	1995	1996	1992	1993	1994	1995	1996	Average 1992-96
Estonia											
Current account	35.7	23.3	−171.0	−185.2	−423.0	3.4	1.4	−7.4	−5.1	−9.7	−3.5
Capital account	25.9	176.0	175.2	259.0	545.0	2.5	10.4	7.5	7.2	12.5	8.0
Of which:											
Foreign investment (net)	79.9	154.2	198.0	185.9	255.0	7.6	9.1	8.5	5.2	5.9	7.3
Medium and long term	9.6	84.4	7.3	47.6	161.0	0.9	5.0	0.3	1.3	3.7	2.2
Short term	−26.5	−82.5	−39.9	27.0	147.0	−2.5	−4.9	−1.7	0.8	3.4	−1.0
Errors and omissions	−5.6	−50.9	26.4	31.8	−21.0	−0.5	−3.0	1.1	0.9	−0.5	−0.4
Overall balance	56.0	148.4	30.7	106.0	101.0	5.3	8.8	1.3	2.9	2.3	4.1
Memo items											
Use of fund credit (net)	26.4	46.2	0.0	12.5	−11.2	2.5	2.7	0.0	0.3	−0.3	1.1
Exchange rate (period average)[a]	11.70	13.23	12.98	11.47	12.03						
Latvia											
Current account	25.0	151.0	−8.6	−159.0	−217.2	1.8	7.0	−0.2	−3.4	−4.1	−0.2
Capital account	76.0	186.0	274.0	249.4	592.1	5.6	8.6	7.5	5.3	11.1	7.6
Of which:											
Foreign investment (net)	43.0	51.0	155.0	243.5	402.5	3.2	2.4	4.2	5.2	7.5	4.5
Medium and long term	33.0	98.0	87.0	63.3	61.4	2.4	4.5	2.4	1.3	1.2	2.4
Short term	0.0	37.0	32.0	−57.4	128.1	0.0	1.7	0.9	−1.3	2.4	0.7
Errors and omissions	33.8	−15.0	−125.2	−188.6	−125.7	2.5	−0.7	−3.4	−4.0	−2.4	−1.6
Overall balance	134.8	322.0	140.2	−98.2	249.2	9.9	14.8	3.8	−2.1	4.7	6.2
Memo items											
Use of fund credit (net)	35.2	74.0	45.8	−2.9	−25.5	2.6	3.4	1.3	−0.1	−0.5	1.3
Exchange rate (period average)[a]	0.74	0.68	0.56	0.53	0.55						
Lithuania											
Current account	n.a.	−85.7	−94.0	−614.4	−722.6	n.a.	−3.0	−2.2	−10.2	−9.1	−6.1
Capital account	n.a.	204.1	254.2	495.9	644.0	n.a.	7.7.	6.0	8.2	8.4	7.6
Of which:											
Foreign investment (net)	n.a.	29.8	35.7	87.7	215.1	n.a.	1.1	0.8	1.5	2.7	1.5
Medium and long term	n.a.	157.6	128.8	295.0	481.7	n.a.	5.9	3.1	4.9	6.1	5.0
Short term	n.a.	16.7	76.8	152.2	−38.2	n.a.	0.6	1.8	2.5	−0.5	1.1
Errors and omissions	n.a.	92.3	−43.4	287.6	54.4	n.a.	3.5	−1.0	4.8	0.7	2.0
Overall balance	n.a.	210.6	116.8	169.2	−4.2	n.a.	7.9	2.8	2.8	0.1	3.4
Memo items											
Use of fund credit (net)	24.3	97.5	67.0	62.6	19.5	1.3	3.4	1.2	0.8	0.2	1.4
Exchange rate (period average)[a]	1.77	4.27	3.98	4.00	4.00						

[a] Defined as units of national currency per US$. Abbreviation: n.a., not available.
Source: IMF (EU2 centralized database); and IMF staff estimates.

As in other countries going through the first stages of exchange rate based stabilization, the Baltic countries attracted a significant amount of capital inflows after they embarked on their comprehensive stabilization and reform programs. Net
capital inflows, as measured by the capital account of the balance of payments,
amounted to more than 10% of GDP cumulatively in 1992–1993 (see *Table 7.2*).[4]
A reversal of capital inflows took place in Latvia and Lithuania in connection with
their banking crises in 1995, but with fiscal tightening and renewed efforts to accelerate structural reform, confidence was restored and capital inflows rapidly resumed
to both countries.[5]

7.2   Nature and Composition of Capital Inflows

The benefits and risks associated with capital inflows and the appropriate policy
response have generated an extensive literature.[6] Broadly speaking, capital inflows are considered a mixed blessing. On the positive side, they help bridge a
resource gap in countries with limited national savings but ample investment opportunities, allowing more immediate consumption, higher rates of investment and
output growth, lower interest rates, and a larger accumulation of international reserves. In the case of foreign direct investment (FDI), the receiving countries also
benefit from the transfer of new technology, know-how, and possibly enhanced access to foreign markets. On the negative side, capital inflows are often associated
with weaker monetary control, inflationary pressures, and real currency appreciation, with adverse effects on external competitiveness. There are often concerns
about the sustainability of current account deficits, linked to whether the inflows
are financing increased consumption or increased investment. Finally, capital inflows can also exacerbate the fragility of domestic financial systems, because they
may provide the basis for excessive and/or risky lending.

Problems may arise, in particular, if the magnitude of capital inflows is considerable, but at the same time there is uncertainty about their nature (and therefore
their reversibility) and their maturity. Flows associated with ownership and management of business and industrial operations, such as FDI and certain portfolio
investments, are more likely to foster productivity and growth. They are also less
likely to cause monetary expansion to the extent that they are not intermediated
through the domestic banking system. By contrast, speculative inflows will be
prone to sudden reversals and may thus create serious destabilizing effects. Therefore, investigating the origin of the inflows and their likely degree of persistence
becomes essential for designing an appropriate policy response, although in practice it may be very difficult to reach definitive conclusions.

The literature distinguishes between exogenous and domestic factors that determine capital inflows. Exogenous factors (such as a drop in interest rates in investor

countries) are more likely to generate short-term, unstable flows. Domestic factors are associated with successful economic policies that attract investment into the country, with unbalanced financial policies (e.g., monetary policy that is much tighter than fiscal policy), or with not fully credible reforms (e.g., price and trade liberalization) that create short-term opportunities for profit until the underlying imbalances are corrected, and thus stimulate speculative inflows.[7] In the latter case, expectations about interest rate and exchange rate developments are the dominant factor behind capital inflows. In light of the experiences with capital inflows in Latin American and East Asian countries in the early 1990s, there is some concern that the predominance of exogenous, more volatile factors in such countries may lead to less desirable outcomes. For example, Calvo *et al.* (1993) argue that, since exogenous factors were more relevant in Latin America, these countries experienced a more pronounced real appreciation of the domestic currencies than East Asian countries.

In the case of the Baltic states, both domestic and external factors influenced the capital inflows observed during the 1992–1996 period. In all three countries, significant inflows were stimulated by the successful introduction of national currencies and the market's perception that those currencies were significantly undervalued, the adoption of effective stabilization programs based on tight financial policies, and the high interest rates prevailing after liberalization. Trade and financial liberalization and other structural reforms added to the low exchange risk and raised the potential for rapid productivity increases. External factors ranged from the proximity to Finland in the case of Estonia to occasional sudden shifts in the political and economic landscape in Russia, which invariably affected capital flows to Latvia and, to a lesser degree, Lithuania.[8]

The relative magnitudes of capital flows into the three countries and, in particular, the relative share of FDI, reflect to a large extent the different pace of reform in each country, as well as investors' sentiments about the credibility of the exchange rate regimes. As the earliest Baltic reformer anchored on a credible currency board arrangement, Estonia has received the lion's share of FDI among the Baltic states, followed by Latvia and, on a more modest scale, Lithuania. Compared to Estonia, both Latvia and Lithuania moved relatively slowly in implementing the structural reforms (most notably regarding the possibility of foreigners' purchasing land) and establishing a credible exchange rate arrangement. In Latvia, the new currency's credibility was earned through the adoption of tight monetary policy and the increasingly strong anti-inflation reputation of the central bank. In Lithuania, although the currency board arrangement helped boost credibility, it was adopted at a later stage of the transition process and its durability has been periodically questioned.

7.2.1   Composition of inflows

The sources of capital flows to the Baltic countries include portfolio investment, FDI, other medium- and long-term capital, and short-term flows.[9] Some reverse currency substitution (i.e., flows into the domestic currency) followed the introduction of national currencies, as evidenced by the decline in the share of foreign currency deposits in 1993 and a gradual increase in the ratio of broad money to GDP (see *Figure 7.1*). Until 1995, capital flows into Estonia were mainly in the form of FDI and provided sufficient cover for the emerging current account deficits. This situation was reversed in 1996, when a large part of the widening deficit was financed with short-term, debt-creating flows. By contrast, although significant short-term inflows were observed in Latvia and Lithuania during the 1993–1996 period (see *Figure 7.2*), more recently they have received increasing amounts of capital flows of a longer-term nature, including FDI.

Foreign direct investment in the Baltic countries has been linked to each country's progress with privatization and its attitude toward foreign investment. In addition, the credibility of the exchange rate regime and overall economic policy has played a crucial role in shaping investors' perceptions of risk and return, and thus is likely to have been a major determinant of FDI inflows.[10] As mentioned above, Estonia got a head start in terms of establishing macroeconomic policy credibility through its adoption of a currency board arrangement, which encouraged FDI flows into the country at the initial stages of the transition process.

Estonia has been one of the main recipients of FDI among all transition economies, because of its geographical and cultural proximity to Finland (a key investor), quick implementation of the legal and institutional framework necessary to support FDI, and particularly rapid progress on privatization to outsiders (investors outside the firm) and on fostering private sector development. The significant amount of FDI (concentrated on export production) may have helped, in turn, to speed up privatization, suggesting a virtuous circle. The magnitudes were substantial during the period examined, both in terms of GDP and on a per capita basis (see *Table 7.3*). Since mid-1995, however, there has been a decline in the relative importance of FDI, perhaps signaling the end of the first wave of privatization in the country, since most large-scale enterprises, excluding utility companies, have already been privatized.

Although a healthy pick-up was observed in 1996, the inflows of FDI to Latvia and Lithuania have been more modest, probably reflecting delays in private sector development, formal and informal barriers to foreign investment and, more generally, less rapid progress on structural reform. In particular, large-scale privatization programs have moved slowly. Until 1996 there were many restrictions on FDI in Latvia, ranging from the exclusion of direct foreign participation in the privatization process to limitations on the sectors allowed to receive foreign

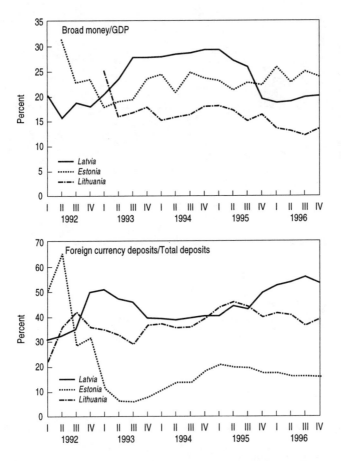

Figure 7.1. Monetary developments in the Baltic states. Source: Country authorities.

investment.[11] These restrictions have been compounded by informal obstacles, including a lengthy and nontransparent approval process. A series of laws was adopted in 1996 to remove legal impediments to FDI, while major efforts are being taken to speed up privatization, in particular that of larger enterprises.

The picture is similar in Lithuania, where foreign investment has been discouraged by slow progress on institutional and legal reform (e.g., the prohibition of foreign land ownership) and in completing privatization, and relatively frequent changes in the trade regime. Weaker commitment to stabilization in the early stages of reform and, subsequently, pressures on the currency board, have most likely also played a role in discouraging FDI.

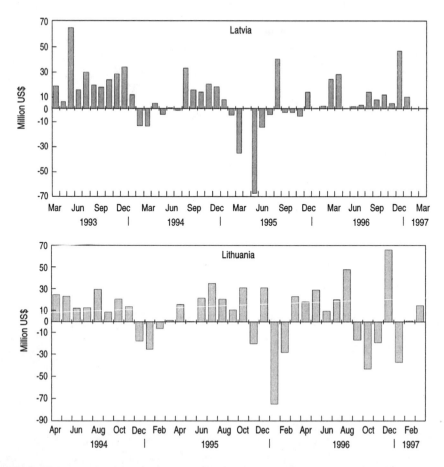

Figure 7.2. Net foreign currency inflows into the central bank in Latvia and Lithuania (in million US$). Source: Country authorities.

In practice it is not always possible to distinguish between *portfolio investment* and direct investment, and for that reason in *Table 7.2* the item *foreign investment (net)* includes both FDI and portfolio investment. In Latvia and Lithuania, this item also comprises flows related to the purchase of treasury bills (T-bills) by foreign investors, which became significant in 1995 in Latvia and 1996 in Lithuania, attracted by the high yields prevailing in connection with the banking crises.[12] Strong domestic and foreign demand, fiscal restraint and, in the case of Latvia, a more liquid secondary market, contributed to a marked decline in T-bill rates in 1996 (see *Figure 7.3*). As a result, domestic investors started to shift funds to short-term securities markets in neighboring countries, leading to capital outflows.

Table 7.3. Annual flows of FDI for selected countries, 1992–1996.

	1992	1993	1994	1995	1996
FDI (in % of GDP)					
Estonia	7.6	9.1	9.1	5.6	2.3
Latvia	3.2	2.1	5.9	3.8	5.4
Lithuania	0.5	0.8	1.1	0.7	1.5
Czech Rep.	0.0	0.0	2.2	5.2	2.6
Hungary	3.9	6.1	2.7	9.6	3.7
Poland	0.3	0.7	0.6	1.0	2.1
Russia	0.8	0.5	0.2	0.5	0.4
Chile	1.7	1.9	3.6	2.8	5.8
China	2.7	6.4	6.2	5.1	5.0
Indonesia	1.2	1.2	1.4	2.3	2.8
Malaysia	7.7	6.8	3.4	4.6	4.3
Thailand	1.5	1.3	1.0	1.3	1.4
FDI (flows per capita; in US$)					
Estonia	50.6	97.2	135.3	129.9	63.6
Latvia	16.1	16.9	81.6	69.5	112.3
Lithuania	2.7	6.1	15.9	14.6	40.5
Czech Rep.	0.0	0.0	84.1	248.3	138.3
Hungary	142.6	227.7	110.9	422.2	165.4
Poland	7.4	15.1	14.0	29.3	70.8
Russia	4.7	6.1	4.0	13.5	13.5
Chile	55.2	64.4	137.7	136.1	297.3
China	9.6	23.3	28.3	29.7	33.4
Indonesia	9.0	10.1	12.6	24.0	31.6
Malaysia	239.8	228.0	125.5	197.4	206.7
Thailand	29.3	28.1	24.0	35.5	43.3

Sources: IMF staff estimates; and IMF *World Economic Outlook*, various issues.

Such transfers are often effected through banks' accounts abroad, in which case no outflow is recorded in the balance of payments.

The significant *short-term capital inflows* in Latvia and Lithuania during the early stages of reform, as suggested by the recorded data and the large "errors and omissions", were partly related to capital flight from Russia and other neighboring countries. The inflow of speculative funds ("hot money"), particularly relevant in Latvia, was attracted by the more liberal exchange rate regime and the very high interest rates in the two Baltic states. In the post-reform unregulated environment, interest rates were kept at high levels by several factors: high credit risk; the lack of collateral for loans; weak payment discipline and other structural deficiencies of the financial and enterprise sectors; and, naturally, the willingness of borrowers to

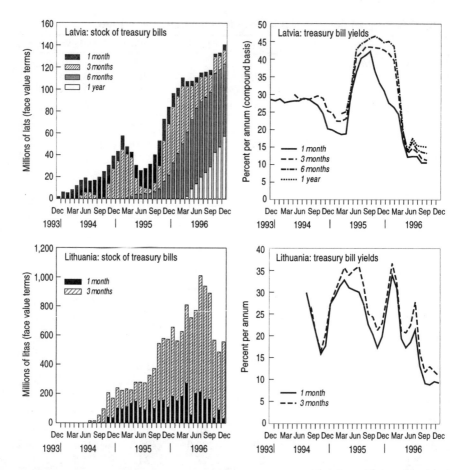

Figure 7.3. Stocks and yields of treasury bills in Latvia and Lithuania. (In December 1996, the exchange rate for Latvia was 0.556 lats per \$, and for Lithuania it was 4 litas per \$.) Source: Country authorities.

pay very high rates to finance highly profitable short-term transactions, including financing arbitrage trade of commodities that had their prices controlled in Russia and other countries of the former Soviet Union. "Transit money" from neighboring countries is still relevant for Latvia today. Barring developments associated with the 1995 banking crisis, a seasonal pattern has been common, with capital flowing in toward the end of the year and out at the beginning, suggesting the influence of bank and business behavior in Russia ("window dressing" to avoid paying taxes).

In Estonia, the recent decline in the share of FDI in total inflows was accompanied by an increased role for bank intermediation, as banks gained access to external financial markets and stepped up their domestic lending. The bulk of capital inflows in 1996 represented external borrowing (mainly by banks) and deposits of nonresident subsidiaries of Estonian enterprises. Although these events suggest growing confidence in the banking system, there is also concern about the short-term nature of the debt, as well as about the rapid growth in bank credit (credit to the private sector increased by 70% in 1996).

Medium- and long-term capital inflows other than FDI have been associated with official borrowing, including from the European Union, G-24 countries, and the World Bank. During 1995–1996 they also included the placement of government bonds on international capital markets and other private external borrowing, reflecting the general trend in the Baltic states, Russia and other countries of the former Soviet Union to borrow increasingly from private external sources. Among the Baltic states, Lithuania has been the most active in obtaining private external financing.[13]

The Baltic states' stabilization and reform programs have been supported by financial arrangements with the IMF. Stand-by arrangements (SBAs) were approved for each of the three countries in the fall of 1992, followed by further SBAs and additional support under the IMF's Systemic Transformation Facility in late 1993. Thereafter, SBAs were approved for Latvia and Estonia both in 1995 and 1996, but those were precautionary arrangements, with no drawings from these loans effected. By contrast, until 1997 Lithuania continued to use IMF resources under a 3-year Extended Fund Facility arrangement, approved in October 1994.

7.2.2 Capital outflows

The main episodes of capital outflows in the Baltic countries were related to the banking crises in Latvia and Lithuania, although in Lithuania pressures on the currency board in late 1994 and developments related to the parliamentary elections in October and December 1996 also led to temporary outflows (see *Figure 7.2*). Large outflows were recorded in Latvia in the spring of 1995; part of the capital that fled Latvia was transferred to Lithuania. As a result of the measures taken by the Latvian authorities to deal with the banking crisis and strengthen the banking system, confidence gradually built up and reflows were observed later in the year. A net inflow was recorded for the year as a whole and large inflows followed in 1996, more than offsetting the current account deficit. Lithuania experienced significant capital outflows following the banking crisis in late 1995; inflows resumed in March 1996.

7.3   Effects of Capital Inflows

The macroeconomic effects of the capital flows into the Baltic countries have been largely as predicted in the standard small open-economy models under a fixed exchange rate regime: accumulation of international reserves; widening current account deficits; real appreciation of the domestic currency; and monetary expansion; we discuss these effects in more detail below. Despite the capital inflows, commercial banks' interest rates came down only gradually, and by the end of the 1993–1996 period real lending rates and interest rate spreads remained high (see *Figure 7.4*). Although it is difficult to determine how much impact capital inflows had on economic recovery, they are likely to have contributed to growth through increases in both investment and consumption. On the other hand, it can be argued that, in the absence of an effective regulatory and supervision framework, the availability of speculative capital encouraged risky behavior by banks and thus contributed to the banking crises in Latvia and Lithuania.[14]

7.3.1   The macroeconomic picture

The wave of capital inflows that followed monetary reform translated initially into a marked accumulation of international reserves, both in terms of US dollars and months of imports of goods and nonfactor services. Subsequently, the ensuing inflows were associated with widening current account deficits, which partly reflected increased imports of machinery and intermediate goods. In terms of the saving–investment balance, the pattern that emerged in the Baltic states during the period 1992–1996 is a marked decline in national saving combined with a sharp increase in foreign saving, while overall investment ratios increased modestly (see *Table 7.4*).[15]

The high saving and investment ratios characteristic of central planning fell significantly with the dismantling of that system. By the end of 1996, the overall saving rate had declined to levels typical of developing countries: 17–18% in Latvia and Estonia, and 15% in Lithuania, compared with rates of around 30% under central planning.[16] The decline in public saving resulted from the collapse of revenue, coupled with increased government expenditures on social transfers. Public saving has been higher in Estonia and Lithuania, where public sector behavior is constrained by the currency board arrangement.

Preliminary work on Estonia suggests that the declining trend in private saving reflects mainly the dynamics of enterprise saving. The same pattern, also observed in other transition economies, is likely to apply to Latvia and Lithuania.[17] The decline in enterprise profitability that followed price liberalization and the severe recession that marked the beginning of the transition period contributed significantly to the fall in enterprise saving. Household saving is likely to have increased

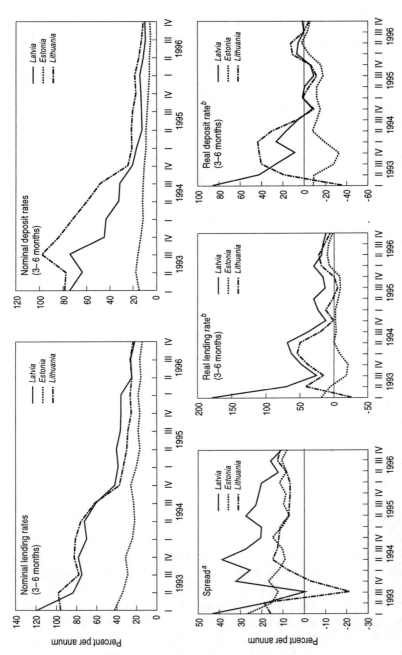

Figure 7.4. Interest rates in the Baltic states (in percent per annum). [a]The spread is defined as the difference between the nominal lending rate and the nominal deposit rate. [b]Real rates have been deflated by the six-month forward inflation rate. Sources: Country authorities; IMF staff estimates.

Table 7.4. Saving and investment balances in the Baltic states, 1992–1996 (in % of GDP).

	1992	1993	1994	1995	1996
Estonia					
Saving[a]	32.0	27.4	21.6	21.2	17.8
Private	21.7	17.7	11.0	13.9	12.1
Public	10.3	9.7	10.6	7.3	5.7
Investment	28.6	26.0	29.0	26.4	27.5
Private	27.2	23.2	24.9	21.7	22.6
Public	1.4	2.8	4.1	4.6	4.9
Current account balance	3.4	1.4	−7.4	−5.1	−9.7
Latvia					
Saving[a]	22.6	19.9	20.6	15.5	16.6
Private	21.1	17.7	21.1	17.4	16.1
Public	1.4	2.2	−0.5	−1.9	0.5
Investment	20.6	12.9	20.8	18.9	20.7
Private	19.1	11.8	16.8	17.0	18.9
Public	1.5	1.2	4.0	1.9	1.9
Current account balance	1.8	7.0	−0.2	−3.4	−4.1
Lithuania					
Saving[a]	n.a.	16.2	16.2	14.5	15.3
Private	n.a.	12.0	14.6	12.6	15.2
Public	4.7	4.2	1.6	1.9	0.2
Investment	15.7	19.2	18.4	24.7	24.5
Private	13.3	15.8	14.5	20.9	21.8
Public	2.5	3.4	3.9	3.8	2.7
Current account balance	n.a.	−3.0	−2.2	-10.2	−9.1

[a] Defined as national savings.
Abbreviation: n.a., not available.
Source: IMF staff estimates.

somewhat in recent years, reflecting both a higher share of household income in GDP and the added incentive for precautionary saving as a response to the collapse of the "cradle-to-grave" protection afforded under central planning. However, after being deprived of consumption opportunities for so long, households also had a strong motivation to try to increase their consumption, so any increase that may have occurred in household saving was not enough to offset the decline in enterprise saving.

Investment ratios did not increase significantly during the 1992–1996 period. Public investment fell sharply after the collapse of the Soviet Union, owing to the higher priority accorded to protecting current expenditures. Private investment was constrained by high risk and the lack of profitable investment opportunities. Following steady progress on structural reform, private investment started to pick up in Latvia and Lithuania in 1995. At the same time, public investment ratios rose above 4% of GDP in Estonia but remained very low in Latvia (see *Table 7.4*).

7.3.2   The exchange rate and monetary developments

In all three countries, increased capital inflows were accompanied by a significant real appreciation of the domestic currency, as expected given their initial underval-uation and the experience of other countries undergoing exchange rate based sta-bilization programs (see *Figure 7.5*). The real appreciation was effected basically through inflation in Estonia and Lithuania, while under the managed float period in Latvia, part of the adjustment occurred through a nominal appreciation of the lats.

As in other capital inflow episodes, significant monetary expansion was ob-served in all three Baltic states. Such expansion was more pronounced in Latvia and Lithuania (before the banking crises); the predominance of FDI for most of the period under consideration probably helped limit the expansion of monetary aggre-gates in Estonia (*Table 7.5*). Part of the increase in such aggregates resulting from the inflows accommodated increases in the demand for money and thus did not contribute to inflationary pressures; however, in the absence of reliable estimates of money demand, it is not possible to quantify this effect. Furthermore, to the extent that the inflows financed increased imports, they had no monetary impact.

Given the magnitude of the inflows, they probably had some impact on infla-tion. However, the downward inflation paths in the three countries suggest that the inflationary impact of capital inflows does not appear to have been significant. As explained below, the inflationary process in the Baltic states is related more to structural factors than to excess demand pressures. The growth in monetary aggre-gates fueled by capital inflows essentially accommodated these structural changes and did not contribute significantly to inflation.

7.3.3   Price developments

Inflation behavior during the 1992–1996 period was very similar in Latvia and Estonia, despite the different exchange arrangements. However, the nominal ap-preciation allowed by the Latvian monetary authorities before pegging the lats to the SDR in February 1994 contributed to a somewhat faster decline of inflation in Latvia. Looser financial policies prior to the adoption of the currency board ini-tially resulted in relatively poor inflation performance in Lithuania. Overall, we observe a steady decline in inflation rates in all three countries, albeit at a slower pace than anticipated. After a sharp drop in 1993, average monthly inflation, as measured by the rate of change of the consumer price index, stubbornly remained between 2% and 3% in 1994 and 1995, before dropping to around 1% in 1996 (see

Table 7.5. Monetary developments in the Baltic states, 1993–1996.

	1993	1994	1995	1996
Monetary authorities[a]				
Estonia				
Net foreign assets	87.5	2.2	23.4	27.5
Net domestic assets	29.0	9.2	−4.3	−5.9
Net domestic credit	−3.8	−2.9	−7.4	−0.4
Reserve money	116.5	11.5	19.1	21.6
Latvia[b]				
Net foreign assets	109.5	7.1	−10.6	47.0
Net domestic assets	−1.9	12.6	12.2	−23.9
Net domestic credit	−6.7	3.5	15.0	−20.1
Reserve money	107.7	19.8	1.6	23.1
Lithuania				
Net foreign assets	190.2	69.1	35.2	3.4
Net domestic assets	−19.9	−7.3	−0.2	−1.4
Net domestic credit	−4.8	−8.8	−2.9	−0.1
Reserve money	170.3	61.9	35.0	2.0
Monetary survey[c]				
Estonia				
Net foreign assets	33.7	19.4	9.6	−4.5
Net domestic assets	24.1	10.2	21.7	41.4
Net domestic credit	21.6	15.3	26.0	50.3
Broad money[d]	57.8	29.6	31.3	36.8
Latvia[b]				
Net foreign assets	46.8	12.5	−10.3	27.7
Net domestic assets	37.2	36.2	−13.5	−7.8
Net domestic credit	64.7	38.3	−16.9	3.3
Broad money[d]	84.1	48.7	−23.8	19.9
Lithuania				
Net foreign assets	51.7	21.0	15.6	5.8
Net domestic assets	72.8	42.6	15.3	−7.8
Net domestic credit	56.7	55.3	8.2	1.2
Broad money[d]	124.6	63.6	30.8	−2.0

[a] Change as a percent of reserve money at the beginning of the period.
[b] Figures for 1995–1996 reflect a break in the series due to the reduction in the number of commercial banks following the banking crisis.
[c] Change as a percent of broad money at the beginning of the period.
[d] Includes foreign exchange deposits.
Sources: IMF (EU2 centralized database); and IMF staff estimates.

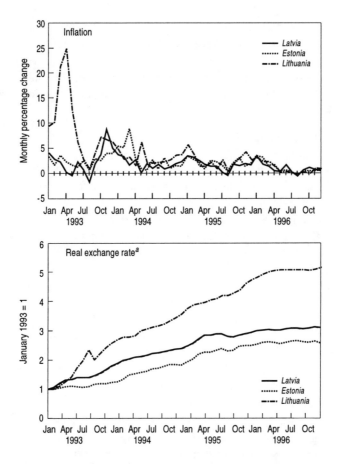

Figure 7.5. Inflation and real exchange rate in the Baltic states. ^aReal exchange rate is based on country and US CPI differentials, January 1993 = 1. An increase in the index indicates an appreciation. Source: IMF (EU2 centralized database).

Figure 7.5).[18] These levels are still considered high by western standards, in particular relative to the inflation rates prevailing in the peg countries, and, given the fixed exchange rate regimes, have raised concerns about external competitiveness. However, in view of the three countries' continuing favorable export performance, competitiveness does not yet seem to be in jeopardy, although margins have been eroded.

Empirical analysis suggests that the dynamics of inflation in the Baltic states can be explained mainly by the process of convergence of domestic prices to international levels, given the initial undervaluation of domestic currencies.[19] Under the fixed rate regimes prevailing for most of the period 1992–1996, this adjustment

took place mainly through inflation. In all three countries there has been a strong correlation between initial price levels and subsequent price increases for the different components of the CPI, particularly with respect to services. The realignment of relative prices and the price level to world levels is still continuing, implying that inflation is likely to remain above western levels during the transition period.

7.4 Policy Response

The source and duration of capital inflows should help in predicting their potential macroeconomic effects and thus are an important guide for the appropriate policy response. In general, faced with potentially destabilizing capital inflows, a country may resort to: (i) exchange rate policy; (ii) sterilized or unsterilized intervention; (iii) fiscal adjustment; (iv) capital controls; and (v) microeconomic policies.[20] Although the policy response depends, to a large extent, on the characteristics of the disturbance, it is also influenced by the overall economic environment and the degree of credibility enjoyed by policymakers. Of course, the nature of the exchange rate regime may also constrain the policy choices.

Conventional wisdom suggests that, in the case of inflows that are expected to persist or have a permanent effect on the economy (such as FDI), the domestic currency should be allowed to adjust in real terms. In the case of short-term or temporary inflows, if the use of exchange rate policy is ruled out, the policy issue is whether to attempt to offset their liquidity impact (by sterilized intervention) or to let these inflows translate into monetary expansion (by unsterilized intervention).[21] There might be a case for sterilizing short-term inflows when fighting inflation has clear priority, although the potentially high costs and low effectiveness of sterilization measures militate against this option in the longer run.[22] Nonetheless, sterilized intervention in varying forms and degrees has been a common policy response to a surge in capital inflows. In practice, it may be difficult to identify the causal factors and the probable effects of capital inflows in time to fashion an adequate response.

In the Baltic states the policy response to the sizable capital inflows experienced during the 1992–1996 period was unsterilized intervention, although in Latvia there was some limited use of sterilization measures and of exchange rate policy before the lats was pegged to the SDR. For all three countries, the pursuit of exchange rate stability was a clear priority; even in the face of potentially destabilizing capital inflows, the desire to preserve the nominal anchor in practice resulted in their making little or no attempt to offset the monetary effects of inflows.

Under the currency board arrangements in Estonia and Lithuania, monetary growth became endogenous and the impact of the inflows was not neutralized.[23] In Estonia, since the inflows mainly took the form of FDI, they were not viewed as destabilizing, while in Lithuania outflows were a more important source of concern. In particular, outflows associated with the banking crisis prompted a policy response (a lowering of reserve requirements and tightening of fiscal policy).

In Latvia, capital inflows influenced monetary developments significantly during the period 1992–1996. They were particularly sizable in 1993, creating a policy dilemma for the monetary authorities under the prevailing managed float, given the conflicting objectives of price stability and external competitiveness. During that episode, the Bank of Latvia (BoL) allowed a gradual nominal appreciation of the domestic currency, thus accommodating the increase in money demand resulting from growing confidence in the national currency. Nevertheless, in view of the magnitude of the inflows, the BoL at times intervened heavily in the foreign exchange market to moderate the appreciation of the lats. At the same time, to discourage further inflows, it gradually reduced its refinance rate and tightened net domestic credit. However, the scope for neutralizing capital inflows was rather limited, in view of the low stock of outstanding credit and the absence of active interbank and money markets to transmit interest rate signals to the rest of the economy. Since February 1994, when the lats was pegged to the SDR, the BoL has attempted to counteract the impact of capital inflows on the monetary base. It has done this by running a tight credit policy and through occasional cuts in the refinance rate aimed at lowering market rates. Although the effectiveness of these measures is known to be limited, the BoL would not consider revaluing the lats unless the inflows seriously threatened stabilization objectives. In practice, the commitment to the peg as the cornerstone of monetary policy is very firm.

Fiscal adjustment in the Baltic states during the 1992–1996 period was pursued in the context of the countries' stabilization programs and was not seen as a means of neutralizing foreign currency inflows. But to the extent that fixed exchange regimes were adopted, there was pressure to rely on fiscal policy to correct underlying imbalances; for example, in both Latvia and Lithuania fiscal policy was tightened in the context of the banking crises. Overall, prudent fiscal policies avoided an excessive increase in consumption that could have resulted from increased inflows.

There has been no attempt to resort to capital controls. However, political pressures for using trade policy to insulate domestic producers from the real appreciation of the lats have resulted in higher import tariffs in Latvia.

7.5   Conclusion

Economic developments in the Baltic states during the transition have tended to follow a pattern in which Estonia is the leader, followed closely by Latvia, with Lithuania trailing somewhat behind. This pattern is also valid with respect to the nature and composition of the capital inflows received by the three countries during the period 1992–1996, with Estonia clearly leading as a recipient of longer-term, more desirable capital inflows. Several factors are behind Estonia's leadership: (i) its early adoption of a currency board arrangement and its positive impact on credibility; (ii) its relatively favorable domestic environment for FDI; (iii) its close relationship with Finland, contributing to an early start for foreign investment flows to the country; and (iv) its successful handling of the banking crisis of late 1992 and avoidance of major banking crises in 1995–1996, when Latvia and Lithuania were suffering the consequences of theirs.

In view of the amount of FDI received and the progress achieved in privatization, it is clear that in Estonia capital inflows encouraged private sector development and economic growth and can be generally seen as having positively contributed to the transition process. More recently, however, the growing imbalance between saving and investment has flashed some warning signs. Capital inflows have financed a rapid expansion of domestic credit to the private sector, which only partly appears to be associated with increased bank intermediation and financial deepening. The Estonian authorities have started to address these issues and have taken measures to restrain the growth of aggregate demand.

The picture is somewhat different with respect to Latvia and Lithuania. Compared to Estonia, in these countries capital inflows have contributed less to private sector development, given the lower amount of FDI that they have attracted and the greater importance of speculative inflows, which has had an adverse impact on the stability of their banking system. Moreover, capital inflows did not result in higher domestic lending during the period under analysis. Despite the sharp decline in T-bill rates, demand for these securities remained strong and, as a result, credit to the private sector has been slow to pick up. Nevertheless, recent developments are encouraging.

In Latvia, credit to the private sector started to grow in real terms in the last quarter of 1996 and increased considerably in 1997. Furthermore, the recent trend toward longer-term capital inflows has coincided with an acceleration of large-scale privatization. This suggests that it may now be Latvia's turn to reap the benefits of the progress achieved in structural reform in the last couple of years and of the success in maintaining macroeconomic stability. Further strengthening of banking supervision and regulation and progress on privatization and enterprise restructuring would be the best line of defense against financial instability arising from future short-term capital inflows. If the pattern established in the past few years is a good predictor of future trends, in principle, Lithuania should catch up soon. In practice, the sustainability of capital inflows and the role of long-term capital will hinge upon the success of the process of exiting the currency board.[24]

On the whole, the impact of capital inflows to the Baltic states during the transition period has been more positive than negative. They allowed an immediate increase in the low consumption levels prevailing at the outset of the reform programs and a desirable smoothing of consumption patterns over time (considering the potential for rapid productivity increases and economic growth in the Baltic states). In other words, the capital inflows helped to finance imports both of consumption goods that were unavailable in the pre-reform period and of intermediate and capital goods, allowing an increase in permanent consumption and investment. In particular, given the Baltic states' high dependence on energy imports, the surge in capital inflows at the beginning of the reform period helped to accommodate the sharp terms of trade shock resulting from the adjustment of energy prices to world levels in Russia, thus helping to avoid a larger output collapse.

As small open economies with liberal exchange regimes, the Baltic states will continue to be strong candidates for large capital inflows, especially from their neighbors. The relative amount of longer-term capital that each of them will be able to attract and, more generally, the likelihood that the inflows will be beneficial to their economic development, will continue to depend on the credibility of their policies, as well as on the development and maintenance of a favorable environment for private investment and of a sound and efficient banking system.

Acknowledgments

This project was initiated by Jorge Marquéz-Ruarte for the Workshop on "Financial Inflows to Transition Economies", held at IIASA, Laxenburg, Austria, on 9–10 May 1997. The author has benefited from comments and suggestions from Odd Per Brekk, Albert Jaeger, Françoise Le Gall, Augusto Lopez-Claros, Andrei Kirilenko, John Odling-Smee, Anthony Richards, Richard Stern, Emmanuel van der Mensbrugghe, Michael Wyzan, and Tom Wolf. Alex Keenan provided valuable research assistance. The views expressed here are the sole responsibility of the author and do not necessarily represent those of the International Monetary Fund (IMF).

Notes

[1] Balance of payments data are far from reliable; despite vast improvement in recent years, there are still significant problems with classification and coverage, as evidenced by the often large and variable magnitude of "errors and omissions".

[2] Estonia initially kept some capital controls, such as surrender requirements and a prohibition on foreign exchange accounts, but these restrictions were eliminated at the end of 1993.

[3] Estonia was the first to introduce its own currency, the kroon, a step that it took in June 1992. Latvia and Lithuania followed suit in a two-step process, first introducing temporary currencies. In Latvia, the Latvian ruble (introduced in May 1992) was replaced by the lats in March 1993; in Lithuania, the talonas (introduced in October 1992) was replaced by the litas in June 1993.

[4] Although the IMF was the major contributor of financial resources in the early stages of reform (a cumulative 5–6% of GDP in 1992–1993), these flows are treated as reserve liabilities according to the IMF's balance of payments methodology, and are thus excluded from the capital account in *Table 7.2.*

[5] A string of bank failures, including that of the largest commercial bank, culminated in a full-fledged banking crisis in Latvia in April 1995. Lithuania's banking crisis took place in late 1995, following the suspension of the operations of two of the largest private banks. For a detailed discussion of the banking crises in the Baltics, including the earlier crises in Estonia, see Castello Branco *et al.* (1996).

[6] See, for example, Calvo *et al.* (1993, 1996), Schadler *et al.* (1993), and Fernández-Arias and Montiel (1996), to cite only a few.

[7] See Begg (1996) and Calvo *et al.* (1993).

[8] This was the case, for example, during the period around the 1996 presidential elections in Russia.

[9] It is also likely that the current account surpluses recorded at the beginning of the transition period included capital flows, but the magnitudes are not known.

[10] Saavalainen (1995) has argued that the availability of low-cost skilled labor also attracted FDI into the Baltic states.

[11] The prohibition of direct foreign purchases of privatization vouchers (in the face of a 50% voucher requirement for privatization) was one important barrier keeping foreigners out of the privatization program. Furthermore, only in the fall of 1996 were certain foreign investors (those from a small number of countries with which Latvia had bilateral investment guarantees) allowed to buy the land on which enterprises were located (but this did not include agricultural land).

[12] In Estonia, except for a few issues of local government bonds, there are no government securities. By contrast, well-functioning treasury bill primary markets have developed both in Latvia and Lithuania in the last couple of years. At the end of 1996, the outstanding stock of T-bills of all maturities stood at around 5% of GDP in Latvia and 3% in Lithuania.

[13] For an overview of government borrowing in the countries of the former Soviet Union, see Kapur and van der Mensbrugghe (1997).

[14] See Castello Branco *et al.* (1996).

[15] The well-known measurement problems involved in the analysis of saving behavior are more acute in the case of transition economies, where national accounts data are notoriously poor. This suggests caution in cross-country comparisons and interpretations of year-to-year fluctuations in saving during the short transition period.

[16] The high saving ratios under central planning largely reflected high enterprise saving, which was channeled to finance directed capital accumulation. Household saving, accumulated in the form of money balances, was "forced" by shortages of consumer goods in an environment of widespread price controls.

[17] See EBRD (1996).

[18] Although the trend is similar, inflation as measured by the producer price index (PPI) has tended to be lower than that as measured by the consumer price index (CPI), partly because of the smaller share of services in the former.

[19] Higher productivity growth in the tradables sector relative to the nontradables sector, the so-called "Balassa-Samuelson effect", can also contribute to inflation. However, this effect is more likely to become significant in the Baltics when the initial under-valuation is eliminated (Richards and Tersman, 1996).

[20] These include financial sector and trade reform, and liberalization of capital outflows (Schadler *et al.*, 1993).

[21] Unsterilized intervention refers to the purchase of foreign exchange through the creation of high-powered money. In a narrow sense sterilized intervention can be defined as measures (such as open-market operations) to neutralize the effects of capital inflows on the monetary base, or, in a broad sense, when it involves measures (such as an increase in reserve requirements) aimed at curbing the effects of inflows on the money supply.

[22] For a discussion of the pros and cons of sterilization policies, see, e.g., Lee (1997), Calvo *et al.* (1996), and Frankel (1994).

[23] Prior to the adoption of the currency board in Lithuania, intervention in the foreign exchange market by the central bank was insufficient to prevent significant exchange rate volatility.

[24] In early 1997, the authorities put forth a strategy for a gradual exit from the currency board arrangement. The primary reason for abandoning the currency board is the desire to strengthen economic links with the EU and prepare for eventual participation in the EU monetary arrangements. A secondary factor is the desire to deploy a wider arsenal of monetary instruments. The authorities have indicated that the exit will only take place under appropriate conditions, including macroeconomic and financial stability, formal independence of the central bank, and completion of the rehabilitation of the banking sector.

References

Begg, D., 1996, Monetary policy in Central and Eastern Europe: Lessons after half a decade of transition, IMF Working Paper 96/108, International Monetary Fund, Washington, DC, USA.

Calvo, G., Leiderman, L., and Reinhart, C., 1993, The capital inflows problem: Concepts and issues, IMF Paper on Policy Analysis and Assessment 93/19, International Monetary Fund, Washington, DC, USA.

Calvo, G., Leiderman, L., and Reinhart, C., 1996, Inflows of capital to developing countries in the 1990s, *Journal of Economic Perspectives*, **10**(2):123–139.

Castello Branco, M., Kammer, A., and Psalida, L.E., 1996, Financial Sector Reform and Banking Crises in the Baltic Countries, IMF Working Paper 96/134, International Monetary Fund, Washington, DC, USA.

European Bank for Reconstruction and Development (EBRD), 1996, Economic transition in Eastern Europe and the former Soviet Union, transition report, EBRD, London, UK.

Fernández-Arias, E., and Montiel, P.J., 1996, The surge in capital inflows to developing countries: An analytical overview, *World Bank Economic Review*, **10**(1):51–77.

Frankel, J., 1994, Sterilization on Money Inflows: Difficult (Calvo) or Easy (Reisen)? IMF Working Paper 94/159, International Monetary Fund, Washington, DC, USA.

Kapur, I., and van der Mensbrugghe, E., 1997, External Borrowing by the Baltics, Russia and Other Countries of the Former Soviet Union: Developments and Policy Issues, IMF Working Paper 97/72, International Monetary Fund, Washington, DC, USA.

Lee, J.-Y., 1997, Sterilizing capital inflows, *Economic Issues*, No. 7, International Monetary Fund, Washington, DC, USA.

Richards, A.J., and Tersman, G.H.R., 1996, Growth, nontradables, and price convergence in the Baltics, *Journal of Comparative Economics*, **23**(2):121–145.

Saavalainen, T., 1995, Stabilization in the Baltic countries: Early experience, in B. Banerjee *et al.*, *Road Maps of the Transition: The Baltics, the Czech Republic, Hungary, and Russia*, IMF Occasional Paper, No. 127, International Monetary Fund, Washington, DC, USA.

Schadler, S., Carkovic, M., Bennett, A., and Kahn, R., 1993, *Recent Experiences with Surges in Capital Inflows*, IMF Occasional Paper No. 108, International Monetary Fund, Washington, DC, USA.

Appendix: Operation of the Currency Boards in Estonia and Lithuania

One of the basic principles underlying the operation of a currency board is that its liabilities must be exchanged on demand, at a fixed exchange rate and without limit, for the currency to which the domestic currency is pegged. In the case of Estonia, the kroon was pegged to the Deutsche mark at the rate of 8:1 in June 1992. Lithuania's currency board is anchored to the US dollar, to which the litas was pegged at the rate of 4:1 in April 1994. In both cases, the liabilities of the currency board include currency and commercial banks' deposits with the central bank and, in the case of Lithuania, government deposits and the litas-denominated correspondent balances of other central banks.

Another key feature of currency board arrangements is the requirement that the currency board liabilities be covered by convertible foreign assets. In Estonia, the foreign exchange cover for the currency board's liabilities is on the basis of net foreign assets, while in Lithuania coverage is provided only on a *gross* basis, that is, it is not reduced by the amount of foreign liabilities. Estonia started its currency board with 90% cover, using the gold reserves restituted by the Bank of England; additional gold restituted by the Swedish government and the Bank of International Settlements allowed for 100% cover soon thereafter. In contrast, part of the backing for the currency board arrangement in Lithuania was provided by resources borrowed from the IMF.

The operation of currency boards entails a number of restrictions on monetary and fiscal policy. In both countries the currency board is not allowed to lend to the government, so budget financing must originate from domestic commercial banks, nonbanks, and external sources. In view of the limited availability of domestic financing, such a restriction encourages fiscal responsibility. In principle, under a currency board there is no room for discretionary monetary policy, which rules out open-market operations and sterilization policies, as well as discount window facilities. While in the medium term nominal domestic interest rates tend to converge to the levels prevailing in the reserve currency country, in the short term interest rate arbitrage is limited, *inter alia*, by the existence of transaction costs, credit risk, and market imperfections. Since inflation rates can diverge between the currency board country and the reserve country, real interest rates will not be equalized. To the extent that there are foreign exchange reserves in excess of the currency board requirement, in practice there is some scope for exercising the lender of last resort function in case of emergencies. Besides the use of surplus reserve funds, other possibilities for smoothing short-term interest rate fluctuations under currency board arrangements include: (i) changes in the reserve requirement; (ii) direct borrowing abroad by the central bank; and (iii) issuance of securities.

Recognizing that the use of the available flexibility might undermine the credibility of their currency board arrangements, both countries have made an explicit commitment to abstain from monetary management (e.g., changes in reserve requirements are restricted under programs supported by the IMF). In Estonia, although central bank bills were introduced in 1993, their objective was to facilitate collateralized interbank lending, rather than to be used in open market operations. In Lithuania, treasury bills were introduced in 1994, but the central bank is not allowed to purchase bills on the primary market. However, since the currency board was introduced, there have been instances of relaxation of the reserve requirement, as well as borrowing by the Lithuanian government, backed by the currency board's reserves.

Chapter 8

Financial Flows to a Small Open Economy: The Case of Slovenia

Velimir Bole

8.1 Introduction

Sudden large increases in foreign exchange inflows (and foreign exchange reserves) can be triggered by substantial foreign capital inflows, as well as by short-lived significant surges in the current account surplus. The consequences of rapid increases in foreign exchange reserves depend on the sources of those increases. Deterioration in economic performance caused by excessive foreign capital inflows is far more frequent, and is thus much better documented and analyzed than the consequences of significant surges in the current account surplus. Such surges could also have a serious impact on the long-term economic performance, although episodes of "Dutch disease" are infrequent.

It is well known that in the 1970s, large-scale financial inflows following financial liberalization did not come to a happy end in the Southern cone of Latin America (see, e.g., Corbo and de Melo, 1985; McKinnon, 1988). Episodes of huge foreign exchange inflows in Southeast Asia in the 1980s, as well as the recent revival of capital inflows to Asia and Latin America, are also extensively documented (see, e.g., Calvo *et al.*, 1993b; Reisen, 1993a,b; Corbo and Hernández, 1996).

In the 1990s, some economies in transition have faced financial inflows of similar scale relative to gross domestic product (GDP) to other developing economies. It is not obvious that lessons from the Southeast Asian or Latin American experience can be straightforwardly adopted by the more developed economies in transition (such as Slovenia) facing increased financial inflows.

The causes and effects of financial inflows to Southeast Asia and Latin America have been thoroughly studied. The literature has also pinpointed appropriate policies, but are those policies appropriate for transition economies? Is it plausible, for example, that for countries in transition, changes in international interest rates have been the dominant factor behind the substantial private capital inflows in the 1990s (the "push" view)? This happened to be the case for an important group of middle-income economies (see Dooley *et al.*, 1996). A similar question can be posed for effects: is it probable that basic (long-term) effects of increased financial inflows in previously centrally planned economies are the same as in other developing countries? One must also take into account that several crucial factors that may mitigate the harmful effects of huge financial inflows (see Calvo *et al.*, 1993a) are not present in transition economies. The fiscal stance is weak, pressure for huge real wage increases and a catching-up of private consumption is persistent,[1] the banking system is fragile, and so on. Finally, the effectiveness of known policy measures (see Calvo *et al.*, 1993a), especially sterilized intervention, is questionable in transition economies, where financial markets are shallow, tax revenues unstable, and the instruments of macroeconomic management still in the making.

The Slovenian economy has been facing significant financial inflows since its declaration of monetary independence. It is a small and open economy (the foreign trade ratio exceeds 1.15)[2] in transition. Accordingly, the harmful effects of inflows may be greater, and the effectiveness of policy responses weaker, than in a much larger and/or less open middle-income economy in Southeast Asia or Latin America facing large capital inflows.

This chapter has three main objectives. The first is to document the dynamics, structure, substitutability, and persistence of inflows to Slovenia. The second objective is to determine the main causes and effects of inflows, and so to reveal the main factors motivating both persistent sterilization efforts and the direct capital controls launched in a later phase of financial inflows. In the context of a second-best argument, crucial microeconomic distortions to the economy are pinpointed as the main reason for austere and permanent policy responses to foreign financial inflows. The third objective is to evaluate the effects of slightly modified versions of policy recommendations familiar from episodes in Latin America and Southeast Asia. Although the need to mitigate a real appreciation of the exchange rate and/or uncontrolled monetary growth is the standard justification for policy intervention, our analysis goes beyond the effects of policy measures on exchange rates and monetary growth. We complement our description of the empirical evidence with a presentation of the results of running various tests of statistical causality.

Table 8.1. Slovenian macroeconomic indicators (% if not otherwise indicated).

	1992	1993	1994	1995	1996
Growth of real GDP	–6.0	2.8	5.3	3.9	3.1
Domestic private consumption (% of GDP)	51.5	58.3	57.3	58.1	57.6
Gross capital formation (% of GDP)	17.3	18.7	19.6	21.1	22.2
General government fiscal balance (% of GDP)	0.3	0.3	–0.2	0.0	0.1
Inflation (December-to-December)	92.9	22.9	18.0	8.6	8.8
Total external-debt-to-exports ratio	21.7	25.1	26.0	28.7	38.2
Reserves-to-imports ratio	16.8	21.6	33.3	32.4	38.8
Imports-to-GDP ratio	54.8	57.2	57.9	57.0	57.3
Exports-to-GDP ratio	63.7	58.9	60.6	55.8	57.0
GDP per capita (US$)	6,186	6,368	7,205	9,348	9,273

Source: *Monthly Bulletin* of the Bank of Slovenia.

The remainder of the chapter is organized as follows. The second section presents empirical evidence on the scale, structure, and dynamics of financial inflows from 1991 onward. We document the current account surpluses, "pseudo current account" items, and the capital account inflows. In the third section, we sketch the possible causes of such movements. In the fourth, we document the effects of financial flows, in the process presenting the basic reasons for the authorities' persistent and harsh policy responses. In the fifth section, we describe the policy measures and illustrate the intensity of instruments. This section also presents various empirical tests and some facts that illustrate the possible costs and macroeconomic effects of the sterilization and capital control measures. We summarize our main findings in the final section.

8.2 Empirical Evidence

8.2.1 Macroeconomic performance

Some Basic Macroeconomic Facts

In this section we briefly illustrate the main characteristics of capital flows and current account surpluses in Slovenia after it introduced its own currency in October 1991. Key macroeconomic developments are highlighted as well.

Some important macroeconomic indicators for the period 1992–1996 are presented in *Table 8.1*.[3] The basic characteristics of the recent surges in foreign exchange inflows (and reserves) are shown in *Figure 8.1* and *Table 8.2*. The main features of macroeconomic performance in 1992–1996 were gradual price stabilization; a leveling off of economic activity and the pick-up of growth in 1993–1994,

Table 8.2. Slovenian balance of payments (% of GDP).

	1992	1993	1994	1995	1996
Balance on current account,					
excluding official transfers	7.7	2.0	4.2	0.2	0.7
Change in official reserves[a]	–5.1	–0.9	–4.5	–1.2	–3.2
Asset transactions, including errors	–3.6	–2.3	–0.3	–1.8	0.4
Net external financing	1.0	1.2	0.6	2.8	2.1
Direct investment and official transfers	0.7	0.4	0.4	0.5	0.5
Net external borrowing	0.3	0.9	0.2	2.3	1.6
Memorandum items					
Total capital flows[b]	1.1	2.9	3.2	3.5	5.2
Net medium- and long-term capital	0.7	1.7	2.6	4.6	4.7

[a]Negative sign indicates increase of reserves.
[b]Increase in total foreign reserves (of BOS and banks) less current account balance and errors.
Note: This table is presented according to the standard IMF classification.
Source: *Monthly Bulletin* of the Bank of Slovenia (BOS); own calculations.

with moderate growth rates thereafter; and huge and persistent increases in the foreign exchange reserves in all years. In this period, the sources of foreign exchange inflows changed from large current account surpluses and small capital inflows in 1992 to a negligible current account surplus and sizable capital inflows in 1996 (see *Figure 8.1* and the memorandum items to *Table 8.2*).

Macroeconomic Policy

The two pillars of monetary policy – exogenously determined monetary growth and a (managed) floating exchange rate regime – remained unchanged until 1997.[4] Although "money landing" had finished a year and a half after the launching of the tolar, the central bank (Bank of Slovenia, BOS) persisted with its tight monetary policy. The exogeneity and steadiness of the money track are illustrated in *Figure 8.2*, where we present annual growth rates of M3. Fiscal policy was also on the stabilization track, the general government budget running a negligible surplus in 1992–1993 and a deficit of the same order of magnitude in 1994–1996.[5]

Of the fundamentals, only incomes policy was not put in place at the beginning of the transition; that had to wait until the second half of 1995. Because of a segmented labor market (and strong trade unions), rapid increases in wages in part of the nontradables sector spilled over to the whole economy. A major jump in real wages occurred in 1992, and the wage bill rose faster than GDP every year thereafter (until 1997). The permanent pressure on the competitiveness of the Slovenian economy was even higher, because social transfers (pensions and other social benefits) were fully pegged to wages.

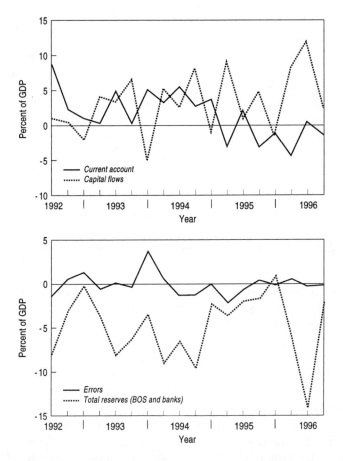

Figure 8.1. Current account, total foreign reserves, and capital flows in Slovenia (BOS = Bank of Slovenia). For reserves negative sign indicates increase.

Current and Capital Account Balances

The general trends in the balance of payments in the 1992–1996 period are illustrated in *Figure 8.1*, while only the key items of the standard International Monetary Fund's (IMF) external financing scheme are presented in *Table 8.2*.[6]

The collapse of the internal (former Yugoslav) market in 1990–1991 and the recession in Western Europe squeezed final demand, turning many enterprises into "distress exporters" in the first year of stabilization.[7] Restrictive monetary policy squeezed domestic demand even more and imports plummeted. Strong exports and weak imports pushed the current account surplus to over 7% of GDP. Because of the squeeze in imports, Slovenia also ran a trade surplus in 1992. In that year,

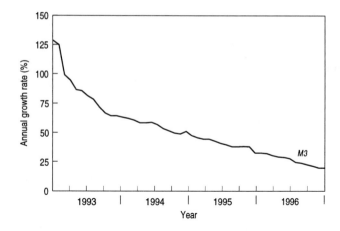

Figure 8.2. Growth of M3 in Slovenia (month on month in previous year).

the current account (net of official transfers) contributed the most to the jump in foreign exchange reserves. Both net external borrowing and net external financing took small values that year.[8]

After 1992, imports increased, while exports, although oscillating, fell every year on average 1.5 percentage points as a share of GDP. Nevertheless, the current account balance remained strong (around 4% of GDP) until the end of 1994. After that, it dropped to zero. In 1995 and 1996, net external financing (and borrowing) made a significant contribution to the increase in the foreign exchange reserves. In 1995–1996, net medium- and long-term capital inflows to Slovenia far exceeded the average values for developing countries and even attained the peak values experienced by the countries of the Asia-Pacific Economic Cooperation Council in the 1990s (see, e.g., Ishii and Dunaway, 1995).

8.2.2 Financial flows: Size, volatility, and substitution of components

Term Structure of Capital Flows

Owing to the persistent efforts of policymakers to contain and neutralize large gross financial inflows, the net items in *Figure 8.1* do not adequately illustrate either the scale or the dynamics of the potential pressure of such inflows on the exchange rate, the money supply, etc. Furthermore, the evolving process of privatization and dramatic changes in currency and sovereign risk after 1991 had different impacts on the scale and volatility of various components of the financial inflows. Therefore, an analytically sensible disaggregation of financial flows must identify components

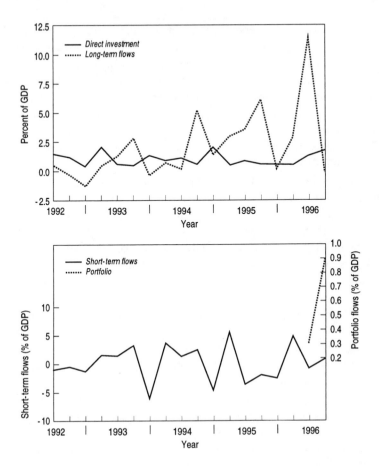

Figure 8.3. Components of financial flows in Slovenia (standard classification).

with distinct causes, characteristics (persistency, volatility), and susceptibility to economic policy measures.

We begin by examining the standard term structure of financial flows. The components of financial flows are presented according to a slightly modified standard classification in *Figure 8.3*. The construction of the components roughly follows that of Claessens *et al.* (1995).[9] Before 1996, there were almost no portfolio flows in Slovenia, so the corresponding values for 1996 are depicted separately on the graph with short-term capital flows.

The analyzed components of financial inflows were positive for the entire 1992–1996 period, indeed, for almost every individual quarter during that period. As illustrated in *Figure 8.3*, the only component that regularly turned negative was short-term flows. Long-term flows and foreign direct investment (FDI) were almost exclusively (in all quarters) inflows in net terms. Descriptive statistics show that FDI is the least volatile component and short-term flows the most volatile one. Thus, the volatility of the various components of financial flows corresponds heuristically to what their labels indicate. However, there is evidence from other countries that the labels "short term" and "long term" do not necessarily indicate the actual volatility of the relevant financial flow components (see Claessens *et al.*, 1995).

Long-term net inflows increased persistently – although with oscillations – in the period 1992–1996. A visible acceleration occurred only in the middle of 1996, after the country finalized agreements with the former Yugoslavia republics' international creditors. At that point, Slovenia received single grade -A from credit-rating agencies and subsequently made its first successful international bonds issue on the Euro market.

Graphs of short-term flows and FDI do not reveal any visible trends in their dynamics. Short-term inflows at the beginning of stabilization were triggered by the privatization of apartments, which was mainly financed through the repatriation of the private foreign exchange deposits of residents abroad (see Mencinger, 1991; Stanovnik, 1994). Direct investment in the first year of monetary independence was made mainly by foreign enterprises that had been present on the Slovenian market before the declaration of monetary sovereignty.

If the components of financial flows are considered substitutes, policy moves taken in response to significant changes in a specific component are at best superfluous. High volatility of a certain component in the presence of substitution among such components does not imply high volatility of total financial flows. It has been documented elsewhere that substitutability among various flow components is common in developed and developing economies. Accordingly, attention should be devoted to the determinants of the total capital account (see, e.g., Claessens *et al.*, 1995).

We can look for evidence of substitutability by examining the simple correlation coefficients among the components of financial flows and the current account balance. On the basis of the figures in *Table 8.3*, we can draw two rather unusual conclusions. FDI is a close substitute for short-term flows, and long-term flows are a substitute for the current account balance. Furthermore, FDI and long-term flows are not highly correlated. We hypothesize that FDI and short-term flows share some important common factors, but FDI and long-term flows do not.

Structure of Financial Flows by Transactor

In the process of financial opening, different institutional sectors were not in equivalent positions. Accordingly, the classification of financial flows by transactor

Table 8.3. Correlation coefficients of financial flows by term structure in Slovenia, 1992–1996.

	Current account	Direct investment	Short-term flows	Long-term flows	Reserves
Current account	1	0.337	−0.358	−0.304	−0.309
Direct investment	0.337	1	−0.342	−0.161	−0.011
Short-term flows	−0.358	−0.342	1	0.088	−0.386
Long-term flows	−0.304	−0.161	0.088	1	−0.565
Reserves	−0.309	−0.011	−0.386	−0.565	1

Notes: Quarterly data used in calculations; flows are given in percentage of GDP.

Table 8.4. Correlation coefficients of financial flows by transactor in Slovenia, 1992–1996.

	Current account	House-holds	Busi-ness	Official sector	Banks
Current account	1	0.416	−0.167	−0.395	−0.080
Households	0.416	1	0.507	−0.216	−0.287
Business	−0.167	0.507	1	−0.066	0.012
Official sector	−0.395	−0.216	−0.066	1	−0.285
Banks	−0.080	−0.287	0.012	−0.285	1

Notes: Quarterly data used in calculations; flows are given in percentage of GDP.

may be more revealing with respect to the causes, volatility, and responsiveness of those flows to measures of economic policy than the term classification discussed above.[10] Four components of financial flows are constructed: household, bank, official and business.[11] Changes in official reserves are not part of the official component of flows, so they must be added to that component to obtain total financial flows.

As *Figure 8.4* shows, the volatility of the financial flows of the banking and business sectors is the smallest and of the flows of the official sector is the largest. The high volatility of the official sector flows stems mainly from the renegotiation of the old Yugoslav debt and the first issuing of bonds on the Euro market. After stabilization began, financial inflows to the business sector were the largest, on average slightly larger than 1.4% of GDP. However, net outflows from the banking sector attained 2.4% of GDP. Until the beginning of 1996, the BOS was successful in using sterilized intervention to increase the attractiveness of the foreign exchange part of bank portfolios. Therefore, it is no surprise that commercial banks absorbed the bulk of inflow to other sectors.

Simple correlation coefficients demonstrate that there was considerable substitutability among the transactor components of financial flows (see *Table 8.4*). Two

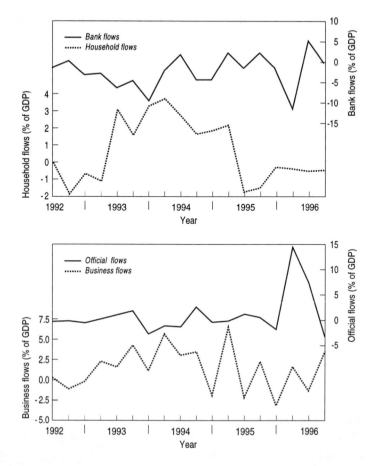

Figure 8.4. Flows to household, bank, business, and official sectors in Slovenia.

relatively highly correlated components, household and official, are worth mentioning. Correlation coefficients are highest in absolute value for flows through the household sector. The central role of this component is confirmed by the gross volume of transactions made in the corresponding part of the foreign exchange market, that is, in foreign exchange offices. In some years that volume reached almost 50% of the volume of total foreign exchange transactions by enterprises.

Official flows have mitigated the volatility of all other components of flows. The correlation coefficients of official flows with all other components of flows are negative.[12] Furthermore, inflows through the household and official components have been considerably mitigated by outflows through banks.

8.3 Causes of Financial Flows

8.3.1 External versus domestic factors

In view of the high volatility of financial flows to developing countries in the last three decades, identifying the causes of these flows is a major step in evaluating the probable evolution of the process and possible policy responses.

If external factors are important (the "push" view), descriptive analysis of the volatility of the flows could be valuable for anticipating possible reversals. In any case, if external factors play a major role, policymakers can only neutralize the effects of past financial flows. External factors have an impact on the external opportunity costs of funds. These factors include foreign interest rates, policies that affect the availability of the capital in creditor countries, and bandwagon effects on international capital markets.

If domestic factors are crucial (the "pull" view), the evolution of financial flows is endogenously determined and more sensitive to direct policy measures. In such a case, policymakers may be able to inhibit future inflows. Analytically, domestic factors can be divided into those operating on the micro (or project) level and those operating on the macro (or country) level (see Calvo *et al.*, 1993a; Fernández-Arias and Montiel, 1996). The former include factors that increase the long-run expected rate of return on real domestic investments (e.g., structural reforms or successful domestic macroeconomic policies); short-run macroeconomic policies that increase the expected rate of return on domestic financial instruments (e.g., restrictive monetary policy); and opening of the domestic financial market under a not-fully credible macroeconomic adjustment program (which would have distorting intertemporal relative prices as its most important consequence). The latter includes debt service reduction agreements, policies that modify the aggregate efficiency of resource allocation, and changes to the international terms of trade.

Financial flows to developing countries in the 1990s have proved difficult to explain. There is evidence that endogenous factors such as debt reduction and policy reforms have affected financial flows. Nevertheless, the effects of external factors, particularly falling foreign interest rates, have been the least disputed. The presence of these external factors also explains why recent capital inflows have not been restricted to economies that have undergone strong restructuring programs (see Calvo *et al.*, 1993a; Dooley *et al.*, 1996; Fernández-Arias and Montiel, 1996).

8.3.2 Factors behind financial inflows in the "distress" period of stabilization

The figures in *Table 8.4* show that some components of financial flows classified by transactor are not highly correlated. Thus, any external driving force had to be intertwined with domestic factors. That is especially because policies for containing and sterilizing capital inflows were launched almost from the very beginning of transition (and stabilization).

There were also differences in access to foreign capital for different institutions (i.e., sectors of the economy). At the beginning of stabilization, because of high sovereignty risk (Slovenia was a new state with an economy in distress and a war near its borders), enterprises were not able even to obtain short-term trade credits. Imports had to be paid for in advance, in cash (Bole, 1997). However, households had long had large foreign exchange deposits in banks just over the border and repatriation of these funds started immediately with the launching of the privatization of apartments. Furthermore, private persons and small enterprises were able to borrow from banks across the border using their personal deposits or life insurance policies as collateral. Up until the end of the second quarter of 1992, net financial inflows through the household sector of around 3.7% of GDP were mainly induced by accelerated repatriation, triggered particularly by the privatization of apartments.

The collapse of the former Yugoslav market and the resulting shrinkage of the internal market turned many enterprises into "distress exporters". Facing a small internal market and a tight monetary policy,[13] these enterprises made severe cuts in (tolar) export prices, in order to keep cash flows positive and buy time for necessary restructuring. In fact, they were partly selling off their assets. Therefore, a portion of the large current account surplus in the first three quarters of 1992 was actually an inflow of capital (see *Figure 8.1*). In the first three quarters of 1992, over one-third of the current account surplus may actually have been an inflow of capital generated by distress exporting.[14]

External Factors of Financial Flows in the Restructuring Phase of Transition

In order to obtain a preliminary idea of how important external factors were in the Slovenian episode (particularly foreign interest rates), we show the components of nominal interest rate differentials in *Figure 8.5*. These two factors are the "currency premium" and the "liquidity premium".[15] Because we have already established the central role of the household sector in channeling financial flows to Slovenia (as evidenced by its high correlation with other components), we present the household financial flows along with the premia in the graphs.

Looking at the liquidity premium graph, we can identify five periods. In the first, the premium did not change significantly. By the end of 1992, monthly interest rates in Slovenia on deposits in German marks were 0.05 points higher than interest rates in Germany on deposits of the same maturity. In the second period, this premium increased; in the third, the premium did not change; in the fourth, it

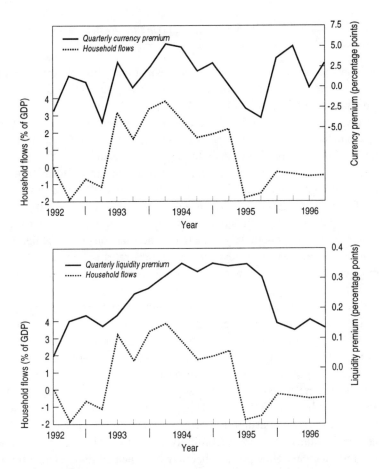

Figure 8.5. Household component of financial flows and components of nominal interest rate differentials in Slovenia.

dropped to around 0.05 again. After the beginning of 1996, there were no significant oscillations in the foreign exchange liquidity premium. The periods evidenced by the currency premium follow more or less the same pattern.

The periods indicated roughly reflect the varying pressures of the flows for a real appreciation of domestic currency, and thus explain the intensity of subsequent policy efforts. Compare, for example, the path of the real exchange rate with that of the financial flows (see *Figures 8.4* and *8.11*). The same relation is illustrated in *Figure 8.5*, where we present the household component of financial flows and the foreign exchange liquidity and currency premia.

*Domestic Factors Behind Financial Flows During the Restructuring Phase
of Transition*

Of the domestic factors that we have mentioned, at least three deserve attention in
the case of Slovenia: the effects of stabilization, a nonsustainable incomes policy,
and agreements for the restructuring of debt.

Because stabilization in Slovenia was money-based, tight monetary policy
could have increased the expected rate of return on domestic financial instruments.
A large fiscal deficit would have done the same. Both could have triggered *ex ante*
positive interest rate differentials, and/or additional demand for loans from abroad
in the case of significant credit rationing in the country. However, there was no
relevant fiscal deficit. Empirical evidence does not support the view that the tightness of monetary policy or financial inefficiency stemming from over-regulation
(financial repression) were unduly large in the stabilization period (Bole, in press).
Nevertheless, in the period of low foreign interest rates and an abundant supply
of foreign credit, the normal (short-term) consequences of stabilization could have
provided an additional push to financial inflows to Slovenia.

In *Figure 8.6*, we illustrate the possible impact of tight monetary policy on
financial flows. We present the growth rates of credit along with the household
and business components of financial flows. The graphs show heuristically that the
growth rate of credit lagged behind both financial inflow variables. We describe
statistical tests of possible causality in the next section.

As indicated in Section 8.2.1, incomes policy was not put on a sustainable track
until the second half of 1995 (Bole, 1997). Rapid increases in wages and social
transfers fueled private consumption, which did not drop as a share of GDP from
the high level attained in 1992. Accordingly, domestic savings (as a percentage of
GDP) did not increase either, a fact that may have helped to accelerate the inflow
of foreign savings. The dynamics of wages also fueled the already rapid increases
in the relative prices of nontradables (Bole, 1997). This resulted in a higher than
expected real appreciation of the exchange rate, which in turn could have further
attracted financial inflows into the country.

In *Figure 8.7* the growth rates of real wages (including other receipts) and the
business component of financial flows are shown. To eliminate possible seasonal
effects, we provide the yearly growth rates (month over month in the previous
year) of wages. The graph shows that the two variables were highly correlated,
although with a lag. To corroborate such a heuristic conclusion, in the next section
we present the results of running causality tests.

As indicated in Section 8.2.2, at the end of the first half of 1996, Slovenia
obtained single grade -A from credit-rating agencies, reached agreement with foreign creditors, and launched a successful bond issue on the Euro market.[16] The

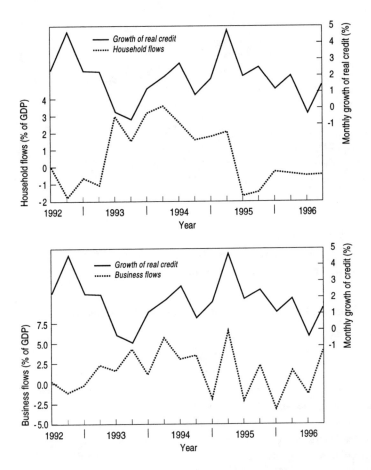

Figure 8.6. Growth of real credit vis-à-vis household and business components of financial flows in Slovenia.

effects of the increased long-run expected rate of return and the significantly improved expected debt service were evident in portfolio inflows, which, as shown in *Figure 8.3*, increased by four times in the second half of 1996.

The country's higher international investment credibility squeezed the interest rates on foreign credits by around 0.7 to 1 percentage points over LIBOR (London Inter-Bank Offered Rate). Consequently, the demand for long-term foreign credits also increased considerably. The authorities had already placed a 40% deposit requirement on foreign credits with maturities of less than 5 years, so the credits demanded were characterized (formally) by longer maturities.

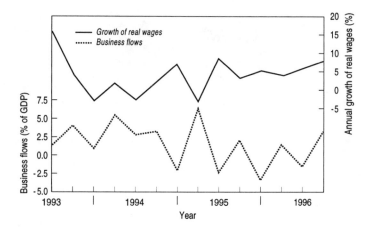

Figure 8.7. Growth of real wages (month on month in the previous year) and business component of financial flows in Slovenia.

8.3.3   Factors behind financial flows: Causality testing

To provide more substantive statistical support for the relevance of the indicated factors, we present the results of running various feedback ("causality") tests. The external factors affecting financial inflows are proxied by the currency premium. To test for the significance of domestic factors, we employ the real lending rate and the growth rate of real credit as proxies for the possible effects of short-run macroeconomic policy (e.g., tight monetary policy). To examine the implications of distorted intertemporal relative prices and noncredible restructuring of the economy, we include the growth rate of real average wages (including all other receipts of employees) and the depth of financial intermediation (as measured by the ratio of broad money to GDP). We include all components of financial flows by transactor, measured in percent of GDP, in our causality testing.

We employ a modification of the Granger-Simms test, which aims to make that test more robust and appropriate for short time series (see Sargent and Wallace, 1973); additional discussion is given in the Appendix. Our data set contains monthly figures for the period July 1992–December 1996.

The authorities began to engage in sterilized intervention in the first quarter of 1992.[17] Direct capital controls, in the form of mandatory deposits on foreign credits with maturities of less than 5 years, were launched in 1995. Consequently, the possible effects of the factors analyzed could have been affected by sterilization measures. To control for such indirect effects, we performed the causality tests conditional on the intensity of sterilization, as proxied by the growth rate of central bank forex bills.[18] To exclude the possible indirect effects of the basic orientation of stabilization policy, we include the growth rate of real base money also as an exogenous variable in our causality tests.

We present the results in *Tables 8.5a* and *8.5b*. We include both F-statistics for the statistical significance of the overall feedback relation and the t-statistics for coefficients a_i on the lead variables. If the overall relationship is statistically significant, as indicated by the F-statistic and the coefficients are significant but of different signs, in the discussion of the relationship the sign of $a_5 + a_6 + a_7 + a_8$ is taken into account. We divide the test results into two tables. In the first (*Table 8.5a*), we present the results of tests of causality from the given factors to financial flows, while in the second (*Table 8.5b*), we provide a test on the reverse causality.

The results show that the currency premium significantly Granger-caused financial flows through the household sector. Because the reverse causality is not significant and the coefficients at the lead variables are positive, the test confirms that the increase in the currency premium caused the rise in household net financial inflows. However, the currency premium did not significantly Granger-cause the other components of financial flows.

The statistical tests allow us to reject the hypothesis of no causality from the real lending rate to the household and bank components of financial flows. A test of the reverse relation rejects the hypothesis that the bank component did not Granger-cause real interest rates. This result supports the view that higher real interest rates increased only the household component of net financial inflows. Although the relationship between real interest rates and the bank component of financial flows is strong, the tests are unable to discern the direction of causality.

The hypothesis that the growth rate of real credits did not Granger-cause financial flows can be rejected for the household, business, and official components. The coefficients on the lead variables are mostly negative for all three components. Furthermore, test statistics for reverse causality are not significant for any of the components. Thus, the deceleration of the growth of real credits Granger-caused an increase in the household, business, and official components of financial flows. The effect can be interpreted as an offset effect under a floating exchange rate regime.[19]

Causality from the variable proxying the depth of (banking) financial intermediation and the household and bank components of financial flows is significant; the t-statistics are uniformly of the same sign in both cases. Both reverse causality relations are insignificant. Thus, our tests confirm that the squeeze put on broad money Granger-caused an increase in the net financial inflow to the household sector, and a decrease in the net financial inflow to the banking sector. Causality from the growth of real wages to financial flows is significant only for the business component of those flows. Because causality in the reverse direction is also significant,

Table 8.5a. Testing causality between financial flows and factors in Slovenia, 1992–1996.

Component of financial flows	F	t_5	t_6	t_7	t_8
Interest rate					
Household	3.1^a	1.76	−0.48	0.01	1.86
Business	1.5	1.13	1.85	2.24	1.45
Official	0.6	−1.14	−1.22	−1.29	−0.68
Bank	3.8^a	−1.05	−2.32	−0.34	−1.79
Currency premium					
Household	3.0^a	1.95	0.11	0.40	−2.61
Business	1.4	−0.70	−1.13	0.33	1.13
Official	0.1	−0.14	0.20	−0.02	0.28
Bank	1.6	0.79	0.06	1.15	1.76
Growth of real credit					
Household	5.1^a	−1.37	0.35	0.09	−3.86
Business	2.8^a	0.69	1.34	0.63	−1.90
Official	2.9^a	−3.04	−0.29	0.86	0.12
Bank	1.2	1.97	0.31	0.44	0.11
Broad money (% of GDP)					
Household	4.0^a	−2.84	−2.49	−1.74	−1.94
Business	0.8	−0.02	0.57	0.74	1.14
Official	1.3	−1.64	−0.65	−0.95	−0.55
Bank	4.6^a	3.94	3.14	1.85	1.29
Growth of real wages					
Household	0.3	0.30	0.16	0.23	−0.06
Business	3.0^a	−0.77	2.69	−0.92	−0.65
Official	0.7	−0.62	−0.37	−1.27	0.82
Bank	1.2	−1.20	−0.69	0.07	0.60

[a]F-statistics significant at 0.1.

Notes: Monthly data used in calculations; flows are given in percentage of GDP.

while the t-statistics on the coefficients are even higher and positive, we can document empirically only a strong dependence between wages and financial inflows and not the direction of causality.

Summing up, our tests support the significance of all three tested factors for at least one component of financial flows. Sensitivity to changes in these factors is the highest for the household component of financial flows. Because of substitutability between the components of the flows, the importance of the factors examined for total financial flows is also confirmed. Given the stance of monetary policy – the supply of base money and the extent of sterilized intervention – net financial inflows offset the limits on the supply of credit. Credit rationing (by domestic banks) was

Table 8.5b. Testing reverse causality between financial flows and factors in Slovenia, 1992–1996.

Component of financial flows	F	t_5	t_6	t_7	t_8
Interest rate					
Household	1.3	0.11	−0.56	1.94	0.56
Business	1.7	−1.86	0.84	1.50	−0.66
Official	1.3	−1.24	1.60	−0.25	−1.64
Bank	5.1[a]	−3.76	0.19	−0.23	1.47
Currency premium					
Household	0.4	−0.46	−0.58	−0.37	0.82
Business	1.2	−1.01	1.18	0.23	−0.24
Official	3.5[a]	−2.65	0.13	0.64	−1.08
Bank	0.3	0.18	0.43	−0.56	−0.24
Growth of real credit					
Household	0.8	−1.28	0.58	−0.19	0.13
Business	0.1	0.33	−0.44	0.10	−0.31
Official	0.2	−0.58	−0.03	0.13	0.79
Bank	0.8	1.01	0.33	−0.92	−0.99
Broad money (% of GDP)					
Household	0.5	−0.65	−0.43	−0.50	1.03
Business	0.6	−0.87	0.95	0.20	−0.26
Official	5.1[a]	−2.97	−0.06	0.50	−1.92
Bank	0.2	0.21	0.29	−0.52	−0.13
Growth of real wages					
Household	1.9	−0.04	0.00	0.26	1.79
Business	5.1[a]	2.05	0.21	1.06	3.46
Official	1.5	−1.87	−0.82	0.20	0.58
Bank	1.2	−0.21	−1.03	−1.15	−1.68

[a]F-statistics significant at 0.1.
Notes: Monthly data used in calculations; flows are given in percentage of GDP.

more important than high lending rates in bringing about such an offset effect on net financial inflows.

8.4 Effects of Financial Flows

8.4.1 Key macroeconomic implications of high growth of net financial inflows

A substantial surge in foreign financial inflows eases the constraint on restructuring and investment resulting from insufficient domestic savings. A brief look at the data reveals that, in recipient developing countries in the 1990s, increased capital inflows have been accompanied by a revival of economic growth and a remarkable increase in foreign exchange reserves. However, while generally welcome, foreign capital inflows raise several concerns, including the possibility of speculative reversals, a reduction in external competitiveness, increased fiscal debt, lost control over the monetary base, and an acceleration of inflation (see, e.g., Corbo and de Melo, 1985; McKinnon, 1988; Calvo *et al.*, 1993b; Schadler *et al.*, 1993).

It is a common conjecture that inflows of short-term and portfolio capital threaten the performance of the recipient economy the most and stable and non-volatile FDI the least. However, there are arguments suggesting that because of the deepening of financial markets and the increased sophistication of financial instruments, the usual labeling of capital inflows does not provide any information about the persistence and volatility of financial flows (see Claessens *et al.*, 1995).

8.4.2   Effects on external competitiveness

In Slovenia, a floating exchange rate regime, combined with a nonaccommodating monetary policy and substantial foreign exchange inflows, may result in increased pressure for a real – and even a nominal – appreciation of the exchange rate. However, the actual deterioration in competitiveness depends on the relevant policy response and the general macroeconomic performance of the country. This is why the recent empirical evidence on the effect of financial flows on competitiveness in developing countries is not clear-cut; while Latin American countries experienced strong real appreciations, in Southeast Asia this was not generally the case (Calvo *et al.*, 1993a).

There are several reasons why the impact of financial flows on the exchange rate varies markedly across countries. The size of national savings and the composition of aggregate demand probably play crucial roles in determining the possible effects of financial flows on the exchange rate. In contrast to investment, an increase in private or public consumption is biased toward the nontradables sector, so a larger real appreciation can be expected if domestic savings are low and consumption high (see Calvo *et al.*, 1993a).

In Slovenia, the effects of financial inflows on the exchange rate are likely to have been large because domestic savings were low. Furthermore, since 1991 the composition of aggregate demand has become even more dominated by private consumption. Accordingly, the relative prices of nontradables increased considerably – on average by about 1.5% per quarter – in the stabilization period. We illustrate in *Figure 8.8* the real exchange rate and the relative prices of services, the latter serving as a proxy for nontradables.[20]

The exchange rate behaved contrary to our expectations based on the large increase in nontradables prices. After a real appreciation of the domestic currency of

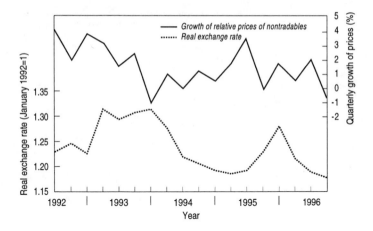

Figure 8.8. Real exchange rate and growth of relative prices of nontradables in Slovenia.

over 10% in the first half of 1992, changes in the trend value of the real exchange rate were modest, although with substantial oscillations. If we calculate the real exchange rate using producer prices, even the strong appreciation in the first half of 1992 almost disappears (see *Figure 8.11*). One of the most important policy targets was containing and neutralizing the effects of the huge inflow of foreign exchange, thus the modest real appreciation after the first half of 1992 is unsurprising.

8.4.3 Effects on interest rates

Strong net financial inflows increase the availability of loanable funds to the economy. If domestic loanable funds are in short supply, net financial inflows will tend to lower interest rates. In the period under examination, there were several important factors affecting interest rates: the stabilization of high and long-lasting inflation, market switching by enterprises, bank rehabilitation, net financial inflows, and sterilized foreign exchange intervention. Therefore, disentangling the effects of any single factor is not straightforward. In a modest attempt to shed light on some of these relationships, *Figure 8.9* presents a time series for the real lending rate and the household component of financial flows.

8.4.4 Effects on savings and the structure of final demand

The real appreciation of the exchange rate also gave a push to the relative prices of nontradables after 1992 (see, e.g., Bole, 1997). The appreciation of the domestic

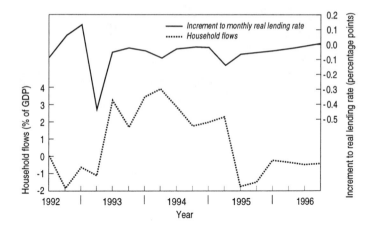

Figure 8.9. Real lending rate and household component of financial flows in Slovenia.

currency held down the domestic prices of tradables, while the prices of nontradables kept rising. Weaker competition enabled enterprises in the nontradable sector to mark up prices almost to the extent of the entire increase in wages. Because of the segmented labor market, the increase in wages in the nontradables sector induced repeated wage increases (through a spillover effect) in other sectors, which perpetuated increased cost pressure on prices in the tradables sector. Nevertheless, the prices of tradables were sluggish, because a buoyant inflow of foreign exchange kept the exchange rate steady and imparted a strong dynamics to imports.[21] Thus, financial flows via a real appreciation of the currency enhanced already existing labor market distortions. The increasing relative prices of nontradables shifted the composition of GDP toward private consumption and nontradable goods.

In the first phase of privatization, selling shares that were received in exchange for privatization vouchers had a strong effect favoring consumption over savings. Households, especially those with considerably greater than average marginal propensities to consume, decided to sell their vouchers, a bias that is particularly strong when share prices are depressed. Thus, we expect that in the first phase of selling "privatization shares", portfolio inflows increased private consumption considerably more than other components of financial flows.

Beginning in August 1996, after Slovenia had received high investment-grade ratings, net portfolio inflows surged (see *Figure 8.3*). Although the empirical evidence is insufficient to draw any firm conclusions, it is worth mentioning that the annual growth rate of private consumption increased in the third quarter of 1996 by

30% and in the final quarter of 1996 by over 100% (both on a quarter-to-quarter basis). During that period, monthly net portfolio inflows surged to around 1–2% of GDP.

8.4.5 Effects of financial flows: Causality testing

Additional causality tests were carried out to seek corroboration for various propositions regarding the effects of financial flows on the appreciation of the exchange rate, interest rates, consumption, the composition of GDP, and savings. The causal relations are examined between the components of financial flows by transactor (measured in percentage of GDP), and the real deposit rate on time deposits, the liquidity premium, the growth of the exchange rate, the growth of real private consumption, the share of private consumption in GDP, the growth of real wages (including all other receipts in cash or goods), and the growth of real broad money. As before, we perform our causality tests conditional on the real growth of base money and the growth of central bank forex bills. Our data cover the period 1992–1996.

We test for causality using monthly series for the period July 1992–December 1996, and present our results in *Tables 8.6a* and *8.6b*. In *Table 8.6a*, we provide test statistics for causality running from financial flows to the studied variables; *Table 8.6b* contains statistics for the reverse causality.

The hypothesis of no causality running from the official component of flows to the real deposit rate can be rejected. However, the relation for testing the reversed causality feedback is not statistically significant. Thus, it can be concluded that the net inflow through the official sector Granger-caused a decrease in real deposit rates in 1992–1996. The test relations for causality running from the other components of flows to the deposit rate are not significant.

Causality from the official component of financial flows to the liquidity premium is significant and all significant t-statistics are negative. Because the hypothesis of no feedback cannot be rejected, the official component of flows Granger-caused a reduction in the liquidity premium. The values of the F-statistics for the other three components of flows are not significantly different from zero.

The values of the F-statistics for causality running from the household and business components of financial flows to the exchange rate are significantly different from zero, while the reverse causality cannot be corroborated. Both of these components of financial flows therefore Granger-caused pressure on the exchange rate to appreciate. The hypothesis of no feedback from the official and bank components of financial flows to the exchange rate cannot be rejected.

Tests of causality running from the household and business components of flows to the growth of real private consumption corroborate the supposition that the

Table 8.6a. Testing causality between financial flows and effects in Slovenia, 1992–1996.

Component of financial flows	F	t_5	t_6	t_7	t_8
Interest rate					
Household	0.9	0.03	−0.96	0.64	1.40
Business	1.2	−1.67	0.98	0.85	−0.49
Official	3.5^a	−2.43	0.42	0.50	−1.81
Bank	1.3	−1.35	0.61	−0.80	−0.09
Liquidity premium					
Household	1.0	−0.23	−0.11	−0.07	1.67
Business	0.6	−0.99	0.91	0.36	−0.46
Official	5.1^a	−3.04	−0.01	0.62	−1.57
Bank	0.9	0.14	0.21	−0.62	−0.64
Rate of change of exchange rate					
Household	2.9^a	−2.50	1.52	−0.16	0.18
Business	2.3^a	1.18	−0.39	−2.42	1.58
Official	0.8	0.89	−1.18	1.15	−1.04
Bank	0.3	−0.79	−0.60	0.10	−0.81
Growth of real private consumption					
Household	2.5^a	0.67	1.07	0.93	2.70
Business	2.6^a	0.13	−1.17	1.58	1.88
Official	1.1	−1.78	−0.89	−0.14	0.07
Bank	2.0	−0.62	−1.70	−1.69	−2.64
Private consumption (% of GDP)					
Household	1.2	−0.91	0.31	−1.32	2.03
Business	0.8	−0.56	0.51	−0.02	0.47
Official	5.0^a	−3.01	−0.01	0.31	−0.87
Bank	0.8	0.83	−0.07	0.03	−1.17
Growth of real wages					
Household	1.9	−0.04	0.00	0.26	1.79
Business	5.1^a	2.05	0.21	1.06	3.46
Official	1.5	−1.87	−0.82	0.20	0.58
Bank	1.2	−0.21	−1.03	−1.15	−1.68
Growth of real broad money					
Household	5.3^a	3.56	1.57	−1.24	1.73
Business	0.1	−0.04	−0.54	0.56	−0.19
Official	0.1	−0.22	−0.28	−0.33	0.36
Bank	2.1^a	−0.43	−2.04	−0.40	−1.44

[a] F-statistics significant at 0.1.

Notes: Monthly data used in calculations; flows are given in percentage of GDP.

Table 8.6b. Testing reverse causality between financial flows and effects in Slovenia, 1992–1996.

Component of financial flows	F	t_5	t_6	t_7	t_8
Interest rate					
Household	2.3^a	0.21	0.66	−0.26	1.58
Business	0.3	−0.84	−0.78	−0.14	−0.73
Official	1.7	−1.33	−1.77	−1.94	−1.36
Bank	0.3	0.26	−1.01	0.30	−0.28
Liquidity premium					
Household	0.1	0.11	0.01	−0.08	0.70
Business	1.5	0.72	0.91	1.45	0.09
Official	0.4	−0.84	−0.43	0.00	0.06
Bank	0.8	0.18	0.67	−0.23	−1.12
Rate of change of exchange rate					
Household	1.6	−0.26	0.14	0.36	1.68
Business	0.4	0.35	0.38	0.09	−0.79
Official	0.6	0.88	0.79	−0.63	−0.14
Bank	1.6	−1.65	−1.34	−0.92	−1.05
Growth of real private consumption					
Household	1.0	−0.77	−0.48	1.58	−1.00
Business	2.8^a	1.36	2.18	0.84	−0.24
Official	0.3	0.47	−0.73	−0.19	0.63
Bank	0.3	−0.28	−0.50	−0.02	0.62
Private consumption (% of GDP)					
Household	2.0	−1.52	0.07	−0.09	−1.26
Business	1.3	1.49	0.74	−0.44	−0.52
Official	1.5	1.20	−0.13	1.77	1.39
Bank	0.6	−0.36	0.09	1.19	0.34
Growth of real wages					
Household	0.3	0.30	0.16	0.23	−0.06
Business	3.1^a	−0.77	2.69	−0.92	−0.65
Official	0.7	−0.62	−0.37	−1.27	0.82
Bank	1.2	−1.20	−0.69	0.07	0.60
Growth of real broad money					
Household	0.1	−0.26	−0.19	0.32	−0.39
Business	1.2	−0.06	0.48	0.37	2.02
Official	0.8	−1.71	−0.48	0.01	0.07
Bank	1.3	0.72	0.64	1.76	−0.13

[a] F-statistics significant at 0.1.

Notes: Monthly data used in calculations; flows are given in percentage of GDP.

rise in net financial inflows accelerated such consumption.[22] Causality running from the bank component of flows to the growth of private consumption is almost significant. Because the hypothesis of no reverse causality can also be rejected, only simultaneous dependence and not causality can be empirically corroborated for the business component of flows and the real growth of private consumption. Causality from the official component of financial flows to the share of private consumption in GDP is significant; most of the coefficients on the lead variables are negative. Because the hypothesis of no reverse causality cannot be rejected, net official financial inflows Granger-caused a decreased share of private consumption in GDP. This means that the official sector, through net foreign financial inflows, crowded out private consumption.

The hypothesis of no causality from the components of financial flows to the growth of real wages can be rejected only for the business component; the F-statistic is high and all coefficients on the lead variables are positive. The reverse causality is also significant. Thus, although there is a strong simultaneous dependence between net financial inflows to the business sector and the growth of real wages, the direction of causality cannot be identified (see Note 22).

We provide test results for the possible effects of financial flows on money at the end of *Tables 8.6a* and *8.6b*. F-statistics for testing for possible causality from financial flows to the growth of real broad money are significant for the household and bank components of flows. For both of these components test statistics for reverse causality are not significant. Thus, net financial inflows through the household sector Granger-caused an increase in growth rate of real broad money. The bank component of net financial inflows Granger-caused a decrease in the growth rate of real broad money. Consequently, a drop in the net foreign assets of banks was triggered by a net inflow of capital. Through such a mechanism, a banking crisis of the Southern cone of Latin America type could emerge. In fact, in the period from 1995/III to 1996/I, bank credit increased at annual growth rates of over 40% in real terms, and the net foreign assets of commercial banks plummeted. The stampede ended with the bankruptcy of a small bank in the third quarter of 1996.

To summarize our results, we can conclude that at least one component of financial flows Granger-caused every proposed effect, that is, statistical tests corroborate that at least one component of financial flows Granger-caused an appreciation of the exchange rate and acceleration of the real growth of both private consumption and broad money. Furthermore, net financial inflows through the official sector crowded out private consumption, while net inflows through the banking sector destabilized banks. Among the favorable effects that we have detected, decreases in the real interest rate and in the liquidity premium should be mentioned.

8.5 Policy Responses to Financial Flows

8.5.1 Activated economic policy areas

Containing and Neutralizing the Effects of Financial Inflows

The authorities in an economy facing sudden and significant surges in financial inflows can employ a variety of policy responses to alleviate a real appreciation of the exchange rate, monetary overhang, and banking instability. These responses depend on the institutional characteristics and performance of the economy, most notably its fiscal stance, exchange rate regime, and the possible existence of micro-economic distortions.

In developing countries, the relevant policies can be divided into measures to neutralize the effects of previous financial inflows and measures to discourage future inflows. The most common policies belonging to the first group of measures include trade policy, sterilized and nonsterilized intervention, increasing marginal reserve requirements for commercial banks, increasing the interest rates on various central bank loans, and reducing access to rediscount facilities. The second category of measures includes tight fiscal policy, taxes and deposits on borrowing abroad, and various types of prudential regulations (see, e.g., Calvo *et al.*, 1993a,b; Schadler *et al.*, 1993).

In Slovenia, where the economy faced considerable labor market distortions, measures for containing and neutralizing financial flows arose in the context of a second-best argument (see, e.g., Dooley, 1996). Of the various types of policy mentioned above, the authorities did not need to adjust fiscal and trade policies for containing and neutralizing the effects of financial inflows. As *Table 8.1* shows, fiscal policy took a strong stance in the period 1992–1996, so that the authorities did not increase the tightness of fiscal policy to curb financial inflows. In 1992, the authorities removed the restrictions on the imports of goods and services and cut custom duties independently of the dynamics of capital inflows. In 1995, the government contemplated introducing subsidies for exporters. However, because of the high share of exports in GDP (around 55%), the fiscal costs of only a 1% subsidy were almost insurmountable and the idea was rejected.

The authorities employed all the other policies mentioned above with varying intensities during at least part of the period after 1991.

Bank Regulation and Supervision

While a real appreciation of the exchange rate is a major source of concern to policymakers in countries facing huge financial inflows, banking crises triggered by high financial inflows prove that banking fragility is no less important a concern (see, e.g., Diaz-Alejandro, 1985; McKinnon, 1988; Calvo *et al.*, 1993a).

Although domestic intermediation is not strictly necessary for inflows of foreign capital, usually the role of domestic banks is crucial during episodes of massive capital inflows. Banks are especially vulnerable when there is a deposit insurance scheme. A surge in lending triggered by capital inflows may increase maturity mismatch, because deposit insurance makes banks neglect the matching of maturities. In developing countries, it is usual to suggest higher risk-based capital requirements and increasing the quality of supervision to insulate the banking sector from possible bubbles caused by sizable inflows of foreign capital. Frequently, different marginal reserve requirements are also used to prevent an uncontrolled increase in bank credits triggered by the monetization of foreign exchange (see, e.g., Calvo *et al.*, 1993a).

In Slovenia, the monetary authorities in 1992 took the first steps toward modifying banking regulation and supervision in order to increase bank prudence with respect to financial flows. The central bank increased the minimum required capital for commercial banks licensed to perform foreign exchange transactions. The minimum required capital was increased in steps; by 1995 (the final step), the requirement for a full license was DM 60 million.[23]

Since 1991, commercial banks have been obligated to have at least a certain percentage of their foreign exchange deposits on their accounts abroad, in government bonds from OECD countries, or in central bank foreign exchange bills. Only foreign exchange deposits susceptible to speculative attack are taken into account in determining whether banks meet this requirement. The size of the foreign exchange cushion for such deposits depends on the latter's maturity. The authorities have changed the percentages several times; at the beginning of 1997 the requirement was that 100% of foreign exchange sight deposits and 0% of foreign exchange time deposits with maturities of over one year must be in the instruments mentioned.

Inflows of foreign credits to domestic banks can trigger an enormous credit expansion through falling net foreign assets, thus threatening the soundness of the banking system.[24] With this in mind, the BOS has enacted a so-called "net foreign assets position", by which banks are forbidden to increase their liabilities toward nonresidents more than their claims against them. Liabilities and claims can be denominated in tolars or foreign exchange.[25] To mitigate the possible adverse effects of financial flows on the maturity mismatch, a "liquidity ladder" was introduced (see, e.g., Marston, 1995). Custody accounts, which are obligatory for nonresident portfolio investors, are also included in the net foreign asset position.[26] Thus, the domestic credit market is insulated from the effects of portfolio capital inflows as well.

Taxes and Deposits on Foreign Credit Facilities

In some developing countries, taxes on short-term foreign borrowing have been used to contain financial inflows. It is well known that ease of circumvention is the main shortcoming of such measures. Another method is to require a variable deposit, which penalizes foreign credits of shorter maturity more severely. The flexibility of this measure enables it to contain unanticipated fluctuations in capital flows; that makes it especially attractive for developing countries, especially those with weak tax enforcement infrastructures (see Calvo *et al.*, 1993a; Lee, 1995).

In Slovenia, the central bank has enacted a variant of the variable deposit requirement. All legal entities are obliged to keep with the central bank an unremunerated tolar deposit against nontrade credits with maturities shorter than a certain threshold. The threshold maturity and the percentage of credit kept as a deposit have been changed twice since 1995. Since the beginning of 1997, all residents must make a 40% deposit against foreign nontrade credits with maturities of less than 7 years; in addition, the nonbanking sector must make a 10% deposit against nontrade credits with maturities of more than 7 years.

Liberalizing Outflows

Relaxation of controls on capital outflows is usually somewhere at the end of the menu of policy measures for neutralizing the harmful effects of excessive financial inflows (see, e.g., Schadler *et al.*, 1993; Williamson, 1994). Moreover, empirical evidence does not confirm that liberalizing outflows contains inflows of foreign capital; rather, lifting controls on capital outflows seems to stimulate net inflows (Labán and Larraín, 1993). Since 1996, banks in Slovenia have faced no constraints when investing in foreign securities and lending to nonresidents, although they are obligated to fulfill standard country and credit risk provisioning.

Sterilized Intervention

Sterilized intervention, which can be practiced under all types of foreign exchange regimes, is defined as a policy effort to attain independent paths for money and the exchange rate (see, e.g., Obstfeld, 1982). While there is no doubt as to the kind of effects that nonsterilized intervention have on an exchange rate, the effectiveness of sterilized intervention continues to be controversial.

It is widely accepted that in the long term reshuffling private portfolios cannot influence the exchange rate without changing the path of money. However, it is less clear whether sterilized intervention is ineffective in the short term. In developed countries, where such intervention has been empirically studied, its possible short-term effectiveness remains controversial (see, e.g., Obstfeld, 1982; Rogoff, 1984). Policy recommendations for developing countries facing huge financial inflows in the 1990s are similarly debatable. For skeptics, the high costs of sterilization and loss of control over the money supply – the latter because of interest payments – are the main obstacles to sterilization. For optimists, however, more pragmatic central banking[27] makes sterilized intervention easier than once believed (Calvo, 1991; Calvo *et al.*, 1993a; Reisen, 1993a; Frankel, 1994).

In Slovenia in recent years, control of the money supply has been the stabilization anchor (see, e.g., Bole, 1997), so nonsterilized intervention has not taken place. However, sterilized intervention began immediately after declaring monetary independence in 1991. It is well known that developing countries usually face significant technical problems with sterilization because of their underdeveloped domestic securities markets (Reisen, 1993a). In addition, due to the absence of government bills, the central bank usually issues its own obligations. In Slovenia, the central bank did the same.

There were two kinds of modifications in the implementation of foreign exchange intervention relative to the methods practiced in developing countries (see Bole, 1994, for details). The first modification directly relied on the currency premium to absorb foreign exchange inflows into the BOS's foreign exchange bills of the central bank; the authorities relied on this method at the very beginning of stabilization. The purpose of this modification was to increase the scope of the BOS's debt management, to decrease the fiscal costs of sterilization, and to prevent any future uncontrolled increases in the money supply (on the last of these, see Calvo, 1991).

The second important modification was the offering of central bank bills – through the intermediation of commercial banks – to nonbank entities. Because the liquidity risk premium was still high at the beginning of stabilization,[28] it was expected that neutralizing financial inflows by offering central bank foreign exchange bills would further reduce the fiscal costs of sterilization. This "portfolio-balance channel", which was more effective for the nonbank sectors,[29] made the necessary reduction in the money supply less costly. Moreover, it was expected that the reduction of the money supply would be more effective (per unit of sterilization costs) because of the money multiplier.

8.5.2   Instruments, strategy, and effects of policy measures

Main Instruments Used in the Sterilization Experiment

The main channel used to offset previous financial inflows has been the BOS's ongoing offering of foreign exchange bills (FEB) with varying maturities to all legal entities. At maturity, those bills are redeemable in foreign exchange.

Limiting access to the rediscount window chiefly to those banks having enough central bank foreign exchange bills in their portfolios has increased significantly the central role of FEB in containing and neutralizing financial inflows. Other measures to sterilize inflows have included the provision of Lombard loans against FEB, the collateralization of liquidity credits using foreign exchange or FEB, the BOS's temporary purchasing of FEB (repurchase agreements), and temporary swaps of foreign exchange. It is not surprising that, after 5 years of sterilization, commercial banks have become major investors in FEB; at the beginning of 1997, over 90% of outstanding FEB were in bank portfolios. In developing countries that have recently pursued sterilization-type policies, it is also common for the bonds used in those policies to accumulate in bank portfolios (see, e.g., Calvo *et al.*, 1993a).

To enhance intervention through repurchase and swap arrangements and loans, the central bank has continually pumped money out of the monetary system. In the first 2 years of stabilization, it did this through so-called "twin-bills", which were bought in domestic currency, but redeemed half in foreign exchange and half in tolars. Later, when the foreign exchange risk premium dropped, the central bank withdrew money from the system mainly by offering a warrant (derivative) through commercial banks to all legal entities.

The Changing Mix of Policies for Containing and Neutralizing Financial Inflows

The mix of policy measures has been changing continually since the establishment of monetary independence. It has been adapted to the changing structure and mobility of financial inflows, as well as to the effectiveness and opportunity costs of the measures at the authorities' disposal.

Sterilized intervention is usually one of the first lines of defense against huge financial inflows, and direct capital controls are among the last. Sterilization measures are easily and quickly implemented, curbing both the monetary effects of inflows as well as possible sudden (speculative) reversals in flows. Accordingly, policymakers use them to buy time to prepare and enact other measures, such as cutting the budget deficit, changing the exchange rate regime and trade policy, enacting impediments to inflows, and implementing financial sector reforms.

In Slovenia, sterilization measures were also used first and capital controls last. Broadly speaking, the authorities have changed the mix of policy measures four times since 1991 (for the dynamics of sterilization efforts see *Figure 8.10*). In the first period (1992–1993, characterized by high current account surpluses), the mobility of foreign capital was small, and the BOS employed instruments that implicitly relied on the high currency risk. By using such instruments, the central bank was able to increase the absorption of foreign exchange into residents' portfolios. In this period, the costs of sterilization were negligible.

In the second period (1994–1995/I), the liquidity risk was still high enough to prevent a massive increase in financial inflows (credits) to the domestic non-banking sector. The high liquidity risk restrained nonresidents from using resident

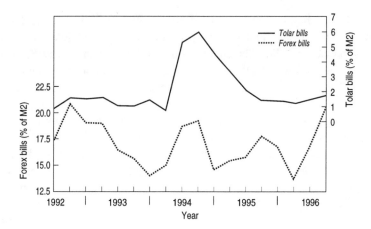

Figure 8.10. Dynamics of sterilization efforts: Movements in stocks of forex bills and tolar bills in Slovenia.

nonbank financial intermediators as fronts to buy the BOS's foreign exchange bills. Thus, the BOS could increase the returns on those bills enough to absorb any excess supply of foreign exchange in residents' portfolios. The BOS's warrant and foreign exchange bills were the basic instruments used in that period. To wipe out any excess money supply created by monetization, the BOS also increased the volume of tolar-denominated bills, but that was less important. The BOS also increased the minimum required capital for fully licensed banks to DM 40 million. In this period, sterilization costs increased considerably.

In the third period (1995/II–1996/II), liquidity risk dropped significantly and the mobility of foreign capital increased considerably. Resident nonbank entities had easy access to inexpensive and long-term foreign credit facilities, and inflows of portfolio capital picked up. In this period, containing financial inflows by the direct use of BOS bills bought and redeemed in foreign exchange became less and less efficient per unit of costs. With this in mind, the BOS launched direct controls on financial inflows: it slapped a deposit of 40% on nontrade credit facilities from nonresidents with maturities of less than 5 years, and increased the minimum capital requirement for new banks to DM 60 million. The costs of sterilization in this period did not change significantly.

The last period (1996/III–present) began when Slovenia received a single investment grade -A from credit-rating agencies. On top of the already large long-term credit inflows, portfolio capital inflows also accelerated considerably. The 40% deposit on nontrade credit facilities was extended to all credits with maturities of less than 7 years. Nonbank economic entities also had to pay a 10% deposit on credits with maturities of longer than 7 years. The BOS also enacted

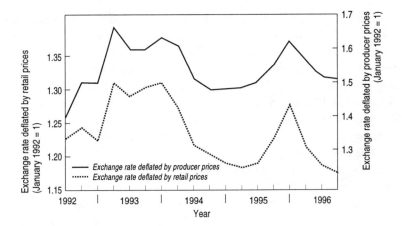

Figure 8.11. Real exchange rates in Slovenia.

the aforementioned net foreign assets position and other instruments to stimulate financial outflows. The volume of forex- and tolar-nominated bills increased considerably, as did sterilization costs.

An Illustration of the Effects of Policies for Containing and Neutralizing Financial Inflows

Policy efforts for containing and neutralizing financial flows were based on a desire to influence the path of real exchange rate in the period after the first half of 1992. Accordingly, an evaluation of policymakers' efforts to contain and neutralize financial flows must evaluate the effects of those efforts on the exchange rate.

In recent episodes of financial inflows, especially in Latin America, sterilized foreign exchange intervention has frequently caused some deterioration in economic performance: monetary control has loosened, upward pressure on interest rates increased, inflation picked up, and financial inflows have been prolonged. To all of this, we must add the usually high costs of sterilization, which are also the most frequent reason cited for having to halt sterilized intervention. Because of the BOS's persistent and concentrated sterilization activities, the deterioration in economic performance known from episodes abroad may also have taken place in Slovenia.

Figure 8.11 presents the real exchange rate, calculated alternatively using retail prices and producer prices according to the method described in Note 20. We present indexes of the real exchange rate for the period when inflation was largely tamed, that is for 1992/III–1996/IV. By the end of 1996, the exchange rate calculated using retail prices had appreciated by around 3% compared with 1992/III, while the exchange rate calculated on the basis of producer prices depreciated by approximately 7%. The differences in the indexes stem from the increasing relative prices of nontradables. The oscillations in the real exchange rate attained the greatest values (around 8–10%) after a large wave in the household component of financial inflows during 1993/III–1994/II. Because of that surge in net financial inflows, in 1994/III policymakers started the most aggressive and costly phase of sterilized foreign exchange intervention by offering a new instrument (the warrant).

In *Figure 8.12*, we illustrate the possible opportunity costs of the policy for the period 1992/III–1996/IV, presenting its detrimental effects on (already high) interest rates, the money path, and inflation. The effects on these three variables are difficult to disentangle from the effects of other policy measures, especially bank rehabilitation and tight monetary policy, without explicitly modeling their behavior. The figure displays the increment in real deposit rates and the increment in the volume of central bank forex bills in percentage of M3. The large swings in the increment to deposit rates through the first half of 1994 had no visible counterpart in the intensity of the use of the central bank's forex bills. Furthermore, the considerable increase after 1993 in the aggressiveness of the central bank's activity in curbing financial inflows is difficult to juxtapose with the oscillations in the interest rate increment below zero.

In *Figure 8.12* we also present the real growth of broad money and quarterly increments in BOS forex bills as a percentage of M3. The figure provides little evidence that the intensity of the sterilization experiment increased the growth rate of real money; in fact, such growth decreased slowly during the period studied. In Section 8.5.3 we presented the results of performing causality tests to corroborate this heuristic conclusion. Similarly to the cases of interest rates and money, graphs do not provide any clear message regarding the possible effects of sterilized intervention on the inflation rate. During the period 1992/III–1996/IV inflation was characterized by greater oscillations than those in the sterilization intensity, and by a falling trend.

Up until 1997, because all policy measures for containing and neutralizing financial flows were made by the central bank, it is easy to estimate an upper bound for the costs of the sterilization experiment during 1992–1996. Namely, they were less than the payments of the central bank on its corresponding instruments (i.e., in gross terms around 0.5% of GDP).

8.5.3   Testing the effects of policy for containing and neutralizing net financial inflows

The graphs of the real exchange rate demonstrate that the policy of containing and neutralizing net financial inflows must have been successful. However, these graphs do not reveal any relationship between the intensity of intervention and the most

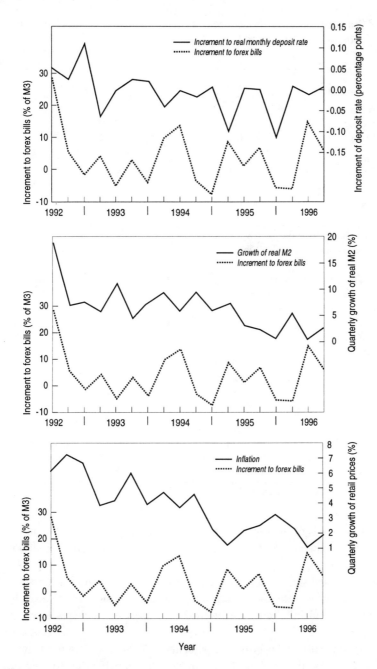

Figure 8.12. Real interest rate, growth of real broad money, and inflation versus increment to central bank forex bills in Slovenia.

Table 8.7a. Testing causality between sterilization measures and economic performance in Slovenia, 1992–1996.

	F	t_5	t_6
Forex bills			
Exchange rate	2.5[a]	2.03	−0.72
Inflation	0.8	0.61	1.03
Broad money	1.5	−1.19	−1.09
Interest rate	0.0	0.02	−0.04
Tolar bills			
Exchange rate	1.1	0.51	1.09
Inflation	0.5	0.71	0.41
Broad money	0.8	1.08	−0.94
Interest rate	0.9	1.25	−0.37

[a]F-statistics significant at 0.1.
Note: Monthly data used in calculations.

Table 8.7b. Testing reverse causality between sterilization measures and economic performance in Slovenia, 1992–1996.

	F	t_5	t_6
Forex bills			
Exchange rate	0.4	0.85	−0.09
Inflation	0.4	−0.16	−0.02
Broad money	1.1	−0.96	1.29
Interest rate	0.3	0.13	0.63
Tolar bills			
Exchange rate	0.3	−0.70	−0.46
Inflation	0.1	0.34	0.50
Broad money	2.1	1.07	1.86
Interest rate	0.9	1.31	0.53

Note: Monthly data used in calculations.

common measures of the opportunity costs of such actions. With this in mind, we carried out statistical tests for the "success-of-sterilization" and "no-opportunity-costs" propositions.

We performed statistical tests of causality running from policy measures to the growth of exchange rate, the increment in the real deposit rate, the growth of real broad money, and inflation. We proxied the extent of measures to contain and neutralize financial flows by the increment to forex bills as a percentage of M3 and the increment to tolar bills as a percentage of M2.[30] Causality was tested for conditional on the growth of base money, the variable that formed the basic target for policymakers. Our tests were performed on monthly data for the period July 1992–December 1996. Results are given in *Tables 8.7a* and *8.7b*. *Table 8.7a* reports the results for testing causality from the sterilization variable to exchange rate, interest rate, money, and inflation, and *Table 8.7b* reports on tests of the reverse causality.

The hypothesis of no feedback from sterilization to the real exchange rate can be rejected for forex bills; only the first lead coefficient is significant; the reverse causality is not significant. Thus, empirical evidence corroborates the proposition that the sterilization variable Granger-caused the depreciation of the exchange rate. All other F-statistics in *Tables 8.7a* and *8.7b* show insignificant causal relations, so that the hypothesis of no feedback from sterilization instruments to inflation, the real growth of money, and the real deposit rate cannot be rejected.

To summarize the results of causality testing, the policy of containing and neu-tralizing financial flows seems to have prevented a real appreciation of the exchange rate of above 3% in the period June 1992–December 1996. Moreover, the volatility of real exchange rate was high, with oscillations exceeding 10%. Our empirical work does not provide any evidence of the alleged side effects of the policy on interest rates, money, or inflation.

8.6 Summary and Conclusions

After 1991 Slovenia faced a strong surge in foreign exchange inflows. The sources of the inflow have changed radically over the years. Driven by distress exporting, a current account surplus of over 8% of GDP was the major source of inflows in 1992. After 1994, capital inflows took the lead: net medium- and long-term capital inflows exceeded 4.5% of GDP.

Descriptive statistical analysis of term structure components of financial flows corroborates their expected volatility: the volatility of FDI was the smallest and that of short-term flows the largest in the period 1992–1996. The differences in the volatility of the transactor components of financial flows were not substantial: volatility was the smallest for financial flows of the bank and business sectors and the largest for the official sector. There was considerable substitutability among financial flows classified by transactor. As the household component of financial flows was the largest component, and it had the greatest degree of substitutability with other components, it played a central role in our analysis of the causes and effects of financial flows.

We pinpointed differences between foreign and domestic interest rates, mea-sures for short-term macroeconomic adjustment (a credit squeeze), and labor mar-ket distortions as the driving forces behind financial inflows to Slovenia after 1991. The effectiveness of each external and domestic factor is corroborated for at least one transactor component of financial flows. The household component of finan-cial flows showed the greatest sensitivity to changes in the factors that we identified as likely to cause such flows. However, substitutability between the components of flows means that the factors studied also had an impact on total financial flows. Offsetting the limited supply of domestic credit was the most common cause of financial flows across transactor components. The importance of this offset effect demonstrates that credit rationing had a more significant economic impact than high lending rates. Financial flows had a favorable impact on the economy by decreasing domestic real interest rates and interest-rate differentials (the liquidity premium).

In the period 1992–1996, financial flows continuously created pressure for an appreciation of exchange rate and an acceleration of the growth of private consumption and the growth of real money. They also increased the vulnerability of banks. In addition, financial flows enabled the official sector to crowd out private consumption. The "unsustainable" phase of financial inflows began in the middle of 1995, when liquidity risk plummeted and long-term inflows (in the form of nontrade credits) began to systematically overshoot the foreign direct investment component. Two additional problems for policymakers appeared during this phase: the effectiveness of sterilized intervention decreased considerably and the fragility of the banking system increased.

The authorities launched policy measures for containing and neutralizing the effects of financial flows in the first year of stabilization. They employed sterilized intervention from the very beginning. They enacted direct controls of financial flows in the third year of the financial inflow episode, after there had been a significant drop in the foreign exchange liquidity risk. To mitigate the vulnerability of banks intermediating huge financial flows, they also made modifications to banking regulation and supervision. Finally, late in the period under study, they adopted measures for promoting financial outflows.

In the period 1992–1996, the real appreciation of the exchange rate was less than 3%, although oscillations therein attained values of higher than 10%. Empirical evidence does not confirm the existence of statistically significant side effects on interest rates, money, or inflation from policies aimed at containing and neutralizing financial flows.

Notes

[1] Kornai's (1997) analysis of a premature increase in present-day material welfare ("goulash postcommunism") is relevant here.

[2] Exports plus imports per unit of GDP.

[3] For a more detailed analysis of macroeconomic developments in Slovenia, see Bole (1997).

[4] For details on monetary and general macroeconomic policy in the stabilization episode, see Bole (1997).

[5] There was an operational surplus.

[6] For definitions of the items see, e.g., the IMF's *World Economic Outlook*, 1993, p. 173.

[7] Many enterprises that lost their markets in the former Yugoslavia had been important exporters to hard currency areas even before the country broke apart. Thus, it is no surprise that the upper quartile of enterprises (ranked by the magnitude of relative sales in the former Yugoslavia before secession) had the highest ratio of exports to total sales in 1992, i.e., after secession (see Bole, 1993).

[8] According to the IMF scheme, nondebt-creating flows and the change in reserve-related liabilities make up the difference between external borrowing and financing.

[9] Details on data classification are given in the Appendix. We have changed only the definition of the reserves component and the corresponding short-term flows. More specifically, to make the effects of sterilization measures more transparent, we have added bank deposits to the total reserves component.

[10] Households, for example, were completely free to hold foreign exchange deposits, to obtain credits abroad, etc., from the beginning of stabilization. However, before enterprises were privatized, they were not permitted to freely sell or buy assets abroad.

[11] We provide details on our data classification in the Appendix.

[12] By definition (see the Appendix), official flows do not include the change in official reserves.

[13] In the first quarter of 1992 inflation was still running at over 10% monthly.

[14] This calculation takes into account enterprise losses weighted by the corresponding enterprises' share of exports.

[15] The foreign exchange "liquidity premium" is defined as the difference between the interest rate on foreign exchange time deposits (in German marks) in Slovenia and that on time deposits of a similar maturity in Germany. The "currency premium" is defined as the difference between the interest rates on tolar and foreign exchange deposits of the same duration in Slovenia.

[16] Grade A was given by Standard & Poor's, A- by IBCA, and A3 by Moody's.

[17] The reason for this policy action was the surge in foreign exchange inflows stemming from the privatization of apartments and from distress exporting.

[18] It should be stressed that such an indicator of sterilized intervention cannot satisfactorily embrace direct capital controls or prudential regulation.

[19] For more information on offset effects, a phenomenon central to the monetary approach to the balance of payments, see, e.g., Marston (1985).

[20] To obtain the real exchange rate, we adjust the nominal rate in tolars for the German mark by an index of relative prices, i.e., by an index of retail prices in Germany divided by an index of retail prices in Slovenia.

[21] There are two possible explanations for the increasing relative prices of nontradables. The first is a slightly modified Kravis-Lipsey-Bhagwati explanation relying on a positive correlation between increases in the relative prices of nontradables and increases in GDP. The second follows from the higher price elasticity of the supply function of tradables and the real appreciation of the exchange rate. See Bole (1997).

[22] To disentangle the actual dependence between the business component of financial flows and the growth of real private consumption, we would have to specify and estimate a VAR (vector autoregression) process. However, the available data series are too short to allow us to carry out such a procedure.

[23] A bank must have a full license to offer foreign exchange deposits and to make foreign exchange payments. The average capital adequacy ratio (of around 20) is well over the Basel norm; it corresponds to suggestions made for economies in transition (see, e.g., Caprio, 1995).

[24] As documented in the previous section, foreign credits to banks triggered a rapid increase in credit (accompanied by falling net foreign assets) in the middle of 1995.

[25] This "net foreign assets position" is not the same as the standard net foreign exchange position, which is also mandatory in banking regulation.

[26] However, investors with control packages of equities and primary market disbursements are excluded.

[27] According to Reisen (1993b), this kind of banking refers to the "use of public institutions such as social security funds, state banks and public enterprises as monetary instruments".

[28] Commercial banks' foreign exchange liquidity was insufficiently credible for residents, who remembered banks' foreign exchange illiquidity at the end of 1990 (while Slovenia was still part of the former Yugoslavia).

[29] Many large companies, especially in retail trade and insurance, bought these bills.

[30] Bole (1994) provides an empirical analysis of other instruments used in the sterilization experiment.

References

Bole, V., 1993, Size of Enterprises and Their Performance: Some Empirical Facts, *Gospodarska gibanja*, Economic Institute at the School of Law, No. 8, pp. 19–30 [in Slovene].

Bole, V., 1994, Sterilization in a Small Open Economy: The Case of Slovenia, paper presented at the conference "Alternative Perspectives on Finance", held in Bled, published in Working Papers 1, Economic Institute at the School of Law, Ljubljana, Slovenia.

Bole, V., 1997, Stabilization in Slovenia: From high inflation to excessive inflow of foreign capital, in M.I. Blejer and M. Skreb, eds., *Macroeconomic Stabilization in Transition Economies*, Cambridge University Press, Cambridge, UK.

Bole, V., in press, The financial sector and high interest rates: Lessons from Slovenia, in M.I. Blejer and M. Skreb, eds., *Financial Sector Transformation*, Cambridge University Press, Cambridge, UK.

Calvo, G.A., 1991, The perils of sterilization, *IMF Staff Papers*, **38**(4):921–926.

Calvo, G.A., Leiderman, L., and Reinhart, C.M., 1993a, *The Capital Inflows Problem: Concepts and Issues*, IMF Working Paper: PPAA/93/10, July 1993.

Calvo, G.A., Leiderman, L., and Reinhart, C. M., 1993b, Capital inflows and real exchange rate appreciation in Latin America, *IMF Staff Papers*, **40**(1):108–151.

Caprio, G.J., 1995, Bank Regulation: The Case of the Missing Model, paper presented at the conference "Sequencing of Financial Reform", Policy Research Department, World Bank, Washington, DC, USA (mimeo).

Claessens, S., Dooley, M.P., and Warner, A., 1995, Portfolio capital flows: Hot or cool? *World Bank Economic Review*, **9**(1):153–174.

Corbo, V., and de Melo, J., 1985, Liberalization with stabilization in the southern cone of Latin America: Overview and summary, *World Development*, **13**(8):863–866.

Corbo, V., and Hernández, L., 1996, Macroeconomic adjustment to capital inflows: Lessons from recent Latin and East Asian experience, *World Bank Research Observer*, **11**(1):61–85.

Diaz-Alejandro, C., 1985, Good-bye financial repression, hello financial crash, *Journal of Development Economics*, **19**:1–24.

Dooley, M. P., 1996, A survey of literature on controls over international capital transactions, *IMF Staff Papers*, **43**(4):639–687.

Dooley, M., Fernández-Arias, E., and Kletzer, K., 1996, Is the debt crisis history? Recent private capital inflows to developing countries, *World Bank Economic Review*, **10**(1):27–50.

Fernández-Arias, E., and Montiel, P.J., 1996, The surge in capital inflows to developing countries: An analytical overview, *World Bank Economic Review*, **10**(1):51–77.

Frankel, J.A., 1994, Sterilization of Money Inflows: Difficult (Calvo) or Easy (Reisen)? IMF Working Paper 94/159.

Ishii, S., and Dunaway, S., 1995, Portfolio flows to the developing country members of APEC, in M.S. Khan and C.M. Reinhart, eds., *Capital Flows in the APEC Region,* IMF Occasional Paper 122, pp. 3–14.

Kornai, J., 1997, The political economy of the Hungarian stabilization and austerity program, in M.I. Blejer and M. Skreb, eds., *Macroeconomic Stabilization in Transition Economies*, Cambridge University Press, Cambridge, UK.

Labán, R., and Larraín, F., 1993, Can a Liberalization of Capital Outflows Increase Net Capital Inflows? Instituto de Economía, Universidad Católica de Chile, Working Paper No. 155.

Lee, J.Y., 1995, Implications of Surge in Capital Inflows: Available Tools and Consequences for the Conduct of Monetary Policy, IMF Working Paper 96/53.

McKinnon, R.I., 1988, Financial liberalization in retrospect: Interest rate policies in LDCs, in G. Ranis and T.R Schultz, eds., *The State of Development Economics*, Basil Blackwell, New York, NY, USA, pp. 386–415.

Marston, D., 1995, Short-term Absorption of Capital Inflows, Operational Paper, IMF Monetary and Exchange Affairs Department, Washington, DC, USA.

Marston, R.C., 1985, Stabilization policies in open economies, in R.W. Jones and P.B. Kenen, eds., *Handbook of International Economics*, Vol. 2, North-Holland, Amsterdam, Netherlands.

Mencinger, J., 1991, The Economics of Apartment Privatization, Gospodarska gibanja, Economic Institute at the School of Law, 1991/11 [in Slovene].

Obstfeld, M., 1982, Can we sterilize? Theory and evidence, *American Economic Review*, **72**(2):45–50.

Reisen, H., 1993a, The Case for Sterilized Intervention in Latin America, NBER, Sixth Annual Inter-American Seminar on Economics, 28–29 May, Caracas, Venezuela (mimeo).

Reisen, H., 1993b, South-East Asia and the impossible trinity, *International Economic Insights*, May/June.

Rogoff, K., 1984, On the effects of sterilized intervention: An analysis of weekly data, *Journal of Monetary Economics*, **14**(2):133–150.

Sargent, T.J., and Wallace, N., 1973, Rational expectations and the dynamics of hyperinflation, *International Economic Review*, **14**(2):328–350.

Schadler, S., Carkovic, M., Bennett, A., and Khan, R., 1993, *Recent Experiences with Surges in Capital Inflows*, IMF Occasional Paper No. 108.

Stanovnik, T., 1994, The sale of the social housing stock in Slovenia: What happened and why, *Urban Studies*, **31**(9):1559–1570.

Williamson, J., 1994, The Management of Capital Inflows, paper prepared for IFC, Institute for International Economics (mimeo).

Appendix

Testing feedback

Due to the short nature of the series, we employ a modification of the Granger-type test of causality proposed by Sargent and Wallace (1973).

We test linear causality from variable A to B (A "causes" B) using the model:

$$A(t) = a_0 + a_1 X(t) + a_2 B(t) + a_3 \Sigma r^i B(t-i) + a_4 r^t + a_5 B(t+1)$$
$$+ a_6 B(t+2) + a_7 B(t+3) + a_8 B(t+4) + e(t).$$

Parameters are indicated by a_i and r, X is a variable containing effects of other (nonanalyzed) variables correlated with A and B, and $e(t)$ is the statistical residual. We assess the possible linear causality from A to B by testing the hypothesis $a_5 = a_6 = a_7 = a_8 = 0$.

Sources of data

All data used in the study are obtained from various issues of the *Monthly Bulletin* of the Bank of Slovenia.

Definitions of the components of financial flows

We aggregate the balance of payments items found in the *Monthly Bulletin* to come up with terms corresponding to the IMF's "Standard Components of the Balance of Payments". Thus, the classification of components is constrained by the available level of aggregation in the *Monthly Bulletin*. In the following two schemes, we indicate only items explicitly available in the *Monthly Bulletin* (the portfolio item is the exception to this rule). For absent items, we provide only net values or values aggregated across such items.

Components of Flows by Term Structure

Long-term flows
    a. Debt securities.
    b. Loans; assets, liabilities; banks.
    c. Loans; liabilities; monetary authority; long-term.
    d. Loans; liabilities; general government; long-term.
    e. Loans; liabilities; other sectors; long-term.
    f. Trade credits; assets, liabilities; long-term.
Short-term flows
    a. Trade credits; short-term.

b. Currency and deposits; assets; other sectors.

c. Deposits; liabilities.

d. Loans; assets; other sectors.

e. Loans; liabilities; other sectors; short-term.

f. Other; assets, liabilities.

Foreign direct investment

a. Direct investment; abroad, in reporting economy.

Portfolio equity

a. Equity securities; assets, liabilities.

Reserves

a. Reserve assets (official).

b. Currency and deposits; assets; banks.

Components of Flows by Transactor

Household

a. Currency and deposits; assets; households.

Business

a. Direct investment; abroad, in reporting economy.

b. Trade credits.

c. Loans; assets, liabilities; other sectors.

d. Currency and deposits; assets; other sectors (less households).

e. Other; assets; other sectors.

Official

a. Debt securities.

b. Loans; liabilities; monetary authority, general government.

c. Other; assets; monetary authority, general government.

Banks

a. Currency and deposits; assets; banks.

b. Currency and deposits; liabilities.

c. Loans; assets, liabilities; banks.

d. Other; liabilities.

Summary

Charles Wyplosz

This book is uniquely rich in lessons, learnt and re-learnt. The concentration of chapters dealing with the same topic with a common approach creates a strong impression of similarities and yet, differences emerge in a picture that becomes progressively less blurred. This summary is structured around the themes that have surfaced repeatedly. Wherever I can, I attempt to establish consensus. Otherwise, I try to present disagreements and to bring some issues that, to my view, have not received as much attention as I would have liked.

Reasons for Capital Inflows

As policy-oriented economists spend much of their time trying to solve disagreements among themselves, it is important to note at the outset that all of the contributing authors to this book agree that inflows are good, especially when compared to outflows. Inflows are often seen as a reward to successful policies such as disinflation and more generally a shift to a stable macroeconomic situation, or liberalization of otherwise repressed goods and financial markets. Inflows are a general feature in countries that have recently improved their economic and political situation.

Beyond that, however, this book attempts systematically to determine exactly what the causes of inflows are. The existing literature (e.g., Calvo *et al.*, 1993; Fernández-Arias, 1994) provides convergent empirical evidence on the push factors; i.e., flows to developing countries tend to rise when interest rates decline in the developed countries, chiefly in the USA. Yet, clearly, domestic factors must

239

also matter. Perhaps we do not yet have a clear grasp of what these factors are. In particular, it would be useful to know whether there is a difference in this respect between economies in transition and "normal" developing countries.

Effects of Capital Inflows

Welfare improvement

By supplementing domestic savings, inflows allow capital to accumulate faster and/or to increase the consumption bonus of successful policies. That much has been well established. What is not clear is how the inflows are divided between investment and consumption. Two distinctions emerge.

First, Asian countries seem to essentially use inflows to boost investment already buoyed by high savings, while Latin American recipients take a larger share into increased consumption. Second, foreign direct investment (FDI) often takes a different form in transition economies. Hungary, for example, has mostly attracted inflows through its privatization program. This may partly explain its lackluster growth performance, relative to Poland which, until recently, has received considerably less foreign capital. Indeed, inflows into privatization do not add to capacities, initially at least. They may lead to a transfer of know-how, but it remains to be seen whether such inflows are as growth-enhancing as greenfield investment.

Macroeconomic effects

All of the chapters in this book establish that certain key macroeconomic indicators worsen when substantial inflows occur. Inflation stops declining. The current account worsens as spending rises faster than output. Even the budget deficit tends to worsen. This may be the temporary consequence of a mismatch between the demand and supply effects (time-to-build) of investment. More work is needed to contrast the experience of Asian countries with that of transition economies.

Policy dilemma

This book shows that one of the key problems posed by capital inflows is to create a policy dilemma between external competitiveness and inflation. Without intervention, the currency tends to appreciate: this reduces inflation but hurts competitiveness. Conversely, stabilizing the exchange rate may require monetary expansion and its corollary, inflation pressure.

The threat of reversals

Clearly, the most worrying issue is the threat that inflows quickly reverse themselves. The financial disaster in Mexico has left a deep impression on all policymakers.

The conditions under which reversals occur are not analyzed actively in this book, perhaps because reversals had not yet (this was just before the Czech minicrisis) occurred in transition countries. The push view of inflows is well established and could be worrying as we enter a period during which US and other major OECD interest rates are likely to be oriented upward. This makes it all the more important to improve our understanding of the pull factors.

Bank fragility

There is also consensus on the implications for the banking system. Abundant liquidities lead banks to increase credit. This process involves a double transformation: foreign currency liabilities are matched by domestic currency assets, and short-term inflows may lead to longer-term credit. This phenomenon has been destructive in Latin America. It is even more threatening in transition countries where there is no banking tradition and limited accumulated know-how. In addition, banks are often weak, plagued by nonperforming loans inherited from the previous regime, and still growing as a result of continuing soft budget constraints. All chapters note the risks ahead if capital flows were to reverse themselves before banks have been consolidated.

Policy Issues

How to deal with the trade-off

Experiments in various parts of the world have provided some useful lessons. As always, diversity is good for discerning what works and what does not.

The Latin American solution has been to deal with inflows by not changing the policy settings, just intervening on the foreign exchange markets and sterilizing the impact of interventions. This policy worked for a while, and then systematically failed. The reason is that sterilizing has proven to be too costly to be sustainable for very long. Surprisingly, the worst costs are not just the true economic costs of low yields on foreign assets and high returns paid on domestic liabilities. The limiting factor is accounting costs, i.e., the fact that the central bank books deteriorate.

The Asian solution has been the same: to sterilize. At the time when the first versions of these chapters were discussed (May 1997), it seemed that it was working. Yet real exchange rates were appreciating. Debating whether real appreciation is caused by nominal appreciation or by rapid inflation is beside the point: real appreciation is the normal market response to sterilized capital inflows. Either way, it is equally unsustainable. The chapters debate the question whether the real exchange rate appreciation could be softly reversed or whether a hard landing would be the outcome. Events have vindicated the darker predictions.

What role for fiscal policy?

There is some debate on the usefulness of a policy-mix response. With two objectives – the exchange rate and inflation – one could envision a combination of easy money to discourage the inflows by reducing the interest rate and tight fiscal policy to prevent inflation from flaring up. A verdict is still undecided due to lack of experimentation. The mix is likely to be politically difficult because fiscal restrictions do not sell well.

Should inflows be resisted at all?

A basic question is whether it is desirable to deter inflows (assuming that it is possible to do so). Indeed, capital flows represent, first and foremost, a positive sign of confidence in the economy. As noted above, they provide financing for productive investment as well as for desirable consumption after years of underspending. Inflows can be compared to chocolate: they are good but too much makes you sick.

This question forces one to think in a more precise way. It is not just an issue between good and bad. The proper approach views the problem as one of sustainability. Can the country go on borrowing at the current rate? With fast present and future growth, the answer may actually be positive. If the answer is negative, we still need to understand whether unsustainability results from policies that have become bad, or from market failures. In the last case, we need to identify the market failures and treat them directly rather than their symptom. For example, loss-making state-owned enterprises may manage to borrow because the government implicitly or explicitly underwrites their debts; the solution is not a blanket attempt to block inflows but privatization.

The authors of this book are in agreement that the reaction to capital inflows must start with caution. Taking time to answer the preceding questions must be better than killing prematurely a favorable development. Inflows do not turn into massive reflux overnight: there is time to ponder and analyze.

Do we have instruments to resist?

If it is eventually decided that the inflows need to be resisted, how can the job be done? One instrument is the interest rate. Bringing it down gently can alter the situation without resulting in a disaster. This option was not explored in the book. Another policy is to make inflows riskier, especially for investors who look for a quick return. This can be done by increasing the volatility of the exchange rate. As has been noted already, most episodes of rapid inflows follow a period of inflation stabilization underpinned by an exchange rate anchor. This may be the time to dispose of the nominal anchor. The inflows respond to a degree of trust in the robustness of disinflation. A nominal anchor is not needed anymore to be a signal from the monetary authorities that they are committed to disinflate. Indeed, many countries have responded by widening the bands of fluctuations that they had put in place earlier. There is mounting evidence that this is the appropriate policy response. The main limitation is that it is not a sufficient condition to repel inflows. It helps, but is not enough.

A controversial response is the implementation of capital controls. Capital controls generate an instinctive repulsion among governments freshly committed to market mechanisms, as well as among most international organizations and market participants. They are denigrated before even being considered. Yet capital controls can play a crucial role, provided that their role is neither inflated nor minimized.[1] Controls can deal with surges, in one direction or the other. Controls also help to sort out short- from long-term flows. Controls are never tight, and do not need to be for effectiveness. They operate by raising costs. This is often enough to discourage the back-and-forth trips that are the hallmark of speculative activity and can swell at the click of a computer key. Capital controls are most desirable in situations where markets move, even though the fundamentals do not justify an attack. Chile is often given as an example of a country that has benefited from a Tobin tax to get out of the Tequila crisis unhurt, although that assessment has been challenged in this book. The latest round of speculative activity in Southeast Asia, spreading to Eastern Europe and South America, again illustrates the phenomenon of contagion and the potential value of controls to guard against it.[2]

The banking system

In line with the broad consensus reported in the section on bank fragility is the importance of strengthening the banking system. There is general agreement that too little has been done in terms of regulation and overseeing. Appropriate prudential rules are needed, as well as institutions able to enforce and adapt the rules. This requires know-how and therefore cannot be done immediately in the middle of a crisis; the earlier it is undertaken, the better. Many countries now aspire to gradually meet the targets of the Basel Agreement on International Capital Standards. It has been noted that these targets are designed for the OECD countries, with mature financial markets and banks, and a relatively stable macroeconomic environment. Transition countries could well aim at significantly tighter rules. It would also be highly desirable if commercial banks engaged in real commercial banking (i.e, lending to firms and households), instead of attempting to survive or make profits out of trading public paper and foreign currencies.

What is Special about Transition Economies?

One of the most useful aspects of this book is the diversity of country experiences reviewed within a similar framework. Inevitably one asks whether the phenomenon of capital flows into the transition economies resembles that seen previously in Latin America or in Asia. In fact, both bear a resemblance. As with Asia, FDIs loom large. And as in Latin America, sterilization is clearly perceived as a limited approach. However, a number of features distinguish the transition economies.

First, data limitation is more severe in transition countries. Various experts have noted that much less is known about capital inflows in transition economies than elsewhere. This is due to the inherent difficulty of rapidly building up a statistical reporting system compatible with free markets, when another (but ill-adapted) system (with significant human capital invested in it) already exists. It is also due to the fact that the banking and financial systems are often weak and poorly regulated. Data limitation makes it harder to design sound policies and plays a role in perpetuating mistakes in policy analysis.

The second distinguishing feature is the fragility of the banking and financial systems, which reduce the ability to cope with inflows and deal with mishaps. This aspect is compounded by the presence of a large number of state-owned enterprises. Many of them are not profitable and therefore cannot easily adapt to a real appreciation or to the sudden availability of funds. Even when they are profitable, the situation may lead to conflicts of interest in governments, which act both as monetary and fiscal authorities and as shareholders.

Finally, the link between FDI and productive investment needs to be better understood. The two are not necessarily connected. The clearest example is in Hungary, the country that has managed to attract by far the largest inflows of direct investment. Most of these flows are associated with privatization. Although a positive step, change of ownership does not necessarily imply the installation of new equipment. Conversely, Poland has been less successful at attracting direct investment but indigenous productive investment seems to be very dynamic. However, it seems the sectors and firms that benefit from FDI adapt better and grow faster. If these relationships could be clearly established, another important and strategic lesson would be learnt about the intricate impact of capital inflows.

Notes

[1] For a theory of capital controls, see Wyplosz (1986).

[2] Empirical evidence of contagion and of the role of controls in OECD countries can be found in Eichengreen *et al.* (1996).

References

Calvo, G., Leiderman, L., and Reinhart, C., 1993, Capital Inflows to Latin America: The Role of External Factors, IMF Staff Papers 40, pp. 108–151, International Monetary Fund, Washington, DC, USA.

Eichengreen, B., Rose, A., and Wyplosz, C., 1996, Contagious currency crises, *Scandinavian Economic Review*, **98**(4):463–484.

Fernández-Arias, E., 1994, The New Wave of Private Capital Inflows: Push or Pull? World Bank Policy Research Working Paper 1312, The World Bank, Washington, DC, USA.

Wyplosz, C., 1986, Capital controls and balance of payments crises, *Journal of International Money and Finance*, **5**(2):167–179.

Index